Survival at Stalag IVB

Survival at Stalag IVB

Soldiers and Airmen Remember Germany's Largest POW Camp of World War II

TONY VERCOE

McFarland & Company, Inc., Publishers
Jefferson, North Carolina, and London

LIBRARY OF CONGRESS CATALOGUING-IN-PUBLICATION DATA

Vercoe, Tony, 1919–
  Survival at Stalag IVB : soldiers and airmen remember Germany's largest POW camp of World War II / Tony Vercoe.
    p.   cm.
  Includes bibliographical references and index.

  ISBN-13: 978-0-7864-2404-7
  softcover : 50# alkaline paper ∞

  1. Stalag IV B.   2. World War, 1939–1945 — Prisoners and prisons, German.   3. World War, 1939–1945 — Personal narratives.   I. Title.
  D805.5.S719V47   2006
  940.54'7243 — dc22   2005034169

British Library cataloguing data are available

©2006 Tony Vercoe. All rights reserved

No part of this book may be reproduced or transmitted in any form or by any means, electronic or mechanical, including photocopying or recording, or by any information storage and retrieval system, without permission in writing from the publisher.

On the cover: photograph — Main Street 1945 (E.J. McGregor); inset — "Stille Nacht" (drawing by Ray Newell)

Manufactured in the United States of America

McFarland & Company, Inc., Publishers
  Box 611, Jefferson, North Carolina 28640
    www.mcfarlandpub.com

Lew Parsons of Essex, U.K., is principally responsible for my undertaking this memoir of Stalag IVB, and for the considerable documentary material he provided at the outset and for his continuing encouragement, I am greatly indebted. Lew's example has generously been followed by many other veterans of that wartime, wire-bound, unforgotten enclosure in Saxony, and all of these are acknowledged elsewhere in the book.

Acknowledgments

References, information and other assistance received from the following, and much to the advantage of this book, are gratefully acknowledged:

Comité International de la Croix Rouge, Geneva, Switzerland
George Czekalowski (U.K.), primary scans of Ray Newell pictures
Rudi de Kinderen, *Flying Colours* (N.Z.), scans of all illustrations
Defence Base Records, Wellington, New Zealand
George Duncan (research website) *www.iinet.net.au/~gduncan*
Gedenkstätte Ehrenhain Zeithain, Saxony, Germany
Imperial War Museum, London, U.K.
106th Infantry Division Association, USA
National Association, American Ex-Prisoners of War, USA
Public Records Office, Kew, U.K.
Royal Air Force Museum, Hendon, U.K.
Second World War Experience Centre, Leeds, U.K.
Stalag IVB Association, Chicago, USA
Stalag IVB ex-POW Group, U.K.

And thanks to *Les Editions de Minuit*, France, for permission to reprint lines from Paul Eluard's "Liberté" (*Au rendez-vous allemande*, ©1945)

Contents

Acknowledgments	vii
Preface	1
Introduction	3
1. M. Stammlager IVB	7
2. Babbelfest	18
3. The Commissariat	31
4. A Half-Life	41
5. Words and Music	52
6. A Secret War	67
7. Doug's Story	74
8. The Escape Imperative	100
9. Discipline/Punishment/War Crimes	118
10. Bartering and Bribery	126
11. Stranger Than Fiction	132
12. The Satellite Camps	143
13. In Limbo	158
14. Deliverance	169
Glossary	183
Chapter Notes	187
Bibliography	193
Contributors	195
Index	197

Preface

The largest of all the German World War II prisoner of war camps is the subject of this book. Stalag IVB, as the war went on, became a crowded, pestiferous monster of a place within whose bleak boundaries the men of many nations were confined and in which they struggled daily to sustain morale and self-respect, or merely to keep themselves clean.

For much of its five and a half years of existence Stalag IVB was a melting pot as more and more men — and occasionally, women — were brought there to spend months or years inside its barbed wire perimeters or to be transferred to some of the hundreds of satellite Lagers which it supported.

Based on the firsthand experiences of the author, thorough research and many absorbing contributions from other veterans, this work is an extensively illustrated evocation of the camp, its background, layout, procedures for the intake of prisoners and the subsequent nature of their lives there. The vital role of the International Red Cross in their survival is acknowledged, and a collateral chapter enacting life in the vast network of satellite and work camps (Arbeitskommandos) is included.

Inevitably, given its great size and multinational character, the author has been able to enrich his case history of Stalag IVB with authentic accounts of a number of strange incidents — some of them frankly bizarre — in compiling a chronicle as unique and dramatic in its own way as those of Oflag IVC, Colditz or Stalag Luft III, Sagan.

Introduction

Standing there, remembering, looking back across time, I see the past rising again. The stark frame of the arched gateway is there, the clock, the armed guard staring down. Main Street stretches away beyond, running straight between the gray-walled huts.

Main entrance to M. Stammlager IVB, drawn by Ray Newell in 1945.

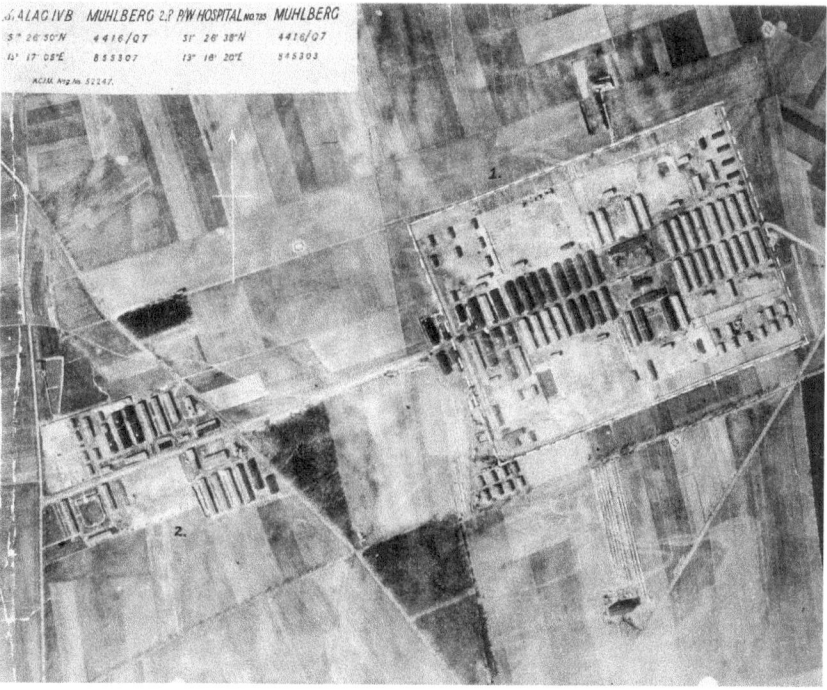

Top: Camp location and Main Street in 2001 (courtesy Alex Franks). *Bottom:* Aerial photograph of camp (RAF photograph A.C.J.U. Neg. No. 52247, declassified).

Introduction

Main Street 1945 (E.J. McGregor photograph).

Men are there, leaning against the barrack walls, gathering at the swap shop, walking to keep the circulation going, all marking time. And that stink — it hangs in the air everywhere. The putrid old Scheissenwagen can't be far away, trundling between compounds; and the Russians...

1

M. Stammlager IVB

> *Es ist die letzte territoriale Forderung, die ich Europa zu stellen habe.*
>
> (Adolf Hitler, referring to Sudetenland, in a speech in Berlin, 1938)

PART ONE

While the world west of the Rhine may have derived some reassurance from this declaration by Hitler that the Sudetenland was to be his last territorial claim in Europe, countries close to Germany's eastern and southern borders could hardly have been put at ease by it. From their viewpoints it was obvious that the military activism of the Third Reich had already far outrun the substance of the statement. They could see an inexorable march under way.

The Wehrmacht occupied Czechoslovakia in March 1939 and by then various separate, though not unrelated, German military initiatives were also well advanced. One of these was the tactical search by the German Army Fiscal Service in many parts of the country for suitable sites at which to establish a network of Stammlagers (muster-encampments, or prisoner-of-war transit camps). It found several in Saxony,[1] leased them and delegated the responsibility for their administration to Wehrkreis IV (War Area IV Command) based at Dresden.

Here are the details for the Mannschafts Stammlager as translated by Heinz L. Herz from a postwar report by the German historian Achim Kilian:

Location: Away from main trafic routes, but not more than 5 kms distant from a railroad station.
Site characteristics: Flat, good visibility, shielded from heavy winds, with sandy, tillable soil.
Size: Minimum of 40 hectares to hold 10,000 POWs.
Water: Source must be readily available and simple to supply.
German Army specifications for a double barbed-wire fence, watch towers etc.

The area of open land that would become Stalag IVB seemed to meet

Locations of German Prisoner-of-War Camps

Listed by camp name with nearest town, from International Red Cross, 31 December 1944

POW Camps

Stalag II A (Neubrandenburg)
Stalag II B (Hammerstein)
Staglag III A (Luckenwalde)
Stalag III B (Fürstenburg/Oder)
Stalag III C (Altdrewitz)
Stalag III D (Berlin-Steglitz)
Stalag IV A (Hohnstein)
Stalag IV B (Mühlberg)
Stalag IV C (Wistritz)
Stalag IV D (Torgau)
Stalag IV D/Z (Annaburg)
Stalag IV F (Hartmannsdorf)
Stalag IV G (Oschatz)
Stalag IV H/304 (Jacobstahl; not acknowledged by Germans)
Stalag V A (Ludwigsburg)
Stalag V B (Villingen)
Stalag VI G (Bergisch-Neustadt)
Stalag VI J (Krefeld)
Stalag VII A (Moosburg)
Stalag VII B (Memmingen)
Stalag VIII B (Teschen)
Stalag 344 (Lamsdorf)
Stalag VIII C (Sagan)
Stalag IX B (Bad Orb)
Stalag IX C (Bad Sulza)
Stalag X B (Bremervörde)
Stalag X C (Nienburg)
Stalag XI A (Altengrabow)
Stalag XI B (Fallingbostel)
Stalag XII A (Limburg)
Stalag XII D (Wahbreitbach)
Stalag XII F (Freinshein)
Stalag XIII C (Hammelburg)
Stalag XIII D (Nürnberg-Langwasser)
Stalag 383 (Hohenfels)
Stalag XVII A (Kaisersteinbruch)
Stalag 398 (Pupping)
Stalag XVIII A (Wolfsberg)
Stalag XVIII C (317) (Markt-Pongau)
Stalag 357 (Oerbke)
Stalag XX A (Tórun)
Stalag XX B (Marienburg)
WK8 — BAB21 (Blechhammer)

Camps for Airmen

Luft I (Barth)
Luft III (Sagan)
Luft IV (Grosstychow)
Luft VII (Bankau)
Stalag XVII B (Krems/Gneixendorf)
Dulag Luft (Wetzlar)

Naval and Merchant Marine Camps

Marlag-Milag (Tarmstedt)

Ground Force Officers' Camps

Oflag IV C (Colditz)
Oflag VII B (Eichstätt)
Oflag IX A/H (Spangenburg)
Oflag IX A/Z (Rotenburg)

---

most of these conditions. Nearby patches of woodland were neither dense enough nor close enough to the camp to cause concern. The location was some 4 kilometers northeast of the village of Mühlberg-am-Elbe in the heart of eastern Germany, within a triangle of the major cities: Berlin, 96 kilometers to the north, Leipzig, 64 kilometers to the southwest and Dresden, some 55 kilometers southeast. The main railway south from Berlin to Dresden and beyond passed through nearby Riesa.

The river Elbe, a few kilometers west of the Stalag, carries enough water to enable large barges to travel it. These deliver supplies, and most of the villages along its banks have small anchorages or jetties for access.

1—M. Stammlager IVB

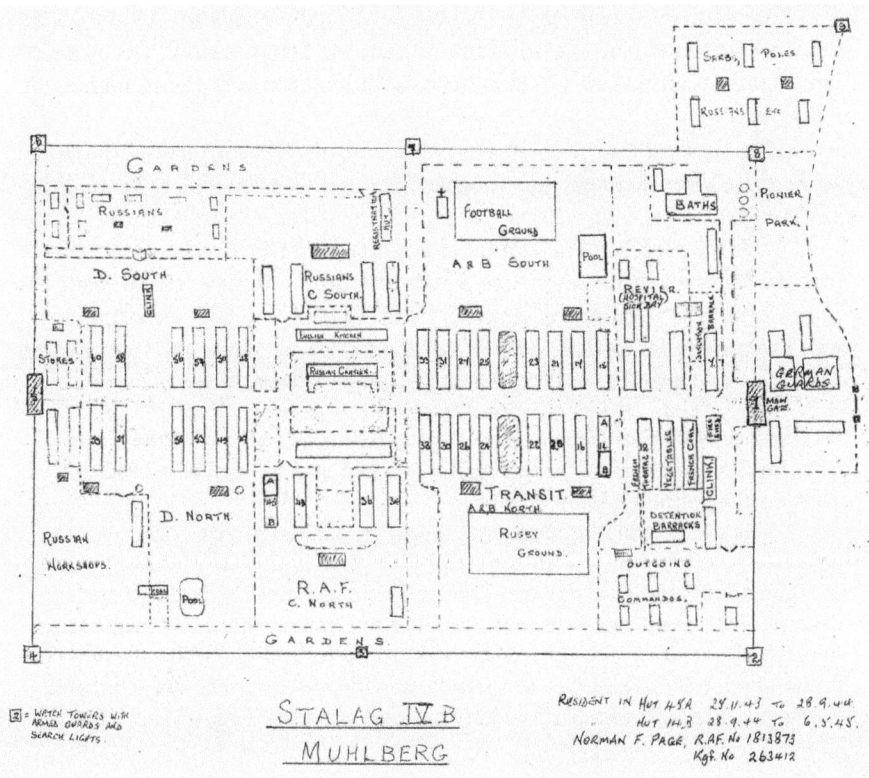

A diagram of Stalag IVB, drawn and supplied by Norman Page.

M. Stammlager IVB had always been planned as a transit camp, but circumstances contrived to cause deferment and modification of this. Outbreaks of diphtheria and typhus from the end of 1941 had to be contained and, as the war went on, the increasing numbers of POWs from various fronts put great strain on German resources for their accommodation.

In spite of the express prescription and methodical planning, the Stalag grew and grew. The first true prisoners of war, the Poles, housed in tents from the start, soon found themselves to be forced labor for the Third Reich. Along with other prisoners who followed, many were set to work on the construction of the camp. Trees felled in forests to the east were stripped and topped to provide fence posts. These were erected in holes dug around the perimeter, heavy duty barbed wire was attached, and the first guard towers built. Inside the fence a number of tents were set up temporarily while the first couple of wooden huts were built. Kilian notes that by mid-June 1940, 60 barracks had been finished, about 40 for living quarters, the rest for administrative use. Other buildings, open spaces and camp roads were being developed.

The position had been well chosen, allowing room for growth. Laid out on that flat expanse, grimly functional, the Stalag waited. (Achim Kilian: "A camp with dark wooden huts, with watchtowers rising high as on stilts.")

This time when the train stops the sliding doors are roughly hauled aside and—'Raus! 'Raus! Aus machen! Schnell!—we're ordered out. Journey's end.

After the near-blackness of the closed truck, the daylight is almost blinding. We know the ground is three feet or so below and we've got to make the jump. Muscles are cramped, limbs are stiff. One or two fellows stumble and fall. The guards harass us into line. We start marching. Grass and trees around us. The countryside here should smell clean and fresh, but…

SERGEANT FRED HEATHFIELD (51 SQUADRON, RAF). "On the warm morning breeze came the most revolting stench and we wondered what on earth could produce such a smell.…

"The camp came into sight and I was amazed at its size. Later, it was measured out to be 800 yards long and 550 yards wide. As we walked along the long south side, the wire was crowded with the most bedraggled and decrepit creatures I had ever seen.[2] I could not believe these had ever been soldiers of any army. We turned the corner and walked along the shorter side to the main gate, a large wooden structure with watch towers and overhead walkway for the guards. In large letters a sign read: M. STAMMLAGER IV B."

Double barbed wire attached to posts every two yards and topped with coiled barbed wire defined the camp perimeters. Floodlights were positioned along this about 50 yards apart. Guard towers loomed at roughly 300-yard intervals along the main sides and at 200 yards on each end. Twenty yards inside the main fence and a couple of feet above ground was stretched a single barbed wire runner. The area between this "trip wire" and the outer fence was no-man's-land. Anyone trespassing onto it would be shot without warning.

FRED HEATHFIELD. "Why were we in an army camp? Goering told the German people that not one single RAF bomber would penetrate the defences of the Third Reich. He hedged his bets by building one small POW camp at Barth on the Baltic coast. I think it was originally designed for about 100 men. By the time the Battle of the Ruhr was at its height, RAF prisoners were dropping into Germany in such numbers the Luft camps were not big enough, despite a rapid building programme, so some of the Wehrmacht camps were asked to take the surplus of NCO prisoners. Our mail was still addressed via Stalag Luft III.

"Very soon after we had settled in a small group of prisoners were transferred from Luft I at Barth and among them was a Canadian Navigator, F/Sgt Jack Meyers, who was universally known as 'Snowshoes,' apparently because of his enormous feet. He had considerable experience of prison camp procedure and was quickly elected as our Camp Leader. This was an official position under the Geneva Convention and Meyers was recognised by the Germans as our Vertrauensmann (Man of Confidence). This was other ranks' equivalent of the Senior British Officer in officers' camps but, by the nature of things, a Man of Confidence usually commanded far more men than any SBO. When the camp grew in numbers with the troops from Italy, and the RAF was greatly outnumbered by the army, Snowshoes remained in charge."

A few miles away, the auxiliary camp (H304) near Zeithain seemed equally unwelcoming to POWs arriving there.³

DRIVER ALEX FRANKS (T/172554 RASC, 2/2 MOTOR AMBULANCE COMPANY). "After that five days–four nights cattle truck ride from Campo 70 at Fermo, I finally stretched my legs at a siding 500 yards south of the railway station: Jacobstahl. From there we marched across fields of swedes and turnips. Some chaps were pulling these up and were rifle-butted brutally."

FRED HILL (A YOUNG SALVATION ARMY OFFICER). "Not a pretty sight—barbed wire, at each corner a sentry box about 30 feet from the ground, guards sweeping the area with searchlights and the barking of Alsatian dogs.... It all added up to the grim picture of Jacobstahl."

PART TWO

The German administration offices at Stalag IVB were situated just outside the main gate. Across from there were the quarters for the guards, some 200 of them. By May 1941 Major Schöltzel, the first Kommandant, had been replaced by Oberstleutnant (lieutenant colonel) Sperl, who was himself succeeded in mid-1942 by Oberst Semf. At the beginning of 1943 Oberstleutnant Stossier arrived to take over. His Lagerführer or Lageroffizier (camp manager) was Hauptmann (Captain) König, and this hierarchy, along with their staff of officers and other ranks, remained little changed until the attempt in July 1944 to assassinate Hitler. In the purge of the Wehrmacht following this, Stossier was replaced by Oberst Lührsen.

It seems that Goering had issued a personal order requiring all German forces to replace the standard military salute with the "Heil Hitler" version as an affirmation of loyalty. Oberstleutnant Stossier, a professional soldier of the old school, was not prepared to make such a change.

After the bomb plot, SS and Gestapo descended on the camp and carried out a general Blitz, rather superficially of the British, more rigorously of the Germans. Oberstlt. Stossier was placed under house arrest. Hauptmann König retained his position but even after the arrival of Oberst Lührsen the real control of the camp was in the hands of an *SS* captain.

The prisoners in each new batch were subjected to a routine induction process. Once through the camp gate they were led off to the right along the inside of the wire to a small compound in the southwest corner, the delousing unit. Here they were ordered to strip naked and place all their clothing in iron baskets of a type used at some swimming pools before the war. Russian prisoners hung the baskets on rails mounted on trolleys and pushed them into large gas ovens. Advised to keep well clear, the new men were shepherded into another room where they saw a strange contraption with a big wheel and supports at each corner. A Russian was seated at the wheel ready to turn it by hand, providing power for a set of shears operated by yet another prisoner.

In his manuscript "With the 4th Battalion, the Green Howards," CSM Richard Hall said he'd been told machines like this were used at home to trim donkeys.

FRED HILL. "Not a word was spoken. The clippers said it all. The first swoop over my head left the impression of a well-worn path across a cornfield. By the third swoop I was as bald as when I made my first appearance into this world."

All men were compulsorily shorn in this manner and then, while still naked, passed through another doorway, 20 or 30 at a time, into an enclosed room: the shower room.[4] There were holes for drainage in the tiled floor and, along the wall and in the ceiling, many water vents. No soap or towels were visible.[5]

KURT VONNEGUT (SCOUT PFC. HQ. COMPANY, 2ND BATTALION 423RD REGIMENT, U.S. 106TH INFANTRY DIVISION). "An unseen hand turned a master valve. Out of the showerheads gushed scalding rain. The rain was a blowtorch that did not warm."

The next phase brought no comfort. A man sat by the door, ready beside him a bucket containing a powerful, acrid disinfectant. Each prisoner had to stand with his arms in the air and feet apart while the operator dipped a cloth-covered brush in the liquid and applied the stuff under each arm and even more generously, it seemed, at the groin. The room was soon full of naked men dancing about, from the sting of the disinfectant and the cold.

The clothing had been steamed and disinfected and, when the gas ovens were opened, the Russians drew out the racks using long poles. They left them in the open air and warned the men not to go near until told it was safe to do so. Lined up in fives now by the guards, they waited.

FRED HILL. "We talked together until a German sergeant came shouting and raving. It dawned on us that he was trying to tell us to be silent. One prisoner slow to obey was made to stand in a corner like a naughty schoolboy."

At last the word was given, there was a rush to recover clothing, and, even though it still felt damp, there was enormous relief at being dressed again. Next the prisoners were hustled along to a medical block to be checked and X-rayed.

FRED HEATHFIELD. "A large wooden calliper was used to measure chest depth and to sort us into four groups. I was in the smallest group, number 4, with the deepest chest measurement. After the X-ray we were injected by medical orderlies who had the rustiest and bluntest needles I have ever seen. Two jabs in the chest, a scrape and an injection in the arm and we were through. Apparently the Germans were very keen to X-ray us as they had a great dread of tuberculosis, and this was actually one sure illness which guaranteed repatriation.[6]

"Registration was the next phase—fingerprints and a photograph were taken, receipt given for money, new metal *Kriegsgefangene* dog tags with number—six-figure numbers at Stalag IVB, all beginning with 2—to be worn round the neck, and forever etched upon the mind like one's service number.

"The identity tag was of aluminium, perforated down the middle and with the number on each piece; one half to be left on the body, the other half to be handed in for records."

KURT VONNEGUT (ARRIVING WITH HIS GROUP OF AMERICANS). "[We] ... came to a shed where a corporal with only one arm and one eye wrote the name and serial number of each prisoner in a big, red ledger. Before they got their names and numbers in that book, they were missing in action and probably dead."

LARRY FALSTEIN (28TH DIVISION, U.S. ARMY, AS REPORTED BY TOM NELSON). "There were so many of them that some British soldiers were recruited to help sign them in. He gave his usual details and, when asked his religion, said 'Jewish.' The army man just looked up at him and said 'Let's put Protestant.' Some time later he discovered that the Jewish GIs were sent to the most dangerous and horrible jobs.[7] Larry said: 'Just three little words, but they might have saved my life.'"

Fred Heathfield reported that the Red Cross parcels his group had brought with them had been marked with their names and numbers and placed in a parcel store. Their wounded and injured had been taken to the Revier, marked with a Red Cross near the main gate, but the German doctors and medical orderlies there refused to treat them, so they had to be brought back and were forced to stand with the rest in the street.

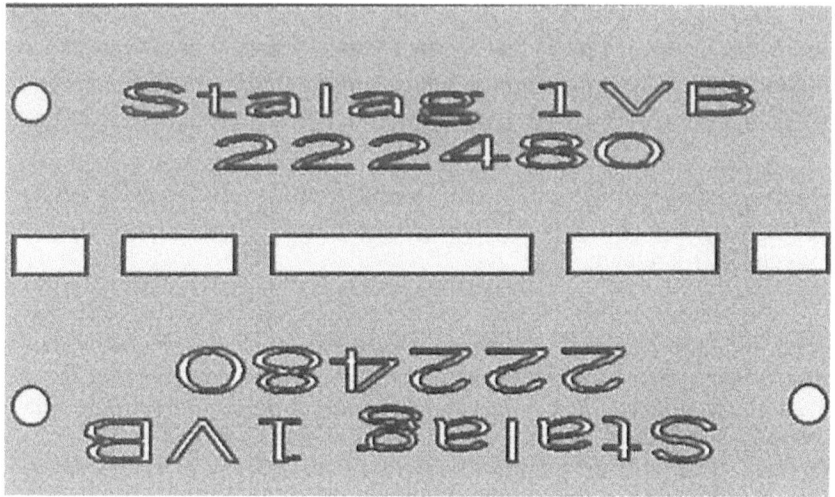

All prisoners of war were issued with metal identification tags by the Germans, and these were commonly known as "dog tags" (courtesy A.F. [Andy] Anderson).

FRED HEATHFIELD. "The day was getting hotter and nothing seemed to be happening for ages. The street and open places were empty, everyone had been confined to their huts. Suddenly, from one of the huts, a Russian dashed out with a can of water. He was followed by others who ignored the rifle butts of the guards to bring us the welcome water. The French, Belgian and Dutch prisoners stayed indoors. Eventually we were told to move into hut 47B in D North Compound, which later became the camp's Empire Theatre."

After registration it was usual for each group to be marched along the main road of the Stalag to the hut which was to become its future home.[8] Only now were the men able to grasp the vastness of the place, passing row after row of barracks on either side, with secondary roads leading off to various compounds, each of which contained a similar group of huts.

Every hut was something like 200 feet long by 35 feet wide and was divided into two parts, the slightly longer end intended to accommodate 220 men, the other 180. Both ends had entrances via a sort of vestibule, in which was located the night latrine, a single-seat cubicle.[9] The washroom area, located centrally between the two sections of the hut, contained two rows of concrete troughs, scarcely adequate washing facilities for the needs of 400 men trying to keep themselves and their clothing reasonably clean. In each hut were two fireplaces for heating purposes, with metal covering plates that would soon be used in resourceful ways for cooking.

Wooden bunk units, three beds per unit, stood three deep on one side of the hut, with narrow gangways between the blocks. Palliasses lay on the bed boards. The two blankets originally issued were later reduced to one. There were no pillows. Along the other side of the hut were wooden tables, with forms for seating.

FRED HEATHFIELD. "I grabbed a top bunk, remembering what my father had told me from his experiences in the trenches of World War I. The top bunk is always the best. Hot air rises and dirt falls. You get warmed by the heat of the bodies below, and there is no one above to drop crumbs and dirt from their boots onto you. I also found there was more headroom than on the middle and bottom bunks, where one could barely sit upright."[10]

Regardless of anyone's position in the hut, each night's confinement was a sort of living hell. The unventilated air, rank with the smell of unwashed bodies and dirty clothing, was further fouled by the stench from the night latrine just outside the door. Many men often had to get out to use this or, finding sleep impossible, tossed and turned, disturbing others in their units. The nights generally seemed endless, and shuffling out into the open air for morning roll call brought real relief.

APPELLS

QMS FREDERICK HEDGES (2/5TH ESSEX REGIMENT). "The Germans hold two roll calls (Appells) per day in the summer, usually at 6:30 a.m. and 8:00 p.m. In the winter both roll calls are likely to be held inside the huts. Occasionally Jerry will have a Blitz, order one or more huts out and thoroughly search the interiors, turning everything inside out and upside down."

Men who had previously been held in Italian prison camps, where they had often been made to stand for long periods— sometimes for hours— on roll call, found the Appell here much more efficient. Delays were uncommon — except in the RAF compound.

There was a diametric difference between army and air force attitudes to appearances on parade — whether the morning roll calls or the other occasions sometimes imposed by the Germans— and it caused some friction. The army's view was that it was a matter of pride always to appear smartly turned out, whereas the RAF types ...

SERGEANT (LATER FLIGHT LIEUTENANT) TOM NELSON (51 SQUADRON, RAF). "I remember the roll calls well and the constant comparison between the Army and the RAF compounds. The army always seemed to turn out as if on parade. The men looked clean and had all shaved and there was instant reaction to an order. As an ex-Army man I could applaud this attitude. By contrast the RAF seemed undisciplined and untidy. Most of us hadn't shaved or made any attempt to clean up. On one of those freezing winter mornings I would watch the Army Appell be over in five minutes while the RAF count would take half an hour. Nor do I remember any special instructions given to us to act like this.... We did it perhaps for the sheer hell of it."[11]

The company sergeant major reckoned the Brylcreem Boys were "an 'orrible shower, a disgrace to the uniform."

The boys in blue thought "the brown jobs" had gone over the top, kowtowing to the arrogant goons.[12]

P/O JAMES BRANFORD (149 SQUADRON, RAF). "Had we allowed it, the bullying, arrogant guards would have made life a pretty good hell. The RAF did all they could to wear them down. Turning up late on parade, talking, booing the guards whenever they kicked anyone for small offences."[13]

Appells were sometimes used by the Germans to spring surprise searches of some huts, usually during early morning parades. If this involved the RAF the men would typically be outside in the compound in deliberately disorganized hut groupings and untidy rows. Suddenly two or three truckloads of guards would arrive. Some would surround a selected group of perhaps several hundred prisoners, while the rest went to work inside the huts, carrying out spot searches, particularly of the bed spaces. They were nominally looking for any illicit or verboten items and would leave beds dismantled, personal items and even Red Cross food items strewn about, or sometimes missing.

This procedure might last an entire morning, and was very uncomfortable during the winter, and the men usually saw it as an opportunity to ensure it wouldn't be the happiest of spells for their guards either.

SERGEANT LEW PARSONS (75 SQUADRON, RNZAF). "We were on Appell one morning and because of our recalcitrant attitude were being kept on parade as punishment. One of our chaps asked if he could go to the toilet block and was given permission. As he walked behind a sentry to go up the steps of the toilets he broke a twig off a bush near the steps. In the toilet he stripped several leaves from the stem and when he came down the steps he popped the twig in the barrel of the sentry's rifle. The result was that everyone on parade was laughing and the sentry couldn't understand why until he looked up and saw the leaves sticking out of the muzzle of his gun. He wasn't amused, took the rifle off his shoulder and threatened everyone in sight, but finally decided that it was best ignored."

FRED HEATHFIELD. "Parading in fives was the normal German practice, both in the early days when we paraded inside our huts, morning and evening, and later when we paraded outside. The NCO taking the count would have a soldier who paced along the rows, saying *"Fünf, zehn, fünfzehn, zwanzig,*" to the end of the parade. He then told the NCO the number, which was entered on a sheet of paper. A second soldier counted the sick in barracks, and this was added to the count, which had to tally with the number on the barrack roll call. It rarely did.

"Once the counting soldier was past the hundred mark, someone in a middle or back row would move to one side into an empty space, or someone would bend down to tie a lace.[14] A man might even wait until counted, then crouch low and run to another place in the back row. The count had to start again. After a while two counters were used, one pacing along in front of the parade and another matching up with him at the rear. Using up extra German manpower!

"With five or six men scattered about the hut, sick, they could also dodge from bunk to bunk in the dark alleyways. By the time the RAF compound had grown to four full barracks, with eight huts on parade we could do anything we wanted with the count. It was virtually a case of the German NCO asking a hut leader, 'How many men have you got?,' and the hut leader *could* have said: 'How many would you like?' If necessary we could make the count last a couple of hours. I doubt if the Germans ever knew how many were in the RAF compound!"

The tally of air crew personnel in the Stalag continued to increase, and in September 1944, aware that their numbers were approaching 2,000, the Germans moved them to A/B North Compound. If they'd hoped this would improve their control of the Appells they were out of luck.

2

Babbelfest

They have been at a great feast of languages and stolen the scraps.
(Shakespeare, *Love's Labour's Lost*, V.*i*)

Had all the languages in Stalag IVB given tongue together they might have rivalled Babel, too. It was a remarkable fact that at least 27 nationalities were represented. English, for a start, was voiced in every possible British Isles dialectic variant (brogue, burr, BBC or Billingsgate) and in Aussie, Kiwi, Springbok vernacular and Canuck idiom, in all the accents of the Indian sub-continent, in sundry U.S. inflections, and in a medley of patois and pidgin from around the globe. Other nationals were of extraordinary diversity: Belgium, Bulgaria, China, Cyprus, Czechoslovakia, Denmark, Egypt, France, Greece, Holland, Hungary, Ireland, Italy, Mexico, Morocco, Poland, Romania, Russia (Tartars, Ukrainians, Uzbeks et al.), the Seychelles, Tahiti, Yugoslavia.

A prisoner from 1939, this Pole was a most unhappy man who, according to Ray Newell at the time he painted him, hated the Germans, detested the Russians and had no time for anyone except, rather to Ray's surprise, the British. He was even annoyed with the Warsaw rebels who had caused him to lose contact with his wife, still in that city (Ray Newell).

IN THE BEGINNING

The Poles were first, in September 1939. Later the same year came French and Belgians. During that winter as many as 100,000 of them arrived, to be processed and most sent on to work camps.

MAJOR ROBERT G. ("PADRE") MCDOWALL, SENIOR CHAPLAIN.[1] "At an inspection on June 10, 1940, the International Red Cross representative noted there were 23,000 French and Belgian POWs."

These were followed, for a short spell, by some British from the west, taken just before Dunkirk. Among them was the young Lieutenant H.V.E. Jessop, captured at the coast in May 1940. He reappears later in our story.

Dutch prisoners came next, while some RAF personnel were quartered briefly early in 1941, before being moved to a Stalag Luft.[2] The first Russians arrived in July 1941 and were held at the western end of the camp. Many had lost limbs and hobbled about on crutches, while at least one had to propel himself with his hands in a homemade wheeled contraption. By September 1941, the Stalag held 15,000 POWs, mostly French, with many Belgians, Dutch, Serbians, Russians, and 1,020 British.

PADRE MCDOWALL. "Toward the end of 1941 and the start of 1942, the east end of the camp was fenced off. This consisted of Blocks C, D and E, while A and B were for other nationalities."

About mid-1943 more RAF personnel began to arrive, finding the Stalag at this time virtually empty. Resulting from the increasingly intensive bombing of Germany during 1943, many British planes were being shot down over enemy territory. The hastily prepared Stalag Lufts were full, so crew members who survived the impact of flak or cannon shells— and not uncommonly the homi-

M. Bonneau had been confined for a month in a Straflager on bread and water for "fraternizing" with a German woman, before coming to Stalag IVB. He suffered from beri-beri, and the flesh on his face was soft and puffy (Ray Newell).

cidal intentions of vengeful Germans when rounded up on the ground — often found themselves confined in Stalags such as IVB. These bomber crews were labelled "Terror Flyers" by the Germans and were held in a special compound in the middle of the camp, initially never allowed outside it. By December 1943 the tally of RAF personnel housed in C North Compound had reached about 800.

A BREEZE FROM THE SOUTH

In a diary entry on 24 September 1943, Padre McDowall noted that the second-in-command of the Stalag had told him it held 33,000 prisoners. Bomber losses in the increasingly heavy RAF raids over Germany meant more captured air crew, while the Wehrmacht's continuing successes on the Russian front produced a chronic need for accommodation. While this enclosed environment enabled its hapless residents the opportunity to learn more of what fellow servicemen had done in civilian life, it wasn't until the British and Commonwealth army lads began to arrive at IVB in the last quarter of 1943 that the cultural situation changed dramatically. They were quartered in D Compound adjacent to the RAF, whose gate was now left open, allowing access to each other.

When Italy capitulated in September 1943, the German reaction was typically swift and decisive. As many as 600,000 former Italian soldiers were rounded up and shipped to the fatherland, to become a pool of slave workers and to be treated little better than the Russians. Some thousands of these Italians were brought to IVB and housed in tents in a compound at the far end of the camp, until most were moved out to the work sites.

The Germans were even more concerned about the considerable numbers of British, Australian, New Zealand, Indian and South African servicemen who had been held in the POW camps in Italy. These army men had almost all been captured by Rommel's forces in North Africa,

After arriving from Italy with other Commonwealth POWs, this Sikh man and his compatriots were isolated and subjected to intense propaganda by the Germans.

though some had been taken earlier in Greece and Crete and, after varying periods in generally wretched conditions at primitive transit camps, had been transported across the Mediterranean to PGs (prisoner-of-war camps) on the Italian mainland. They'd used the time there — as much as a year or more in some cases — to set up camp and barrack organizations.

The Allied lines were by then in Southern Italy, and the Germans wanted to ensure that these men didn't get back to "fight another day." Many enterprising fellows had escaped from the Italian PG or work camps, but most were hustled into cattle trucks and taken north via the Brenner Pass. From about the end of September they began to arrive at IVB, where they were quartered in D Compound.

These army servicemen quickly began establishing the systems, routines and procedures they had developed in Italy, electing Hut Commanders (usually the senior W/O or NCO), drawing up rosters for dealing with a variety of duties, and detailing representatives to meet with other compounds or bodies. With their production of camp newspapers, interhut sporting fixtures, entertainments and other activities, it was inevitable that the RAF prisoners would find their lives changed and stimulated as these new interests began to involve them. The process was accelerated when the gate between their compound and the rest of the camp was no longer kept closed.

SERGEANT S.G. ("WALLY") WOLHUTER (SOUTH AFRICAN FORCES). "As I could speak a fair amount of German and understood it well, I became one of the Dolmetschers [interpreters] in the British compounds. Whereas in Italy life generally was dull and soul-destroying, in Germany I had something positive and helpful to do and found the work interesting. It brought me into contact with all the many different nationalities including the German personnel from the commandant downwards."

By this time, during a walk along Main Street or around the perimeter, it had become almost commonplace to see uniforms from all over Europe and beyond on display, but the possibility of surprises continued, as when one passed a Bulgarian trooper, a Cameron Highlander Pipe Major, a young naval man from Holland or an older member of the Dutch merchant marine.

Gunner Ray Newell (Royal Artillery) had been an art student before the war and found the extraordinary variety in national dress and physical features irresistible: "I drew examples of every nationality in camp and got on well with them all."[3]

Some of these men must have found Ray's interest in painting them a unique period of human communion: for the sole representatives in that crowded camp from Casablanca, China, Egypt, the Seychelles, or the Uzbek from Astrakhan, the prattle of unintelligible talk around them could surely

Top Left: There was at least one camp (Marlag) for marine prisoners in Germany. It's not known how this sole Dutch sailor came to be in Stalag IVB (Ray Newell). *Top Right:* This Uzbek man had lived all his life in Astrakhan (Ray Newell). *Bottom:* A Chinese merchant marine sailor (Ray Newell).

only have increased their feelings of loneliness.

From the first the Russians were treated by the Germans as subhuman, Untermenschen, scarcely the equivalent of Jews and Gypsies. Those mobile enough were forced on minimal rations to perform the foulest, most menial jobs about the camp, were frequently brutally beaten by guards and could be shot on the slightest provocation. [4]

S.G. WOLHUTER (on Christmas 1943). "In view of the pitiful condition of the majority of Russians, we gave all our German rations for the day to them and invited Leonard, their Vertrauensmann, [5] as well as their doctor, to have tea with us in the morning. We put up a grand show with real Ceylon tea and chocolate biscuits from our extra Red Cross parcels.[6]

A few Russian prisoners, members of the most numerous and worst-treated of all the nationals in the Stalag (Terry Hunt photograph, courtesy Joe Tombling).

"In the evening ... a Russian choir came along and sang in beautiful stirring voices accompanied by balalaikas. This was followed by a performance of Georgian and Ukrainian dances, which included the splendid 'Dance of the Apple.' Their reward, apart from our enthusiastic applause, was a meal for every performer contributed by the inmates of our hut."

SERGEANT CYRIL G. JENKINS (Royal Armoured Corps). "Twenty-three Russian officers excite our sympathy; they declared themselves as 'Other Ranks' on capture, with the intention of effecting escapes; we are taking it in turns to provide them with some extras."

THE WARSAW UPRISING

In August 1944 the Polish resistance in Warsaw rose against the Germans. The Poles were certain that the Russian army, now on the east bank of the Vistula, would support them, but Stalin had a different agenda, and the Russians did nothing, watching unmoved while Warsaw was destroyed and vast numbers of its inhabitants were massacred. The resistance battled heroically for 63 days until starved into surrender.

Polish women rebels at their barracks in Warsaw, 1944 (courtesy Lew Parsons).

On 2 November a group of about 1,200 Polish girls and women, aged from 12 to 50, began arriving in Stalag IVB, having been forced to march several kilometres in foul weather from the station. They had been resistance fighters in Warsaw and most were still in their uniforms. They were starving, wet and cold, but were not prepared to appear dispirited and were singing as they entered the camp.

They were crowded into a small transit compound near the guards' barracks, which was short of bedding and with generally poor facilities. As soon as was practical, the British and Polish prisoners began collecting food and other articles for the girls and women. One enterprising POW named Adelstein bought rings, brushes, a manicure set and other items from the women and showed these round the huts. At the RAF compound the men contributed 1,500 cigarettes, chocolate, soap and other articles and sent the lot back to the women. When the British Man of Confidence, with the permission of the camp commandant, delivered these gifts to the Polish women, they swiped all his buttons for souvenirs.

Yvonn Lucyna Kozakiewicz was 18 when, as a member of the Resistance before the uprising, she was carrying messages and hiding weapons at her home. On one occasion, when the Germans came to search the house, she removed the weapons from under her bed, hid them under her pillow and lay against it. The Germans did not look there, perhaps, as Yvonn believes, because she appeared very young for her age. She did not know then that her mother was also working for the Resistance and hastily had to hide weapons, too.

During the uprising Yvonn was a corporal in a unit known as "the 330th." At this stage the carrying of messages could involve travelling via

Yvonn Lucyna Kozakiewicz, Vis automatic at her belt, with two fellow Polish resistance fighters Warsaw, August 1944 (courtesy Gaynor Greenwood).

the sewers as one of the safer ways of getting about. Inevitably the Germans discovered this and, lifting the manhole covers, would call down in Polish to try to lure the resistance fighters. Tending the wounded was another of Yvonn's jobs.[7]

Following surrender, the Resistance fighters were badly treated by the Germans and very hungry. Their spirit remained unbroken, and one of their captors remarked that if German women were like these Poles, Germany would soon rule the world.

FREDERICK HEDGES. "One girl of 16 had been wounded 22 times. A Polish prisoner in the camp met his wife among them, the first time he had seen her for five years.[8]

"They left the camp yesterday afternoon in trucks, to the accompaniment of rousing cheers from the British, French and Polish prisoners here."

As they were cheering many chaps wondered what fate awaited these gallant women and girls. These were not the only captives from the Polish capital brought into IVB.

SERGEANT NORMAN F. PAGE (78 Squadron, RAF). "About 250 Polish boys, ages ranging from approx. 9 to 19, arrived on 22 November 1944. They were in a pitiful state. Again we were able to help with food handouts."

PADRE McDOWALL (22 November 1944). "Bandy [a German guard] was busy sorting up to about 250 Poles from Warsaw, of whom 116 were 15 and under—and one 8 years old!"

During the following month about 1,500 members of the Danish police force were brought in. They were tall, blond, fit-looking fellows who had been involved in a mistimed revolt in Denmark. Despite bringing lavish supplies of food parcels with them, and receiving at intervals more sent overland, they were not prepared for the tough conditions of camp life in that hard winter and many fell ill, victims of the various maladies.

YANKEE DOODLE DANDY

The counterassault launched in the west by von Runstedt on 16 December 1944 was both well-planned and a surprise. Facing him in the Ardennes were largely untried American troops and, in driving a wedge 45 miles deep toward Liège in cold and foggy conditions he took several thousands of them prisoner. During this action, which came to be known as the Battle of the Bulge, Larry Falstein was in the vicinity of Bastogne and recalls it vividly: "The Germans overran two American infantry divisions on December 16, 1944, divisions that were either brand new like the 106th that had just come on the line a few days before, or the 28th, which had been devastated the month before in the Hürtgen Forest and was sent to the Luxembourg border to rest, recuperate and be reinforced. I was lucky being in the 110th Regiment of the 28th Division."

KURT VONNEGUT. "The shelling stopped, and a hidden German with a loudspeaker told the Americans to put their weapons down and come out of the woods with their hands on the top of their heads, or the shelling would start again. It wouldn't stop until everybody in there was dead."

Von Runstedt's offensive proved effectively to be the last counterattack the Germans were able to make in the west. It was halted at Monschau and Bastogne, and six weeks later the Allied line was again complete. This was of no benefit to the U.S. prisoners, however, as the immense tactical and transport problems now faced by the Germans and the bitter winter conditions resulted in grim experiences for many of them. They were taken across Germany with little food or hot drink, sometimes on long marches in the intense winter cold, sometimes by rail in closed freight cars with the most primitive sanitation.

Corporal Ervin Szpek Sr., of Company 1, 3rd Battalion, 423rd Regiment, U.S. 106th Infantry Division, tells of marching until nightfall and sleeping in a field. There was no food or water, only snow to eat. He recalled: "The following day was more of the same. We came across one of our tanks that had been destroyed. Next to it was an ambulance. The soldier on the stretcher was dead, along with two medics who were carrying him. All were missing their socks and shoes. It was quite an ordinary sight to see the Germans with our equipment, from boots to tanks.

"I saw other frozen casualties and there were rumors that the Germans were executing prisoners. We were worried."[9]

One day during their eastward trek Szpek and his group passed a launch area for V-1 flying bombs and also glimpsed an Me262 in flight. This early jet was the fastest thing they had seen. He continued: "Again we marched until dark and slept in a barnyard. The following morning we arrived at a rail station and received food for the first time. Our meal was a piece of bread, with sawdust as an ingredient and a bowl of watered-down turnip soup."[10]

GEORGE K. ZAK (also of U.S. 106th Division). "Our train arrived at a dismal, grim-looking prisoner-of-war camp known by the Germans as Stalag IVB. It was surrounded by a high barbed wire fence and wooden guard towers and searchlights."

On December 23, 1944, snow lay thick about the camp. It was another harshly cold day in the most rigorous of winters for many years.

POWs looking out late that afternoon were surprised to see a long column of men streaming through the main gate. These were allies of theirs, Americans, and, as they were crowded into the Vorlager, many seemed close to collapse.

Though the British in the Stalag were aware via "the grapevine"[11] that Americans were on their way to IVB they had not known the numbers involved nor the severity of the privations they had suffered during their journey eastward. Nor was their ordeal finished, as they were left overnight in the Vorlager, where they could only sit in the snow. Some did not survive that bitter night.

During the previous three months or so the men in the RAF compound had been carefully saving articles from their food parcels—virtually starving themselves along the way—in preparation for a mighty feast at Christmas. They'd intended this to be spread over most of the day and to relish every mouthful.

Next day, Christmas Eve, the Americans were moved into the already overcrowded huts in the camp. The British doubled up on the bunks, freeing up others onto which the new arrivals could slump. The RAF men were shocked by their condition and immediately did whatever they could to help them. Later, in a critical meeting, they debated whether to go ahead with their planned Christmas dinner or forgo it and hand their carefully hoarded food to the Americans.

There were a few dissenting voices suggesting "give half, keep half," but in the end the "give all" vote was overwhelming. The RAF boys knew in their hearts that the Americans needed it so much more, and the store of food was distributed to them. They quickly disposed of it.[12]

George K. Zak and Kurt Vonnegut recorded accounts of this remarkably warm welcome, but unfortunately, for many of the new arrivals in their debilitated state, its richness proved too much.

KURT VONNEGUT describes the subsequent scene at the outside latrine: "[this] … consisted of a one-rail fence with twelve buckets underneath it (and) was crammed with Americans who had taken their pants down. The welcome feast had made them as sick as volcanoes. The buckets were full or had been kicked over."

Some time later Vonnegut noticed men digging holes for upright timbers near the prison hospital: "Englishmen were building themselves a new latrine. They had abandoned their old latrine to the Americans—and their theater, the place where the feast had been held, too."

S.G. WOLHUTER. "The British and American compounds were under the overall control of a Vertrauensmann, or Man-of-Confidence, who was officially recognised by the detaining power as our representative and spokesman. He had authority to deal with both Germans and the International Red Cross in Switzerland.

"Our man was Warrant Officer Meyers of the RAF, a Canadian who was nicknamed 'Snowshoes.' A few hundred RAF crews shot down over Europe had arrived in camp before us and that is how … Snowshoes became the Man-of-Confidence, a position he retained up to the end of the war."

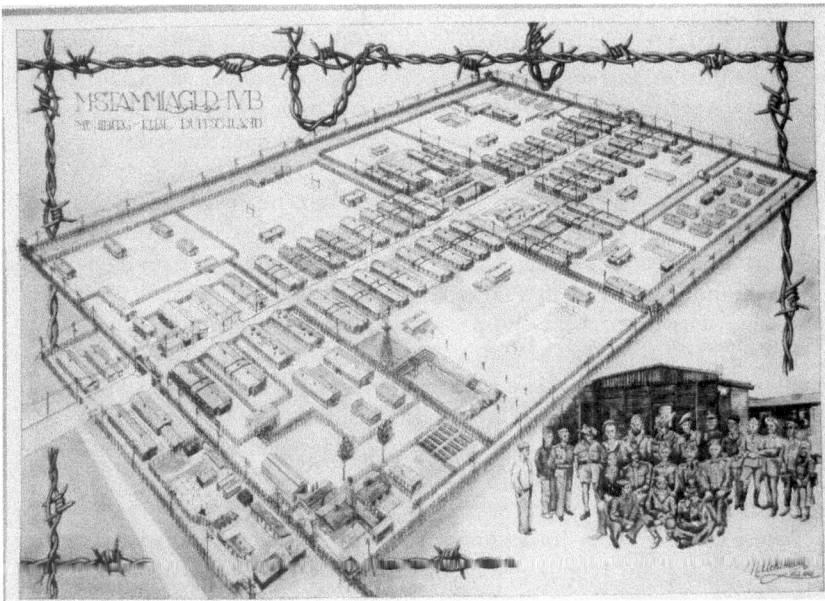

The Dutch artist N. Uchtmann completed the large color original of this diagram in March 1945 and took orders and payment for it from other POWs on the basis that he would supply their copies postwar. They duly received true facsimiles after their return home. Examples of most of the nationals in Stalag IVB are depicted at lower right (courtesy Lew Parsons).

A few observations on the international passing show:

S.G. WOLHUTER. "Oberfeldwebel Ulbrich, a crusty First World War character who disliked anything non-German and in particular the British habit of slouching around with their hands in their pockets, once remarked that: 'The Dutch walk around the camp as if they own it. The French walk around as if they would like to own it. The English walk around as if they don't care a damn who owns it!'"

PADRE MCDOWALL. "Here comes a wagon pushed by about a dozen Russians with ash cans ... there two Dutchmen, an Italian, two more Russians, looking in my window with a "What have you got to give me" look, some chaps off to a football match with a stool on which to stand or sit; four Russians with barbed wire to do some mending on a fence, two Frenchmen to the office next door, a little Italian, two more Dutch, two French, two English chaps pulling a little cart, a Dutchman in clogs, a German, a bunch of Russians and two Germans, about 1,200 English carrying empty Red Cross boxes—Canadian—to the German stores, a party of Italians, a flashily dressed sergeant with a homemade hat."

GUNNER RAY NEWELL, on another of his portrait subjects. "Malych taught at Minsk University, spoke very good English, but said he had never heard an Englishman speak before. He asked if he could sit in and listen to colloquial English in the barrack room. I don't know what good it did for his vocabulary but it was very useful to me to have a permanent private interpreter!"

CSM RICHARD HALL (4th Battalion, the Green Howards) has this anecdote about conversations with a French friend and a Russian doctor: "I thought in English, translated it into French, Henri translated my French into German, the doctor took that German into Russian, and so on.... Often we ended up in laughter as the end product did not make any sense!"

SERGEANT SAM GILLETTE (C Company, 242nd Combat Infantry Regiment, U.S. 42 Division). "The Ghurkas were astonishing in their tenacity, insisting on cooking their own food over outside fires. The Russians would try to cast a shadow over this. The idea was that the meal would then be discarded because it was befouled."

After the Americans had settled in, GEORGE K. ZAK noted the layout of the camp and the variety of its inmates: "During daylight hours we were free to roam the British compound.... The camp was overloaded, and included about 8,000 British, 4,000 American, and 10,000 prisoners of other nationalities. The British prisoners came from not just England but from Scotland, Wales, Northern Ireland, Australia, Canada, New Zealand and elsewhere...."

3

The Commissariat

"*If only it were as easy,*" he said, "*to banish hunger by rubbing the belly.*"
(In Diogenes Laertius, *Lives of Eminent Philosophers*, "Diogenes," ca. A.D. 230)

THE FOOD

OFFICIAL REPORT (WO 208/3274) *Secret Camp Histories*—Stalag IVB.[1] "The food started by being good and sufficient; all the cooking was done in a huge central kitchen on great brick stoves. There were large, well-stocked canteens, but by January 1942 things had deteriorated greatly and the camp was isolated owing to a suspicion of typhus. There was no canteen at all and the lighting which hitherto had been normal was very poor indeed, and the water supply was extremely insufficient. This may have been due to 1,665 Ors [2] being lodged there while at working camps, who overlapped with 1,863 RAF who were shortly leaving for an RAF camp. 167 Indian NCOs were also sent there for punishment because they refused to do camp work at Annaburg. All these extra men overcrowded the camp considerably. They were sleeping in three-tier bunks with only one blanket."

Agreement among the 47 signatories to the 1929 Geneva International Convention had provided not only that prisoners of war were to be confined in conditions not inferior to the standards applicable in their captors' own base camps, but were also to be supplied with food rations of similar standard. Payments in the holding powers' currencies were to be made to all prisoners. High ideals had informed the agreement in respect of these and other provisions. A decade and more on, in the reality of war, precept and praxis would often prove different.

Typical German rations issued from the kitchen: A few small potatoes five or six times per week, boiled.

Soup, made usually of millet or occasionally, barley, pumpkin or tomato and, once a week, pea soup — always the most sought after, the only kind tasty and filling.

Margarine: a small issue used mainly for cooking.

Bread: a 2,000 gm loaf daily among five to seven men. This was that famous staple Scharzbrot, asserted by the Germans as sehr nahrhaft [3] despite the obvious nature of much of its content.

The following recipe is reputed to be quoted from the official records of the Food Providing Ministry published (top secret) Berlin 24 November 1941, the ministry directors Herr Mansfeld and Herr Moritz having agreed that the best mixture for the baking of black bread was:

50 percent bruised rye grain
20 percent sliced sugar beets
20 percent tree flour (sawdust)
10 percent minced leaves and straw

At least one POW claimed to have seen bits of glass and sand in his bread.

Sometimes there was cheese, but the German cheese was commonly viewed with suspicion and in the view of many men, should be approached with caution. Often rancid with maggots, the cheese was eaten by some, notwithstanding.

SAM GILLETTE. "The cheese—yellow strips with white topping—was so strong the smell went upwind! We didn't get much, but we ate it."

More often it bore a passing resemblance to a small rissole. Once the rubbery outer layer was removed the most revolting stink was released and — even holding their noses — many fellows weren't up to eating it, even at their hungriest. Fred Heathfield has recalled that it used to be said that no one needed bother collecting the cheese issue: "You just whistled and it crawled over to you! We did experiment with it by toasting it and frying it, but it made very little difference."

Perhaps three days per week, with luck, there was an issue of meat paste — a couple of kilos to 30 men. The tea, if any, was herbal — ersatz, anyway, usually lukewarm and tasteless. The coffee was slightly more palatable, though made from roasted acorns.

WARRANT OFFICER A.F. ("ANDY") ANDERSON, RAF. "Disciplining how we ate what little we did get was essential, not only to our morale, but also to our health. Eating everything when we got it would mean having nothing at all for long periods."

On a few occasions an opportunity to augment the monotonous diet with meat in some form might present itself to anyone quick enough off the mark to seize it.

3—The Commissariat

FRED HEATHFIELD. "Once I was walking behind a Frenchman who turned a corner into the passage between two huts. The grain was being harvested beyond the wire and a hare ran into the camp and across the far end of the passage. The Frenchman's reaction was instant. He bent down, pulled off one of his heavy wooden clogs and hurled it at the hare, killing it stone dead. Then he ran forward and picked it up, to bear it triumphantly back to his hut!"

JAMES BRANFORD. "In the next barracks to us they got so desperate that they killed a cat and ate it."

FREDERICK HEDGES. "There used to be, running around the camp, lots of cats. It's a very significant fact that these cats are now conspicuous by their absence."

FRED HILL. "Timimi, the three-legged dog brought from Italy, turned up with a litter of puppies. Unfortunately she strayed into the Russian compound and was eaten."

Clearly neither the number of its legs nor the nature of the beast affected the Russians' taste for dog. The Germans were rash enough one evening to turn a couple of their fierce Alsatian dogs loose in the Russian compound. The furious barking with which they set about their work was abruptly switched off, leaving only silence. Next morning two pelts hung on the compound fence.[4]

The Russians were by now the largest national group in the camp, also the hungriest, and would go to any lengths to obtain food, often taking considerable risks in the process.

PADRE McDOWALL. "There were several Russians yesterday at one of the tin dumps, peering eagerly into the old tins, running a finger round them and sucking off whatever they got.

"A Russian went tearing by just now, hugging his food can, an Italian dixie tied to his belt behind. Hunger drives them anywhere. They go past the window—a young lad has just gone by in rags—one after the other. A German sentry is roaring, another has come along on a bicycle and has caught a Russian, taking him off to the stand nearby. Those they catch have to stand from one to six or seven hours."

The supply of clothing was an ongoing problem and by August 1943, when other conditions, including the water supply, had improved, the stocks of items such as uniforms, underwear and shoes were being exhausted by the growing influx of prisoners being transferred from camps in Italy, as well as the increasing numbers of RAF personnel. The situation was aggravated by a frequent lack of agreement between the Man of Confidence (nominally in control of all materials coming via the International Red Cross) and the German NCO in charge of distribution.

FLIGHT SERGEANT JACK DAVIS, 429 Squadron, RCAF: "Our flying boots were taken off us and we were given wooden clogs. Six months later the Red Cross sent us some shoes."

TOM NELSON. "We were starving and had only the clothes we were shot down in. Many of us did not even have shoes....

"Clothing, blankets, etc., began to arrive around November 1943 and from then onwards we were reasonably warm and dressed."

THE INTERNATIONAL RED CROSS

Neutral Switzerland, home to *le Comité International de la Croix-Rouge*,[5] based at Geneva, was known as the Protecting Power. In 1929 a revision of the original Geneva Convention of 1864 extended its coverage to prisoners of war and the safeguarding of their rights to humanitarian treatment. At the time World War II began the convention had been ratified by nearly 100 countries, including all of the British Commonwealth and European countries, the United States, and many Asian states, but not the U.S.S.R.

In Germany the work of the International Red Cross, which extended almost from the beginning of hostilities until the end, covered regular if infrequent visits by its representatives to all Stalags and the reporting to the international committee on the conditions and the treatment of those held there. More importantly, it arranged the supply of commodities of extraordinary diversity to the prisoner-of-war camps.[6] The distribution of food parcels alone, to the camps spread throughout Germany, responsible as it was for the saving of innumerable lives, surely amounted at the time to an almost incredible feat of logistics. It required the active cooperation of the German authorities and, while they knew that, for the sake of their servicemen in allied hands, the system needed to work both ways, it is fair to say that such cooperation was forthcoming for most of the period and in most areas.

Only during the final months of the war, as the toll from bombing and the inevitable strain on German transport resources were being felt, did the distribution begin to falter. By that time, too, the dwindling reserves of many commodities throughout Germany inevitably caused an escalation of pilfering wherever opportunities occurred.

S.G. WOLHUTER. "Red Cross food and cigarette parcels came in sealed trucks from Geneva in Switzerland and were accompanied by guards from the German border to the various camps. Yet, despite the strict precautions, some cigarette parcels had invariably disappeared by the time they reached the camp."

Food parcels were often similarly affected.

3—The Commissariat

Copie conforme

ARCHIVES DU CICR

STALAG IV B (Mühlberg)

visité le 14 mai 1941 par Descoeudres-Exchaquet

Commandant du camp : Oberstlt. Sperl.
Homme de confiance : Adj.-chef Lamothe Armand, No 4073.

Fonction du camp

    Le Stalag, autrefois vaste camp avec nombreux Détachements de Travail, comptant près de cent mille hommes, a été transformé depuis le 1 février 41 : il n'est plus qu'un "Sammellager", c'est-à-dire un camp de rassemblement pour plusieurs catégories de prisonniers : sous-officiers, sanitaires, prêtres, malades devant être rapatriés, etc. Tous les Kommandos qui étaient régis par ce camp ont été rattachés à de nouveaux Stalags (IV A, C, D, E, F, G), dits "Schattenlager" ou camps de passage (voir à ce sujet les rapports détaillés de ces divers camps).

Situation

    Le camp de Mühlberg est un grand Stalag classique, et de taille gigantesque. Il ne compte pas moins de 44 baraques, pouvant abriter chacune de 350 à 380 hommes. Sa capacité maximale est de 13.000 hommes. Les baraques sont alignées des deux côtés d'une allée centrale, dans une vaste plaine, et à 5 kilomètres de la ville de Mühlberg, au sud-est de Leipzig. Il est très bien entretenu, propre et manque totalement de charme !

Effectif

    Le 14 mai 41, le Stalag abrite 5666 prisonniers, dont 4714 sont Français. Parmi ceux-ci se trouvent 3030 sous-officiers, 11 médecins et 58 sanitaires.

    Mais bien d'autres nationalités sont représentées :

    962 Serbes   )
     39 Belges   )   AYANT COMBATTU
     97 Polonais   )   AVEC L'ARMEE
     52 Ukrainiens   )   POLONAISE.
     21 Russes blancs)

Red Cross document, 14 May 1941: Page 1 of a typical report as made by an International Red Cross representative. Inspections of all prison camps were carried out on a near-annual basis and covered several aspects in addition to numbers, living conditions, rations and health care (courtesy ICRC, Geneva).

FREDERICK HEDGES. "We have learnt that, with the Red Cross food parcel each week, a man can live fairly well on these rations; but, without the parcel, health and strength would very quickly be at zero."

The English parcels, packed in different towns, had some variety of content, but generally those from New Zealand, Canada, the United States, Scotland and so on — while different from each other — followed standard content patterns. So-called "bulk" issues, derived from foodstuffs collected by British residents in Argentina and sent via the Red Cross, were also made from time to time.

Over the course of several months Sergeants Norman Page (78 Squadron) and Fred Heathfield (51 Squadron) RAF, noted the contents of some Red Cross food parcels:

American "A" parcel	*English parcel*
1 pound powdered milk (Klim)	1 large Nestlé'(s milk
1/2 pound sugar	2 ounces sugar, 2 ounces tea, 4 ounces cocoa
1 small tin butter	1/2 pound margarine or butter
1 tin liver paté	1 tin meat and vegetables
1 tin peaches	1 tin meat roll or bacon
1 tin orange jelly	1 tin salmon or pilchards
1 tin dehydrated onions	1 tin vegetables (peas, carrots, etc.)
1 tin dehydrated corned beef hash	1 tin egg powder or flakes
1 packet breakfast cereal	1 tin midlothian oats
1 packet biscuits	1 tin service biscuits
1 packet bouillon cubes	1 small jam or syrup
2 packets chewing gum	1 packet fruit (prunes, apricots, etc.)
3 packets noodle soup	1 bar chocolate
2 packets egg powder	1 tin cheese
1 bottle multivitamin pills	1 small pudding
1 tin opener	1 packet custard or Yorkshire pudding mixture

Canadian parcel	*Indian parcel*
1 tin "Cowbell" milk	1 tin milk (Nestlé'(s or full cream)
1 packet sugar	2 blocks sugar
1 pound butter	1/2 pound margarine
1 tin salmon	1 tin pilchards
1 tin corned beef	1 packet rice
1 tin sardines	1 tin curry
1 tin York roll	1 packet flour
8 ounces prunes	1 tin celery cuts
1 packet biscuits	1 tin biscuits
12 ounces raisins	1 tin lentils
1 pound jam	1 tin peas or carrots
1 block cheese	1 tin pineapple crush
1 packet tea	1 packet sultanas
1 packet salt	1 bar chocolate
1 block soap	2 ounces tea
100 cigarettes	1 bar soap

3—The Commissariat

MUCKERS

This extraordinary by-product of POW life came about because of the need, under these straitened circumstances, to ensure maximum benefit from the available resources, especially food. Fundamentally a British term, "muckers" implies very close mates, and it became an affiliation common to all POWs everywhere. Usually two, sometimes three or four, men pooled their food and worked out a series of menus generally for a week at a time.

The mucker relationship was based on trust and often developed strong familylike ties. Everything was shared — not merely food, clothing, and that prime currency, cigarettes, but also news from home, hopes for the future, physical or mental problems arising from confinement as POWs, in fact their innermost thoughts, until the life of each group member was like an open book to the others.

This Russian partisan had been captured by the Germans in the Pripet Marshes early in 1942. Looking much older than his 50 years, he had a job clearing the night latrines in the camp (Ray Newell).

Inevitably there were tiffs or quarrels, occasionally even the breaking up of an alliance — and extremely distressing for the parties this would be. But the bonds were usually very strong, enduring until the end of confinement and frequently lasting far beyond.

One air crew group of four muckers — Lew Parsons, Dougie Box, Bob Quelch and Dick Benham — was known as "the Bubbly Boys," arising from a ditty composed for it by Bob:

> We are the Bubbly Boys,
> We share our troubles, share our joys;
> When we're in trouble or in doubt
> We all shout
> "Whoop my old bubbly, aye aye!"

TOM NELSON reports on one of many useful devices conjured up by the brilliant Eric Gargini.[7] "Gargini also came up with what we called 'the element.' This was a small tin can with a piece of wood stuck in the bottom of it. One wire went to the side of the can and the other was attached to the

Germans opening/censoring parcels in the postal depot located near the Main Gate. Some POWs stand by, ready to collect their goods (Terry Hunt photograph, courtesy RAF Museum, Hendon).

wood. When dropped into a Klim tin of water it would boil in a couple of minutes, so we all took turns to use it. I am still at a loss to understand how the huts did not burn down. The fuse wire had been replaced with a strand of barbed wire and the circuits were terribly overloaded. Gargini must have been even more of an expert than we imagined!"

At one stage, believing they could prevent their prisoners from conserving food to assist them in escapes, the Germans decided to puncture all tins received in food parcels. This meant everything had to be eaten immediately, or the contents would go bad. The procedure was applied for some weeks and only after a number of strong representations made by the Man of Confidence was it discontinued.

PADRE McDOWALL (mid–February 1945). "The atmosphere of the camp has changed much and Russians, who were earlier booted about by the Germans, are becoming very cocky ... raiding the supply wagons of potatoes and turnips as they come down the road."

RAY NEWELL'S remarkable range of sketches and paintings in the Stalag includes several Russians. He recalled: "Novachenkov—cheery driver of the

3—The Commissariat

MENU and RATION SCALE for W/E APRIL 8th, 1945

ARTICLE	GRAM PER WEEK PER MAN	EASTER MONDAY MON	TUE	WED	THUR	FRID	SAT	SUN
MEAT (FRESH or TINNED BRAWN or SOUSE)	222	-	30	50/25	30	30	30	47
COOKING FAT	60	9	8	9	8	9	8	9
POTATOES	2000	-	400	400	400	-	400	400
TURNIP	500	-	-	500	-	-	-	-
DRIED VEG.	105	-	35	-	35	-	35	-
FRESH VEG	530	-	-	-	-	-	-	530
PEAS	150	75	-	-	-	75	-	-
RYE FLOUR	122	50	-	11	-	50	-	11
MARGARINE	133	-	30	28	30	-	18	30
COFFEE	15·5	2	2·5	2	2·5	2	2·5	2
BREAD	1950	400	200	250	250	400	200	250
CHEESE	41·6	-	-	-	-	-	-	41·6
SUGAR	155	20	20	20	25	20	25	25
TEA	6·3	·9	·9	·9	·9	·9	·9	·9
JAM	155	80	-	-	-	-	75	-
" (back issue)	200	-	-	100	-	100	-	-
SALT	70	10	10	10	10	10	10	10
TOTAL PER MAN/WEEK	6512·4							

E. BUSHELL.
1.4.45 Stalag IVB, MÜHLBERG/ELBE, GERMANY.   HUT 'Q' 50B
N.B. If BRAWN 50gr, if PASTE 25gr

Chart scrupulously prepared by prisoner E. Bushell just a fortnight before liberation, showing the German rations being supplied at the time (courtesy Lew Parsons).

'Bombay Belle'[8] sewage cart drawn by one mule and a cow. He and a man from Siberia did a lot of trading while they spread the sewage on the neighbouring farms—bringing in fresh vegetables and bread."

Understandably the guards kept their distance from the Scheissenwagen, and these Russians developed a system for smuggling food into the camp, using the empty tank, which the guards weren't keen to investigate closely.

S.G. WOLHUTER. "Although forbidden, a great deal of bread was bartered off the Germans, but some loaves were suspended inside the tank of the Scheissenwagen by string and transported that way. Whether they were wrapped in paper or not is difficult to say, but we hoped so!"
CORPORAL JOE TOMBLING (12 March 1945): "Danish police have given each hut six or eight tins of milk. Very good of them."

JOE TOMBLING (7 April 1945): "On vegetable fatigue instead of coal fatigue. Pushed cart down to Mühlberg and brought it back loaded with swedes and turnips. Eight men to a cart (und ein posten). Managed to smuggle in 10 potatoes and half turnip in slices. One or two chaps were caught at it and put in clink."

A member of the military branch of OGPU, a Soviet anti-insurgency organization, eventually absorbed into the NKVD. Few of these men survived either the Germans when captured, or the Russians, with whom they were very unpopular. This fellow worked all week in the camp factory and only put on his uniform on Sundays (Ray Newell).

4

A Half-Life

In power of others, never in my own;
Scarce half I seem to live ...
                    (John Milton, *Samson Agonistes*)

FEELINGS

Illogical as it may seem, many servicemen made prisoners of war felt a strong sense of shame. They had allowed themselves to fall into the hands of the enemy and were at his mercy. Worse, being unable to continue with their duties as fighting men, they were letting down their comrades in the field and, somehow also, their families at home.

Reaching Stalag IVB they found the oppressive atmosphere generated by the massively bridged entrance, the double barbed wire fences, the uniformed guards, and the searchlight towers manned by machine-gunners. The drab barrack buildings only emphasized the reality of their situation.

Then there was the sight of their fellow prisoners—those who had been there longest, and especially the Russians—ragged and emaciated images of neglected humanity, who offered the new arrivals no lift to the spirit.

RAF air crew initially found it more difficult as a rule to adjust to prison camp conditions than army men, who had been accustomed to living rough in the open while campaigning through the countryside. RAF men had been living with few restrictions, eating well and sleeping comfortably on base in England. Then, when shot down over Germany, they were thrust in violent contrast into the extreme austerity of Stalag life.

TOM NELSON. "A sacking mattress filled with straw and one thin blanket each. There was one cold tap to wash with. Other than that one shower a month was the ration. We were lousy, literally. In summer it was just about tolerable. In winter it was smelly, filthy and muddy. Snow melted, boots cluttering up the place and it was desperately cold."[1]

It several respects it was not so different for the many thousands of U.S. servicemen captured later in the Battle of the Bulge. They'd hardly had time to become used to living in the field before finding themselves force-marched or transported in miserable conditions halfway across Germany to life behind the wire.

Reactions to prison camp life could range from gloomy thoughts to desperate acts contemplated or carried out.

FREDERICK HEDGES. "Can think of nothing else but our reunion with our families these days, and make all sorts of plans for our rehabilitation into the postwar world. It's not going to be easy after three years of this life, living like dogs in a half square mile of barbed wire."

CORPORAL REG ("MICKEY") READ (8th Battalion, Royal Tank Regiment). "We sat up in our beds and wished each other 'Happy Christmas.' Sitting near me was a sergeant major from the Royal Artillery, with tears in his eyes. He was a much older man than me. I said 'Cheer up Sar'nt Major, we'll be home by next Christmas.'

"He looked at me with his watery eyes and said, 'Mick, I'm just thinking of my kiddies undoing their Christmas stockings.'"

The wait for letters from home often seemed endless, and sometimes it might have been better if they'd never come: *"I suppose you're having a good rest there, while the heroes are still fighting."*

Some letters were insensitive enough to unbalance even the most stoical or indomitable spirits:

"Forget we're engaged. I'm having this other chap's baby soon."

FREDERICK HEDGES. "An old member of our hut attempted to cut his throat yesterday. Fortunately he never made a proper job of it. He is now in hospital."

A.F. ANDERSON. "Another sad occasion was early on the morning of 19 March 1944, when a South African soldier was found hanging in one of the washrooms."

Yet, despite the severity of camp life, the Spartan rations, the tenacious lice, the fierce bed bugs, unhygienic conditions and all the rest, many men could see that it would suit the Germans well if poor morale and despondency were prevalent among their captives. "Let's not make things easier for them" became a developing philosophy, a reversal of attitude.

FRED HILL gives his description of Christmas 1943. "After a fancy hat competition, there was a cake competition—the cakes being made from bread crumbs. Following a Zulu dance by the South Africans, Father Christ-

Inside Hut 53B, where decorations (mostly cut from Red Cross tins) were being prepared for Christmas 1943. Ray Newell mentioned that his 'studio' is at left, middistance, with an RAF type waiting to be drawn (Ray Newell).

mas was carried into the hut in a Red Cross container by four men dressed as fairies, their qualification ... being that they had the biggest feet!"

Decorations for the tree had been supplied by the "tin bashers"—stars and other shapes cut from Red Cross tins—and, like manna from heaven, a mass of tinfoil strips dropped by the RAF on a night flight to confuse the German radar.

FRED HILL. "As we celebrated Christmas, I was able to accompany the carol singing on a new accordion sent out from England by the Red Cross."

SGT. FRED HEATHFIELD. "We had to have two firewatchers awake all night in each hut, so card-players often took on this duty. The Germans occasionally checked to see they were alert. One night a German officer came into the hut for this purpose. In the darkness he spotted the glow of a cigarette on a top bunk. He yanked the offender to the ground and marched him, stark naked, along the street to the main gate.

"He ordered the prisoner to stand under the great archway, guarded by the two Postens in the sentry boxes at the side. It was a freezing cold night and the poor chap had to stay there about six hours, jumping up and down and flinging his arms about to try to keep his circulation going. The sentries in their heavy coats stood in large boots of straw to keep their feet warm, but even they were freezing and took pity on him, allowing him to stand inside one of the boxes when there were no patrols about. He returned to the hut about 6 a.m. absolutely blue and expecting a lot of sympathy from his neighbours. He got none.

"Soon after he had been marched away, one of the firewatchers saw smoke and flames rising from his empty bunk. He had dropped his cigarette into his blanket. The firewatchers now sprang into action as firefighters. Grabbing buckets of water they flung them onto the top bunk and put out the flames. They also thoroughly soaked the two men underneath and the man alongside the smoker, and these were not very welcoming when he got back."

"There was another bunk accident when Big Jim Klim, a giant of an Australian, fell through his diminished bedboards and crashed through the two lower bunks, breaking an arm and not doing much good to the two unfortunates below him. Jim was a keen knitter, begging old socks and sweaters to unravel for his great project, a six-foot by four-foot map of Australia, in relief, for a winter blanket. His needles were lengths of straightened barbed wire from the hut windows. He had been taught knitting at a little bush school where the girls knitted while the boys did gardening. Jim said he was too lazy to be interested in gardening so he opted for the knitting!"

Then there were offerings such as these satirical verses produced by the camp's poet, "Ruddyot Klimtin."[2]

LAGER LAMENT[3]
(Inspired by a well-known poet and author)

Achtung! Kriegsgefangenen.
Here for you I have ze "gen"

First—salute *mein offiziers*,
Or unpleasantness occurs.

Nein! You shall not promenade
On my lovely boulevard;
If along it you must come,
March in fünfs and not ze scrum.

Now we leave ze winter cruel
I shall give you nichts more fuel;
And at ten when lights go aus,
Go to bed and hunt ze louse.

Mit die Ruskies deals you made.
Stop them—give my guards ze trade.
I must have ze box, Cross, Red,
Makes good sawdust for your bread.

Do not tease my Posten brave
Ja, they've one foot in der grave;
But if you are aus after eight
Some dim bugger might shoot straight.

Maybe freedom you would like
But do not climb ze wire and hike.
If to fight again you dare
Be a St. George legionnaire.[4]

Then we find you hero's place
Mit das great brave master-race
In Valhalla's lofty halls ...
Was ist das you answer? (Gepruft!).

HEALTH CARE[5]

The Lazarett, or military hospital, at Stalag IVB was located outside at a prudently isolated distance from the main gate, on the road toward Mühlberg village. This was used for cases of serious illness. Inside, near the gate, was the Revier, or sick bay, intended for those with less severe complaints or those recuperating.

It had become clear, from the time of the earliest outbreaks of diphtheria and typhus, that the physical restrictions of camp life, the mixture of nationalities and the ever-increasing numbers held there would foster ideal conditions for further epidemics. From the end of 1943, cases of typhus and diphtheria were reported. On the advice of medical staff, and with the aim of preventing an epidemic the German administration banned entertainments and all gatherings. Much activity in the camp ground to a halt.

JOHN MCMILLAN of RTR was one of a team of advertising men who had been discussing ways of using their talents to the general advantage. This seemed a real opportunity to make a constructive start.

"Our advertising men lost no time. Cooperating with the Senior British Medical Officer, they planned a campaign comprising a two-way appeal—on the one hand stressing the unwelcome quarantining restrictions, on the other giving practical health hints drawn up by the medical men.

"A terrifying lay figure, '*Mr GERM,*' was introduced in posters and advertisements in the camp press, which consisted of hand-done newspapers and magazines on public show. Striking posters appeared inside and outside the barrack huts, and a huge coloured hoarding, reading 'Cleanliness—Fresh Air—Exercise—Keep You Fit' was erected on the main road through the camp.

"There was a perceptible influence on men's habits, keeping them outdoors and keen on such things as open windows and scrupulously clean barracks. It brought results. Six weeks later the situation had eased so much that the quarantining ban could be lifted.

"Later in the year another threat to health developed with the warm weather. This time it was dysentery, and publicity set out to deal with the chief carrier, the common fly.

"Once more the advertising men got busy. Placards were placed throughout the camp and posters stuck up—most appropriately—in the latrines. Play was made on a film title with the caption: 'Dysentery Rides Again.'

"A prize competition was announced, offering cigarette awards for the best anti-fly slogan, the best poster, the most practical fly-trap. The results of this campaign were more difficult to assess but at any rate, fly-swatting became one of the season's popular sports!"

An International Red Cross report dated 5 February 1945 gives the British staff at the Lazarett as follows: Major A.G.D Whyte, RAMC; Major J.Q. Ochse, SAMC; Captain C.P.M. Neethling, SAMC; Captain A.R. Duff, RAMC; Captain T.L. MacDonald, RAMC; and Captain J.G. McGavin, RAMC.

The British dental officer was Lieutenant V. Jessop. Lieutenant Jessop had been a combatant soldier and was, in a way, coming home. He'd been captured near the end of May 1940 on the sands at Bassin des Chasses and, with others, had then spent some time in Stalag IVB before being moved to an Oflag.

By this time two American medical officers had also joined the staff: Captain W.P. McKee and Captain E.C. Yeary, both USAMC.

4—A Half-Life

Forty-three medical orderlies—British, Commonwealth and U.S.—were employed at the Lazarett. The average number of ambulant patients attending daily for treatment was 500. The average number in the British infirmary was 150.

The report was critical of the grossly overcrowded nature of the living quarters in the camp, citing a sharp rise in the incidence of diphtheria, due to the bad hygienic conditions. Among the recently arrived Americans who were suffering from debility and exposure, an epidemic of pneumonia had occurred. Other prevalent disorders included respiratory tract infections, septic conditions of the skin, diarrhea and actual dysentery, the latter being linked to the great scarcity of proper cooking and eating utensils.

FREDERICK HEDGES. "The job of MO in Stalag IVB is done by one Major Whyte, quietly and very efficiently, and the whole camp will be indebted to him for his untiring efforts."

Major Whyte (inevitably dubbed "Chalky") and his team, quartered close to the camp hospital, had set up effective routines and made the most of the limited resources available, though not without occasional difficulty.

FRED HEATHFIELD. "Occasionally small operations were performed in the ward with the patient lying on a single bunk. The rest of the patients crowded onto the top bunks opposite to get a good view and to be in a position to offer advice to the surgical team. The first operation I saw was on a man's face. Captain Duff gave him an injection of sodium pentothal but the patient fought against the anaesthetic and appeared to remain conscious throughout the operation. He struggled violently, and Jack Lawler, the huge South African orderly, had to sit at the top of the bed and clamp the man's head between his thighs. As he took a firm grip on the patient Jack asked Major Whyte to be careful where he used the scalpel! Two other orderlies held the man's arms and another sat on his legs before the incision could be made. The doctors assured us he was not feeling a thing! When the patient recovered he confirmed that he had felt nothing and did not remember struggling.

"The next operation was on a sergeant with a bullet in his back. The bullet had hit his shoulder blade and skidded along inside, so Major Whyte had quite a bit of groping with the bullet forceps before he could fish it out.

"Another involved digging some shell splinters from the leg of a Guards sergeant wounded at Anzio.

"One of the strangest procedures was on a man with a very bad back pain. Major Oesche[6] consulted with the German doctor who supplied him with a spirit lamp and a set of small glass bowls, like tiny goldfish bowls. The bowls were warmed inside with the spirit flame then immediately pressed onto the patient's back, where they stuck. As they cooled, the flesh swelled up inside the bowls. I had heard of cupping and bleeding and I had always thought the cupping collected the blood from the bleeding. Major Oesche explained that the cupping drew the blood to the surface to relieve congestion below the skin. As the cups cooled they dropped off, and the man's back was covered with purple patches about 2 inches in diameter. I cannot remember if he was cured."

PFC RUSSELL KUEHN (1 Company, 110 Infantry Regiment, U.S. 28th Division). "I arrived at Stalag IVB on 30 December 1944 after being captured in Luxembourg during the Battle of the Bulge. At that time I received a head wound that was very slow in healing and, although my name was on a work list to go to Dresden to clean up the bombings of 13 and 14 February, the British doctor would not approve my going."

FREDERICK HEDGES. 16 January, 1945 "Everybody is suffering with colds. This is due to the hut being very damp and not being able to keep a fire going. The roof is continually dripping water. One chap in the hut placed a bucket on his bed and in a few hours the bucket was full of water."

The greater proportion of blokes faced up to the fact that in these polluted, unhealthy conditions personal hygiene — as far as it could be achieved — was vital to survival. The rats, lice, fleas and bed bugs were always with them, could never be eradicated, any more than could the unseen menace of germs and bacteria. So they keep themselves as clean as possible. Well, most of them...

Jack Lawler, the big South African medical orderly, had some methods of his own for securing cures, one of which he applied to an American sergeant from the Normandy landing. The sergeant was not wounded but in a very sorry state and just lay on his bed hardly speaking. He had avoided the showers when he came into camp and would not wash or shave. After a few days he began to smell and his neighbors complained. He was told to go to the showers at the end of the corridor and also to get shaved. He did nothing and ignored a second order. Jack Lawler appeared wearing only shorts, but carrying a large bar of soap and a floor-scrubbing brush. He jerked the American out of bed and frog-marched him down to the showers. The sergeant came back fifteen minutes later scrubbed raw and clean shaven.

FRED HEATHFIELD. "After Arnhem we had a paratrooper with a very painful bottom. Major Whyte opened up and drained a deep-seated boil or ulcer, and told the lad he would soon be fit. The lad did not believe him. He was convinced he had cancer and was about to die. No one could reassure him. He refused to eat or to speak to anyone and fell into a decline. The doctors did their best but he would not change his mind.

"One evening Jack Lawler came into the ward carrying a chair, a book and a small oil light. He settled himself by the paratrooper's bed and opened his book.

"Someone called across: 'What's going on, Jack?'

"'Oh! He's expected to die tonight and I don't like laying out corpses when they have gone stiff,' said Jack. 'I would rather do it while they are still warm.'"

Now the patient was looking at Jack in alarm, no doubt having second thoughts. He survived the night, ate a hearty breakfast and was discharged a couple of weeks later.

SOME FURTHER NOTES ON THE RUSSIANS

They were to be seen everywhere, operating the Scheissenwagens, hauling other carts about the camp, or foraging at the rubbish dumps; but it wasn't merely their numbers that ensured they could not be overlooked. It was their presence, their ubiquity. It was their extraordinary tenacity for survival. Perhaps most distinctively, it was their appearance.

S.G. WOLHUTER. "With very few exceptions Russian prisoners were deprived of their uniforms and given the most ill-fitting and humiliating of garments. Stamped in large white letters on the backs of their jackets was 'S.U.' for Sowyet Union, branding them as outcasts. Their boots were also taken away and they had to wear clogs, with rags called Fusslappen wrapped round their feet instead of socks."

TOM NELSON. "Want had turned them almost subhuman. I remember their thin, parched faces; I remember the few who were not out on work parties hanging sunken-eyed around the kitchens, falling desperately on a potato peeling, any scrap of food. Theirs was an awful existence."

JAMES BRANFORD. "The conditions under which the Russians lived were appalling. They received the bare German rations, which were totally inadequate. Tins which we would throw away on the refuse pile were systematically scraped by the Russians for extra bits of food."

Vast numbers of Russian soldiers had been captured during the rapid German advances through their country during 1941 and 1942. Unfortunately the USSR had declined to become a party to the Geneva Convention. Thus it was not possible for Russian prisoners to be supplied with Red Cross food parcels, nor could the International Red Cross inspectors either enter their compounds or make representations on their behalf.

Their situation was aggravated by the German insistence on treating

Appell in the Russian compound. Poorly garbed, starving, and many hobbling with the aid of sticks, these unfortunate men still did their best to parade as soldiers (Terry Hunt photograph, courtesy Joe Tombling).

them as political, rather than military prisoners, relegating them to a lower-than-animal status. To that extent Stalag IVB was also a concentration camp, and these Russians were used as slave labor, forced to do the toughest, the most menial, the filthiest jobs about the camp.

The death rate from malnutrition and disease among the Russians was extremely high and because of this they were shunned by many of the other prisoners. Avoiding them altogether was difficult, as they were everywhere about the camp, wearing or carrying their pathetic possessions with them. In the worst cases, these poor creatures, hollow-eyed and skeletal, already dangerously infected and emitting a powerful stench of decay, stood unmoving like gaunt scarecrows or drifted slowly by as upright, shuffling corpses.

Once the British and Commonwealth Army men and those in the RAF compound had rationalized their attitudes beyond the negative effects of finding themselves prisoners of the enemy, they were beginning to think of positive ways of helping each other and of cooperating with other nationals. Their sympathies for these downtrodden Russians, their allies, had been aroused from the outset and soon they were working on methods of helping them.

FREDERICK HEDGES. "The British personnel of the camp have formed a Russian Aid Society and undoubtedly do a great deal towards alleviating the sufferings of their less fortunate comrades."

FRED HEATHFIELD. "When we received parcels regularly we had hut levies to send some food over to the Russians. Soon after we got to IVB a young Russian appeared in our hut and asked if anyone spoke French. I was near the door and responded. Boris said he was the Russian doctor and he had come to ask for help and so the levies were started. He often came to see me and sat on my bed drinking coffee and talking. It was interesting to see how thoroughly brainwashed the Russians were. When we told him about our way of life he did not believe us and just said 'That is capitalist propaganda.'"

"He was actually a medical student, not fully qualified, and he said he had been a pilot, shot down while carrying wounded in a small single-engined biplane. He invited me to see his hospital and I went over with a box of food. He had a barrack hut with about 40 single beds and had a cubicle for himself in a corner. The room was swept clean and looked very neat. The patients were on palliasses like ours, covered with the same blankets and they all looked very weak and ill. I was interested to see above each patient's head a board with his diagnosis in Latin. They got no treatment from the Germans, but a German doctor inspected the ward from time to time. Although unqualified, Boris had to perform operations when necessary and, when I asked about drugs and anaesthetics he just shrugged. I believe our medical officers sent some help in this respect."

As POWs were not permitted to leave their barracks after curfew, the almost continuous use of the night latrine was inevitable. This facility was a single-seat cubicle adjacent to the entrance. It meant that the air in every hut was permeated by a nauseating smell throughout the night, and for the men whose bunks were nearest the door their lot was many hours of sheer, unrelieved purgatory.

The main latrine in every compound was a brick building out in the middle. Commonly known as "the 40-seater," it consisted of two wooden rows each with ten holes facing one another. Most of the time it was possible to find someone to talk to there.

A. F. ANDERSON: "I recall an amusing episode, when one freezing cold winter's day I was sitting in the latrine entirely on my own. I looked across to the door and saw another prisoner looking back at me. I wondered what the hell he wanted. I soon found out when I vacated my seat—he ran in and sat down on the warm seat!"

5

Words and Music

What, a play toward! I'll be an auditor —
An actor too, perhaps, if I see cause.
              (Shakespeare, *A Midsummer Night's Dream*, III.*i*)

A SMALL CITY

Stalag IVB has been called "a small city,"[1] and, though its boundaries may have been more finite, its administration more authoritarian, its standard of living inferior to that of most cities, the metaphor is apt enough in many ways. A large group of "permanent residents" consisted of Commonwealth — and later, U.S.— senior noncommissioned army ranks, RAF personnel and a broad range of other nationals. The "floating population," "casuals" or "tourists" comprised the frequent batches of new intakes, from which some would stay, while others were moved to satellite camps or Arbeitskommandos.

As in any city, commercial ventures flourished as, in due course, would cultural ones—the arts, theater, education, newspapers, clubs—also sports, games, gaming and, inevitably, rackets. From this environment would emerge the bracing counterpoint to the dismal tedium of Stalag routine.

DOUG GILLAM. "In our community of several thousands of men, we could find almost every trade and profession that was required, somewhere. It is therefore not surprising that bricklayers and carpenters were found. Finding an architect or theatre manager was not so easy, but they were there and use was made of them. Once the Germans were talked into giving permission to convert an unoccupied hut into a theatre, work began on the construction of the Empire Theatre, Mühlberg-on-Elbe. The hut chosen for this enterprise was the larger end of the first hut, just inside the army compound."

5—Words and Music

This was Hut 47B, D North Compound, and it only became available after considerable lobbying by keen fellows and representations made through the Man of Confidence.

The German administration had reservations about the scheme, as about any innovations promoted by POWs. But they agreed and the Empire Theatre, as it would become known, was prepared and ready for opening in April 1944.

DOUG GILLAM. "From the outside it looked no different from any other hut, but inside, the floor had been completely relaid. The new floor was on several levels, which gave an elevated view of the stage for those customers in the back rows. The stage was brick-built, and was equipped with a proscenium arch with an orchestra pit in front. At the back of the stage, using the area near the washroom, were wardrobe room, scenery workshop and changing rooms. For the audience, there were no plush, upholstered armchairs, all seats being plain wooden benches. The total seating capacity was somewhere between three and four hundred.

"Such a vast undertaking required a fully professional staff. The theatre manager had managed a theatre in the Midlands before he joined the forces. Other full-time staff regularly working in the theatre included scenery constructors and dressmakers. No payment in money, or kind, was involved for these people. The work was done for the love of it. They all believed that, as well as filling their own time, they were doing something to improve the lot of thousands of their fellow prisoners. All raw materials had to be scrounged (or stolen). To supplement this supply, items could be purchased from the Germans; therefore a method had to be found which would provide some form of income. The solution to this problem was really quite simple. All seats in the theatre were free, but an advance booking office was opened. Every seat was numbered and could be booked in advance for each performance; there was a booking fee of one cigarette.

"In the early stages, there were two completely separate companies prepared to present shows in the theatre. One was known as the CADS, which stood for Camp Amateur Dramatic Society. The other was a group working with a man who had been a professional entertainer in the clubs before the war. He was an army corporal who had been captured in Crete, and already had much experience of camp theatre work in Italy. His name, Bill Rae, will always be remembered by anyone who was in Stalag IVB. His company presented revues and variety shows.

"The first show ever presented in the Empire Theatre was a revue entitled *Rae's a Laugh*, starring, of course, Bill Rae. This was followed by the CADS production of the play *Dover Road*. This show introduced us to one of the very best female impersonators I have ever seen. He was Charlie Phelps, an army sergeant, who gave some superb performances throughout 1944.

The Barretts of Wimpole Street. Despite the difficulties of producing dresses, wigs and makeup for the many female parts as played by men, not to mention the men's own period costumes, this play was staged early in July 1944, its season, understandably, perhaps, achieving packed houses. This rare German photograph, taken in the Empire, showing cast on stage and orchestra in pit, was used for propaganda purposes. Courtesy Douglas Gillam (seen fifth from left as Bella).

"The whole concept of female impersonation deserves some comment. All female parts were played straight. No attempt was made to ham them up. The success of our impersonators was probably due to the fact that none of the audiences had ever seen a real woman for many months, or even years.

"Every production usually ran for two full weeks. This meant six evening performances with a matinee on Saturday afternoon, each week. After a show closed on the Saturday night, the theatre was closed for the demolition of the scenery of one show, and the construction of the settings for the next. On the Sunday afternoon during these closures, the theatre was used for various experimental productions, or for musical concerts."

JOE TOMBLING (on *The Women* at the Empire, 10 March 1945). "Whole cast composed of women (nag–nag–gossip–divorce). It was a great success and nice change from watching men for so long."

Eric Hurst, from Leeds, was a multitalented character who, along with other activities, edited the camp newspaper and wrote two musicals performed in the theatre.

5—*Words and Music*

WILF SUTTON (of CADS). "Our first major production was a musical called *Music in the Cage*, written and produced by one of the inmates, Eric Hurst. The plot revolved round British troops on leave in Cairo and, among other requirements, we had to find about a dozen gorgeous dancing girls. The theatre was always jammed to capacity for every performance."

The opening night of *Rae's a Laugh* happened to take place soon after the D-Day landings in Normandy, the news of which was already known in the camp. Fred Heathfield recalled that the German commandant and some of his officers had arrived to attend the performance. A novel touch devised to open the show involved the Man of Confidence, "Snowshoes" Meyers, descending by parachute and flourishing some outlandish props. After the audience had settled down he pulled aside a curtain to reveal a large placard, which read: "Reserved for Montgomery and Eisenhower."

FRED HEATHFIELD. "There was thunderous applause and laughter during which the German officers stamped out of the theatre."

Along with all the other facets of running a repertory company, the role of advertising was not overlooked at the Empire. The same talented team that earlier had devised the fearsome but effective "Mr. Germ" in alerting the camp to the looming possibility of epidemic now took up this challenge. Their view was that the Empire's high standards of production demanded publicity of matching quality.

JOHN MCMILLAN. "Many of the hand-produced posters used to advertise the shows would have graced a West End production.

"Instead of the usual plain theatrical bill, much more play was made with background colouring and stippled effects, with results at once striking and artistic. Care was taken to produce posters in keeping with each presentation, for the programmes included comedies, 'straights,' musical shows, swing sessions, classical concerts, and experimental theatre productions.

"There were even pre-performance advertisements to catch the eyes of the waiting audience. These were presented in the form of cards placed in a frame and changed every 15 seconds: very simple, but quite effective, for each changeover took place with the semblance of a 'wipe' effect on a cinema screen. Clients taking advantage of this service included the camp shop, the watch repairers, the Stalag newspapers and the camp authorities for official announcements."

A shortage of scripts for production was overcome by the International Red Cross, which supplied a useful tally of titles, British and American.

RAY NEWELL. "We disagreed with Padre McDowall when he tried to censor the entertainments, although some of the texts had come from the YMCA.

"The commandant was quite interested in cultural activities in the camp—asked to purchase some of the Sketch Club work, attended theatre, etc."

After the removal of Oberst Stossier as Kommandant, SS and Gestapo personnel continued to be seen about the camp.

FRED HEATHFIELD. "I remember queuing for the theatre one evening and two civilians talking in German in the line before me were so obviously Gestapo that I said involuntarily, 'Gestapo?'

"'Ja! Ja! Gestapo' they replied quite cheerfully. I suppose to them it was an honour to be a member of such a detested police force.

"They went in to the show but I could not see if they paid the three cigarettes admission price."

THE IMPORTANCE OF BEING FRIVOLOUS

In those pioneering days, a most valuable natural quality on which the British and Commonwealth POWs drew was laughter, and once tapped, this became self-sustaining. The grimmest situations could be seen to have their funny sides and, though the Germans were never able to understand this, and were themselves frequently the butt of pranks and jibes, somehow it worked to increase their respect for the British. Guard-baiting was a popular, if sometimes dangerous occupation while the RAF were easily able to turn an Appell in their compound to farce.

A German workman's bicycle had disappeared. The camp authorities weren't at all keen on mysteries— this being by no means the first — and their displeasure was only aggravated when bits the machine were picked up outside the perimeter. Suspicion focussed on one particular hut.

In truth, the bicycle had been nabbed, spirited away and carefully reduced to small pieces. The inner tube was then used as a catapult to fire all but one item over the wire.

When the occupants of the suspect hut were lined up under guard and interrogated, no explanation was forthcoming. The Germans gave up, but, as they marched away, some of them may have wondered if they might be hearing the sound of a ringing bell.[2]

Corporal Bill Rae of the Royal East Kent Regiment ("the Buffs") and of *Rae's a Laugh* fame was one of a kind, a great character and an irrepress-

5—Words and Music

APPELL

RAF *Appell*: This cartoon, signed d'après Bear, '44, skillfully typifies the attitudes of RAF personnel to German regimentation (courtesy Norman Page).

ible comic who contributed much not only to entertainment but to morale generally.[3]

FRED HILL. "One bleak January morning a group of men were standing outside the barracks, roaring with laughter at Bill, who was sitting in the middle of an icy puddle splashing about and telling jokes."

In that typical bit of tomfoolery Bill was pretending to row himself home.

Bill's own passage to Stalag IVB had been far from comical. He'd been taken prisoner in Crete when German parachutists captured the island in 1941, transferred north into Greece and held with others in abominable conditions for a lengthy period in a small camp. The story of what occurred there was recounted at the 1985 Stalag IVB reunion in Edinburgh by the then Chairman of the association, M.M. "Robbie" Robertson.[4]

Robbie described how, in those conditions, in a place crawling with lice and all the fellows in it suffering from dysentery, morale was on the low side. The camp leader came to Bill and asked whether he could do anything to cheer the men up. Bill wasted no time, reeling off some opening patter, telling a few funny stories and getting the lads going on a sing-song. Their spirits had risen.

ROBBIE ROBERTSON. "But the Germans didn't like it. They resented the fact that people who appeared to be down and out could raise themselves up by their own efforts. They resented, and perhaps envied, the spirit of the British in this situation. They resented it to the extent that they took our

To Norman all the Very Best.
Bill Rae

HATS OFF TO THE R.A.F BOYS,
YOU'VE DONE YOUR JOB WELL,
THERE'S PLENTY IN DEUTSCHLAND.
WHO WISH YOU IN HELL,
BUT WE WHO ADMIRE YOU,
FOR BRAVERY AND GUTS,
TAKE A TIP FROM THE ARMY,
— "GET YOUR HAIR CUT."!

"May we meet again under pleasanter circumstances"
B.

The spirited comedian Bill Rae produced this little verse and caricature for Norman Page's notebook in the *Stalag* (courtesy Norman Page).

friend inside, stretched him out on a table, and with a pair of pliers pulled out his big toenails—all for entertaining the boys."

Some weeks later, when leaving the camp, the men had to walk about six miles, a tough trek in their weakened state. Bill Rae was hobbling along as best he could in makeshift footwear and had dropped a bit behind. A German guard smashed his rifle over the back of Bill's head, knocking him flat on his face and causing further injury.

ROBBIE ROBERTSON. "But that didn't deter him. Such was the spirit of the man that he kept on entertaining the boys.... And he continued doing so in Stalag IVB."

FRED HEATHFIELD provides an anecdote about a novel activity, making use of the small pond in D North compound.

"One fine day a prisoner appeared there carrying a pointed plank on which he had fixed a mast and a paper sail. His primitive sailing boat attracted attention and inspired some to higher things. The following days saw a procession of prisoners carrying increasingly more sophisticated sailing boats.

"Then one man appeared among the crowd of mariners. His boat was no better than the others, but he had cunningly made for himself an excellent copy of a blue blazer and a yachting cap with gold braid. A meeting was called immediately by the pond-side and the Stalag IVB Yacht Club was duly founded, with the newcomer as the first Commodore. It flourished for some weeks and regattas were held. At one of these Eric Gargini[5] appeared and, when the race was under way, he launched a motor boat, driven by the spring motor of an old gramophone. It ran amok among the fleet and Gargini was mobbed and thrown into the water."

Nor was this to be the last of Gargini's involuntary baths, as Fred explains:

"Some weeks later he went in again. He had annoyed hut mates by continually predicting a date for the invasion. When the date came with no Allied landing, he was paraded through the camp, held high on some bedboards, then thrown into the pond."

JOE TOMBLING. "Cinderella show in hut at 6 p.m. Very good indeed."

This musical version of *Cinderella* was later performed for a batch of U.S. soldiers by the British, who had first greeted their arrival with a rousing chorus from *The Pirates of Penzance.*

KURT VONNEGUT. "These lusty, ruddy vocalists were among the first English-speaking prisoners to be taken in the Second World War.... They had not seen a woman or a child for four years or more. They hadn't seen any birds either. Not even sparrows would come into the camp."

The Americans had been captured in the Battle of the Bulge and many were in a poor state after a cold, slow journey on foot and by train across Germany. These Brits had heard they were coming and had prepared a mighty feast for them from Red Cross foodstuffs they'd been hoarding, along with a variety of other comforts they'd made by hand.

The stage for *Cinderella* had been colorfully prepared, with pink arches, blue drapes, a huge clock, two golden thrones, and of course a bucket and mop.

Kurt Vonnegut was in the audience of Americans and later recollected the show's hilarious presentation and some pungent lines:

"The women in the play were all really men, of course. The clock had just struck midnight, and Cinderella was lamenting:

"Goodness me, the clock has struck — Alackaday, and fuck my luck."

After almost exactly a year since its first presentation, the Empire Theatre's final show, the comedy *Tons of Money*, opened on 20 April. It was very good, according to Joe Tombling, but the war news was so heady that concentration on the play was difficult.

The remarkable tally of productions mounted for and by the Empire was listed by Sergeant Norman Page:

Blithe Spirit	28 November 1943 (in French theatre)
Outward Bound	8 April 1944 (at the Empire)
Music in the Cage	5 May
Dover Road	16 May
Let's Rae's a Laugh	9 June
The Man Who Came to Dinner	3 July
The Barretts of Wimpole Street	July
Kriegie Cocktail	9 September
You Can't Take it With You	7 October
The Petrified Forest	15 November
Springsong for Jennifer	5 December
No Time for Comedy	31 December
Cinderella	1 January 1945
Keep it Dark	6 January
Rope	26 January
Mexican Gold	8 February
The Women	9 March
Tons of Money	20 April

Although a small proportion of men in the camp had persisted in isolating themselves in cocoons of self-pity and idleness, the majority found positive interests and activities. Clubs of wide variety were formed, some more durable than others. Though it may seem unlikely, one of the more vigorous and successful was the Mühlberg Motor Club. From the half-dozen who turned up at the first meeting the membership grew rapidly to 200 or so.

As the founder and president, Sergeant Tom Swallow, has recorded: "The MMC's aims were to bring motoring enthusiasts together, to find work for idle hands and minds and to educate the 'new motorists.'

"At one committee meeting I suggested that the club should produce

5—*Words and Music*

A sample illustration from one of the newsletters produced by the Mühlberg Motor Club and published postwar in the book *Flywheel* (courtesy Tom Swallow).

its own motoring magazine to keep its members abreast of the motoring times."

The magazine was called *The Flywheel*, its aim being to "Keep the Works Going Round on the Idle Strokes." How apt this aspiration as a slogan for the Stalag at large. Arthur Pill was chairman of the MMC and also took on production management of the magazine. According to Tom, Arthur performed miracles in what was an extremely difficult assignment.

TOM SWALLOW. "There was nothing to write on and nothing to write with, but by adopting a system of beg, borrow, buy or barter (stealing from Jerry was taken for granted), he slowly began to get his act together. Arthur begged a pen-holder, borrowed a nib, bought some ink with Lagergeld (camp money) and bartered cigarettes for something to write on. Someone 'liberated' some quinine tablets from the German sick bay for colour, but heaven knows how he managed to acquire the millet soup, which was our staple diet at the time. He must have gone short himself.

"Millet soup, it was discovered, began to ferment after four or five days and became very gooey. It was used to stick things in the school exercise books that became the magazines and they are still stuck after 43 years."

Ten editions of *The Flywheel* were compiled and circulated — on loan to each hut for half a day — and the eleventh was in production when Cossacks of the 1st Ukrainian Army arrived to liberate the camp.[6]

OTHER ACTIVITIES

FRED HEATHFIELD. "On this first evening the Russian prisoners from a nearby hut appeared ... and gave us an impromptu concert, with fine singing and Cossack dancing. They may have thought we could reward them with food, but we had none. I am sure it was really a spontaneous gesture of comradeship from them, which we had not the talent to return other than with enthusiastic applause."

RICHARD HALL. "The camp was fortunate to have Alan Boult, Sir Adrian Boult's nephew and himself a talented musician. Each piece was explained (before performance) by Alan Boult, creating a much greater appreciation of the music."

JOE TOMBLING. "Light symphony orchestra in evening at Empire. Conductor William Irving. Very good. Ballet music from *Faust, Merrie England, Chu Chin Chow*; selection of Grieg's music."

FRED HEATHFIELD. "The theatre was also reserved on some Sunday afternoons for serious lectures and the finest I remember was by Lieutenant Jessop, the camp dentist, on Heraldry, which he illustrated with beautiful paintings large enough to hang on an easel. I had studied the subject before the war and I could appreciate the work he had put into it."

FREDERICK HEDGES. "A talk from an ex-borstal boy may be followed by the experiences of a big-game hunter, or someone will tell us about the diamond and gold mines of South Africa, followed perhaps, by a chap who will tell us about the great submarine disaster involving the *Thetis*—and so it goes on. Bankers, accountants, draftsmen, commercial travellers, engineers, artists, ex-cons, radio experts, dog-breeders, jockeys, chaps from outposts of the empire—all come forward to tell us about their lives and experiences."

TOM NELSON. "I really enjoyed the 'experts' who came round to each hut and told us about their jobs in civvy street. I remember a hypnotist who put several fellows under his spell and then showed us how to do it. We practised for some time later but with only limited success.

"There was an Assistant Coroner from the City of London who gave us the full and most gory details of every major murder in which he had been involved. There was a cameraman from one of the film studios who gave us the lowdown on the major British films and the actors in them, and there was an undertaker who described the embalming of a body in full and explicit detail. What a great way to pass an evening!"

Tom Nelson's hypnotist was Douglas Denton, who practiced one of the more unusual diversions in the Stalag. Doug was an army man transferred to IVB from Italy. He would come around to the huts, performing extraordinary feats of "autosuggestion," as he preferred to call it.

5—Words and Music

After making some preliminary tests to determine the more susceptible among his audience, Denton would get to work with his demonstrations, as in the following examples.

A chosen subject was required to lie across two stools, his shoulders on one, his feet on the other, a box under his buttocks. Autosuggestion and magic chanting done, Denton removed the box, leaving the subject stretched between the stools. He then performed the "impossible," sitting squarely on the man's stomach. The chap remained as stiff as a board.[7]

HARRY MCLEAN. "Another time, a sergeant in the Parachute Regiment was his stooge. This man was built square and was *tough*. He was a most unlikely candidate. Denton had him sat on a stool, with his back to the chimney breast, telling him that he was an angler, sitting on a river bank fishing. Suddenly 'You've got a bite,' and Denton went on progressively, telling him he'd got a very big fish that was difficult to land. It got harder and harder until finally, it pulled the angler into the water. And the sergeant fell off his stool! While he was still lying on the floor Denton brought him round and the sergeant immediately wanted to know 'Who pushed me off the stool?' It was quite tense for a few moments."

As a private, Doug Denton faced the prospect of being detailed to an Arbeitskommando. Not wishing to work for the enemy, he managed to evade this for a time, but was eventually nosed out by the Germans and ordered to report to the Vorlager with his kit. As No. 51 on their list he just missed inclusion with a group being sent to Leipzig and was ordered to wait there for the next detail. A timely reprieve this time was provided by Sergeant Joe Seddon of the Escape Committee, who happened to spot him walking beside a fence separating the Vorlager from another compound. Joe asked what he was doing in there and, learning the details, said:

"I am not promising anything, but

Many years after the war Ray Newell was in Portsmouth, in southern England, for an exhibition of his work. Afterward Ray was seated, resting, when a man stood in front of him, saying "Look into my eyes!" Ray's first thought was "Who's this nutter?," but then Douglas Denton identified himself, bridging the gap back to IVB (Ray Newell).

A *New Times* front page from a 1944 edition produced in the camp (courtesy Ray Newell).

An example of the arts page from another edition of *The New Times* (courtesy Ray Newell).

be here at 3 o'clock. Meanwhile I'll go and see the French Man of Confidence."

True to his word Joe was back at 3, and carefully placed in Doug's hand a perfectly made pass authorising his release from the Vorlager, and said:

"Pick up your kit, go to the gate and give this to the sentry. Do not on any account hurry."

Doug sauntered to the gate and handed over his pass. The guard read it, smiled and opened the gate, saying "Englander, ja?" Doug confirmed that and slowly walked back into the main camp. Subsequently he was obliged to change huts a number of times as attempts were made to locate him. Eventually the hunt ran out of steam and Doug settled down again to camp routine.

HARRY MCLEAN provides this anecdote about a young airman named Metcalfe who proved to be one of Denton's most responsive patients.

"On this occasion he had Metcalfe sitting on a stool and gave him a mug of water after hypnotising him. Denton persuaded Metcalfe that he was enjoying the drink, and was beginning to feel drunk. After this had gone on for a few minutes we noticed that Metcalfe had wet his pants. He had been unable to hold it back.

"Denton brought him round and Metcalfe then demanded: 'Who's poured water down my trousers?' He was persuaded that no one had done it, and that he had just 'pissed himself.'"

Another Denton feat involved convincing a subject that he was a famous Italian opera singer and inviting him to sing. He obliged, giving a stirring performance in what seemed perfect Italian!

S.G. WOLHUTER. "Wall-newspapers of interest to everyone were started, and it was difficult to believe that anything of so high a standard could be produced with the limited materials available in a prison camp. The printing had to be done by hand; artists produced illustrations, and professional journalists who formed the editorial staff wrote the articles. The contents had to be censored by the Germans, but despite this these unconventional newspapers contained a wealth of information. News was obtained from letters from home, new prisoners were interviewed and members of other nationalities contributed articles and short stories."

The camp newspaper, *The New Times*, was produced weekly and circulated around all the huts. Wilf Sutton said it was "beautifully printed, in colour, absolutely magnificent."

6

A Secret War

Man is practised in disguise; He cheats the most discerning eyes.
(John Gay, Introduction to *Fables*, 1727, 1738)

THE EAST

Between the two world wars, espionage in Europe developed to an extraordinary degree. Germany was at the heart of it, gathering military and industrial information from all the surrounding countries, among which France, Poland and Czechoslovakia particularly, employed agents of their own and set up radio monitoring stations to intercept German military messages.

Austria was taken over at Hitler's order in March 1938. The secession of the Sudetenland followed at the beginning of October the same year. In the middle of March 1939, German troops invaded Czechoslovakia.

Many Poles had continued to hope, given the nonaggression pact of 1934 with Germany, that peace would hold, but the danger signs had been mounting steadily, and for the Polish government and defence chiefs, the invasion of their country by the Wehrmacht on 1 September, 1939, came as no surprise.

More than a decade earlier, the Polish general staff in Warsaw, well aware that German spying into their country's affairs after World War I was an almost routine process, had begun the planning of cryptographic work with the aim of keeping abreast of German intelligence activities. In 1929 some 20 of Professor Z. Krygowski's brightest German-speaking mathematics students at Poznán University were invited to attend a course in cryptology. They were sworn to secrecy.

The Poles had acquired a cipher machine used commercially in Germany by business firms, but this bore little relation to the military model. Eventually, however, their work, with information obtained late in 1932 by French intelligence from a German offering to sell documents, opened the way for their duplication of the military version of the Enigma machine, and less than a month into 1933 they were reading German messages intercepted by Polish monitoring stations. With a great deal of painstaking analysis, trial and error and inspired guesswork, three of these mathematicians — Marian Rejewski, Henryk Zygalski and Jerzy Różycki — had solved the theory of the cipher system and the methods of operation of the Enigma keys. Without delay the building of copies of the military Enigma had been assigned to AVA Radio Manufacturing Company in Warsaw.

On 3 September 1939, Britain and France kept their commitment to Poland by declaring war on Germany but, unable to be of direct help in the east, they had opted to muster their largely outdated and unprepared armies along the enemy's western frontiers.

By mid-September the Germans had advanced quickly through western Poland and bypassed Warsaw. For Rejewski, Zygalski and Różcki the timing was now critical. Determined to get their copies of the Enigma machine out of the country, they headed in what seemed the only direction offering hope — southeast. With their precious green crates they made for Romania and then west from there. After several close calls, difficulties with customs inspections and other incidents, they reached France via Yugoslavia and Italy.

They were installed in a château some distance from Paris, where they continued their work, the results from which went to the French and the British. The British were by now building their own electromechanical decrypting device, based on plans received earlier in Warsaw from the Poles, whose work can hardly be overestimated.

THE WEST

While the strange period of military inactivity — the so-called "phoney war" — dragged on, a separate, more cerebral and livelier initiative was under way in the west.

Existing British intelligence organizations were MI 5, charged with safeguarding internal security, and MI 6, responsible for external intelligence operations. In wartime both were expanded, and an inevitable overlapping of duties required their cooperation. In MI 5's case a section to be known as BIA was established, its purpose being the entrapping of German agents and, while ostensibly allowing them to continue their work for the enemy, "turning" them to British advantage primarily through the transmission of false or fudged information.

Another remarkable organization set up in London in November 1939 was MI 9. Along with functions such as assisting with the escapes of British and Commonwealth POWs, its aims included the collection of information about the enemy and the sustaining of morale among captured servicemen. MI 9[1] was prepared to use all practical means in carrying out its work and steadily developed a variety of ingenious ideas for the purpose. Radio was an obvious medium for coded messages and, once aware which prisoner-of-war camps were able to receive them, MI 9 began initiating careful transmission routines. The BBC's ready cooperation — with as few people as possible there in the know — was enlisted. Regular scheduled programmes seemed least likely to arouse enemy suspicions, enabling the concealment of messages within their normal content. Code users in the camps needed to have been alerted in advance that messages would be broadcast at certain times. By mid-1941, MI 9, through its code section MI 9y, had set up code communication with all the Oflags,[2] and the Stalags would follow.

Earlier than any of that was the need to ensure that code users would be on hand in the Oflags and Stalags able to receive and translate the messages. The premise "better to be prepared" was adopted, and promising candidates from the various services were chosen as prospective code users and instructed in advance, in case they were captured. This forethought would be shown to be amply justified, though inevitably it followed that some camps would be better off than others while some would have no code users at all.

THE CAMP

From *Secret Camp Histories*, WO 208/3274. "There were eight code-users in Stalag IVB, but only two were regular writers, Lance Sergeant Ballauff and Lance Sgt Turner, both of whom were responsible for forwarding all messages between the camp and the War Office.

"The first letter was written by Signalman Malcolm R. MacArthur on 9 August 1943 and received on 9 September 1943, and from that date until 20 October 1944 eleven letters were received by the War Office."

The same report refers to further information passed to the War Office by Sergeants Ballauff and Turner — some of it gathered by listening to the careless talk of the guards — and carried from there by POWs of other nationalities passing through the camp in transit.

In conveying advance information by letter to the camps about codes to be used, MI 9 found it essential to enlist the cooperation of parents, wives and other close relatives who, while naturally keen to participate, were sworn to secrecy. Codes could be implanted in messages in various ways. Letters received by family from the POWs which, for example, bore certain dates would indicate that they contained coded content. Others may involve references in the text to particular persons, whether known to the recipient or not, or to hypothetical activities. These would go to MI 9 (or in some cases the Air Ministry) for reading the encoded messages.

Secret ink and microphotography were other resources employed according to the circumstances.

The Germans suspected that codes were in use, knowing that one of their purposes was to facilitate escaping. However, as with radios, they were never able to isolate the codes or identify their users.[3]

FRED HEATHFIELD. "Quite early on in our prison camp life I met a navigator whom I had known in England. He approached me one day in the compound and told me he was a code-writer and able to send any important messages I might have back to England. I had heard that there were such people. They were generally navigators or bomb-aimers, who naturally had the best chance of escaping from a stricken bomber, and they were chosen by intelligence officers to learn complicated but virtually unbreakable codes for use if they should end up as prisoners. They were supposed to report the fact that they were code-writers to the S.B.O. or Camp Leader so that official messages could be sent. The codes were limited to about twenty words on a letter form and replies or requests for information from England came in the same way, so two-way messages could take months."

After his Halifax had been severely damaged during a raid on Krefeld the night of 21–22 June 1943, and his crew had all bailed out, Fred crash-landed the plane at the edge of a woods in Belgium, set it on fire and started walking. Eventually he arrived in Brussels, where he was introduced to an evasion organization and sheltered for a few days in Swiss Nurse Collet's small apartment. Nurse Collet was unaware that the Gestapo had infiltrated the line, and Fred was collected from her flat by Prosper de Zitter, a Belgian Gestapo agent posing as a captain in the British secret service.

Arrested in Paris by the Gestapo and held in prison in Fresnes before being transferred first to Dulag Luft and later to Stalag IVB, Fred told the code-writer that he was very suspicious about "the Captain" and asked him to convey this in a message to England, suggesting he mention the man's distinctive missing finger joint.

FRED HEATHFIELD. "My unease about 'the Captain' came from the apparent ease with which he drove about Brussels in his Citroën—taking airmen out to have their hair cut by local barbers, producing passports, and his insistence on removing our identity tags: finally, the casual way in which we were taken through the frontier control into France, with just a nod from the German frontier officer."[4]

In Stalag IVB, as in other camps, knowing that illicit radio receivers existed, particularly in the British and French compounds, the Germans

6—A Secret War

instructed all guards to be on the lookout for them. Despite a few close calls the POWs' early warning systems ("Goons up" in the British huts) worked smoothly, and their radios were never discovered.

More thorough *Gestapo* searches were also carried out every so often, with maps, compasses, illegal papers and other escape aids in mind along with wireless. These, too, generally proved fruitless.

The D-Day allied invasion of Europe was confirmed when heard on the camp radios.

RICHARD HALL. "Sometimes a couple of soldiers with an NCO would just wander around the huts, nosing about. I was in a hut in D compound when this happened: the usual warning had not been heard or understood. A wire was hanging from the roof trusses ... those around started to sing and the sentry, in typical German fashion, stupidly jerked the wire, which came loose. Had he climbed onto the bunk he would not only have found the wireless but also the operator."

ANDY ANDERSON. "The radio in our hut ... survived searches by the Germans because it had been installed on the underside of the toilet seat."

In the RAF compound the Germans' penchant for poking about suspiciously could occasionally be turned to diverting effect.

LEW PARSONS. "On one occasion the Feldwebel 'McAlpine'[5] came into the hut and found a wire just protruding from under the brick floor. 'Haha!' he said and proceeded to pull up the bricks, following the wire for several feet before coming to a box. Again 'haha!' in triumph. He was very deflated when he took out the box and opened it only to find a brick with a piece of paper and a message reading 'NIX.'"

TOM NELSON. "Eric Gargini, a radio expert ... built most of the radio sets in IVB, often from the most surprising things. The radio in our hut was looked after by four different people, and it was stored in different places each day. Our barrack commander, Bob Hale, had been a shorthand expert before the war and every night he would take down the BBC news, read it out to our hut and then pass it on around the camp. We always knew the latest news."

FRED HEATHFIELD. "For his next trick he [Gargini] needed a penny. He was told the lavatory was free, but he persisted and someone produced a copper coin. He had brought a broken gramophone record from Dulag Luft and a piece of the silver foil from American cigarette packets. I don't know what else he used or how he did it, but in no time at all he announced that he had heard the BBC news. From that day until the end of the war we never once missed an evening news broadcast. The Germans soon got to know we had a wireless set and they searched and stripped the hut time after time but never found it."[6]

Of the several illicit radio receivers (Schwarzradios) held in various compounds in the Stalag, this example was compactly stored in a Red Cross food parcel box (Terry Hunt photograph, courtesy RAF Museum, Hendon).

This radio receiver in the photo had been brought in by 50 POWs when transferred from Italy. The set had been dismantled and each small piece divided among these POWs and concealed in their possessions.

Among other radio experts active in the *Stalag* were Harry Watson[7] and Walter Biggs.

FRED HEATHFIELD. "Sergeant Walter Biggs, a ground radio and radar technician, captured during the Dodecanese campaign, arrived a few months after us and he went in for radio work in a big way, building sets for other British barracks and for other nationals. I understand he went out to Mühlberg as a member of a French working party to obtain his materials. I never found exactly where or how our set was hidden."

Help was often forthcoming from German guards, bringing in batteries in return for cigarettes, while new valves were sometimes smuggled into the camp in loaves of bread. Another source was from a Dutchman regularly employed by the Germans to service their radios. A surprising number of defective valves in these sets needed frequent replacement, while the British radios remained serviceable.

S.G. WOLHUTER. "News time in the evening was, apart from the weekly issue of Red Cross parcels, the highlight of our existence. No-one was allowed to talk or cause a disturbance while the news was being read and it was always awaited with hushed expectancy. There was a sequence for reading the news in the huts: particular people were appointed to do so and a well-organised guard system was evolved to deal with the possibility of German snoopers catching us in the act. If any German so much as left the Kommandantur or any other of their offices, a system of warning signals from our own sentries was flashed from hut to hut and this always worked well."

It was known by MI 9 that transmitters were built, or partially built in some camps. IVB was among these.

SECRET CAMP HISTORIES, IVB (WO 208/3274). "A message received from S/Sgt Simmons, RASC states: "The camp has a short wave receiving set and broadcasts are heard on the 25 and 31 metre bands at 17.45 and 21.45 hours regularly. POWs also have many parts for a transmitter and it is hoped that they will be able to transmit soon on the 31 metre band."

Notwithstanding the enterprise demonstrated by these POWs, the transmission of messages by wireless from POW camps was strongly discouraged by London, because it was regarded as being too risky for all concerned. It seems fairly certain that no such transmissions were made.[8]

7

Doug's Story[*]

INTO CAPTIVITY

The part of my life which was spent in Stalag IVB was so different from anything I had experienced so far that I have tried to cover it in some detail. It begins with the journey from Frankfurt into Saxony. It was this trip which shattered any illusions that I had about what a prison camp would be like: illusions which had been created by the short stay in Dulag Luft, following my release from solitary confinement. The reasonable condition in which I had been kept, and the adequate food from the Red Cross, were suddenly forgotten as I endured the most frightful journey I have ever undertaken.

There were about 150 of us, all NCOs of the Royal Air Force, and we were handed over by the Luftwaffe to the care of the German Army. We marched out of Dulag Luft to a goods depot at a railway marshalling yard. From now on I became just an item of freight. There were to be no more passenger trains with my own guards for company. The only comfort was the fact that I could now understand what was said to me and join in a conversation; all the RAF spoke English.

Most of my fellow travellers were in small groups of two, three, or even four. Each group consisted of survivors from a bomber crew of seven. Unfortunately I was on my own, trying to find a friend amongst the crowd. I was pleased when I found another lonely chap; he was about my size, a little younger than me, and as glad as I was to find someone to talk to. He was one of four survivors from a Stirling crew, but the others refused to recognise him: he wasn't their regular rear gunner and was blamed by them for allowing an enemy fighter to get close enough to fire at them. He was Sergeant Scandrett and he came from Birmingham. We became friends on

---

[*] *Sergeant (later Warrant Officer) Douglas J. Gillam was navigator on a Bristol Beaufighter of RAF 141 Squadron, shot down over France in August 1943 and subsequently confined at Stalag IVB. This chapter consists of generous extracts from Doug's well-observed postwar account of his experiences, printed here with his permission.*

that train. It was a friendship which grew in closeness throughout our captivity; we came to rely on each other, and learned to share everything we possessed. To me he was just "Ronnie" and although it is now 53 years since that trip in a goods train, the close relationship started then still persists to this day.

My own condition at this time is worthy of comment. It was several weeks since Robbie[4] and I had taken off from Ford, and I was still wearing exactly the same clothes, including my underwear, nothing having been washed or cleaned. This highlights the unhappy physical state I was in and this, when added to a strained mental state, shows that I was in a pretty miserable condition. My mind was still in a state of shock; the transition from RAF senior NCO at Wittering to being a prisoner of an enemy had been far too sudden to be easily assimilated.

On the way to the train it started to rain and none of us had such luxuries as coats or hats. We were pleased to get to the siding and board the transport, a train of good-sized cattle trucks. The last cargo in my truck had been dry cement, so a crowd of soggy, wet airmen soon looked a filthy mess after they scrambled on board and tried to find enough room to sit down on the floor. When the trucks were filled, the sliding doors were closed and sealed and we were shunted into the goods yard until the train set off for our unknown destination, which turned out to be Saxony.

The journey was fairly slow; the whole trip took over two days. We went through several other goods depots but the only place I can remember was the town of Gotha. The only other abiding memories of the journey are the appalling smell inside the truck by the time the trip was over and the difficulty of trying to find enough floor space to lie down on at night. Everybody tried to get a patch as far away as possible from the latrine bucket in the corner. Let's just say we were glad to get out, form up and march to our new home. We were filthy and my long hair was thick with cement dust. What would I have given for a bath?

At Mühlberg-am-Elbe we disembarked, stretched our legs and formed a long crocodile of hungry, bedraggled and miserable airmen. We walked, or shuffled, from the railway sidings until we saw the impressive main gate to our destination.

I became POW No. 222515, instead of RAF No. 1310814. I still have the photograph they took. It is difficult to accept that it is me; it portrays nothing but hatred and loathing. I look as if I am about to commit murder.

My new identity tag was metal. It was made in two parts. We were told that, if we died, one half would be sent to the Red Cross, the other would be fastened to the coffin. That fact didn't really do much for our morale.

This then was the home into which we were ushered to begin our incarceration. Our sole possessions were the clothes we wore and we were so tired that we actually looked forward to settling down on the wooden bed boards with a thin palliasse, and cover ourselves with a single blanket. I am sure nobody in the hut will ever forget that first night. By dawn, everybody had been eaten alive by bed bugs. Some chaps were covered from head to foot with bites, while others seemed to get off fairly lightly. No-one escaped. We spent the next day walking round the compound while the Germans sealed the doors and windows of the hut and filled it with poison gas. When we got back inside we shovelled the bugs up by the million.

Apart from the four huts, the only other structure in C North compound was the latrine block, right in the middle of the compound. In addition to the basic purpose for which it was constructed, this building became a very well-used social centre. It was commonly known as "the 40-seater." It was a solidly-built brick edifice with four rows of ten seats, holes in wooden benches. Each row of seats faced a similar row, so if you didn't want to converse with the chap sitting next to you, you could always discuss serious issues with the person sitting opposite. It still amazes me that such activities quickly became acceptable behaviour.

During an unpleasant induction process, men arriving at the camp over a period of several months were subjected to indignities including being completely shorn of their hair, then photographed by the Germans for their records. The photographs show clearly, as in this one of Douglas Gillam, how the men felt about this treatment (courtesy Douglas Gillam).

When I arrived in the RAF compound, one of the huts was already occupied by airmen who had been there for two or three weeks. During the next few months, other trainloads of men arrived from Dulag Luft at various times, until the RAF compound was filled. In the early stages we realised that we were all of the same, or similar, ranks. It is strange that members of the armed forces are conditioned to expect, and obey, orders from above. Here were 2,000 men without recognised leaders. Our first task, therefore, was to elect a "Hut Commander." The men who had been installed in the RAF Compound before we arrived had already elected their Hut Commander and also a "Man of Confidence." This latter post was the most important position in the camp. He was the only official link between the British prisoners and the "Detaining

7—Doug's Story

Power." The post was filled by a warrant officer of the RCAF, W/O Meyers. He, with his deputy and a secretary, moved out of his hut into the German administration block. He served as Man of Confidence until the war was over; by which time there were 20,000 British and Commonwealth prisoners.

My memories of the following two years form the basis of the next part of my story. However, it is quite impossible to write these down in any date order. Life as a prisoner is the most boring existence it is possible to envisage; every day can be just a repetition of the day before, and the following day repeats it all over again. I have therefore tried to give an impression of the nature of my captivity by recalling a collection of incidents, not in any particular order.

I will start with my recollections of what we had to eat, either provided by the Germans, or provided by the various Red Cross Societies. I make it clear at this stage that, without food sent to us by the Red Cross, many prisoners would have fallen victim to the dangers of malnutrition or even starvation.

The basic rations provided for us came in two parts, bread and skilly. For the issue of such food, it was necessary to divide the company into smaller groups, and we therefore formed ourselves into fives. This arrangement was very handy, because the bread ration was usually "one loaf to five men." The loaves were distributed from the Hut Commander's corner, then each group began the ritual of cutting. In a group of five, one man measured the loaf and cut it into five pieces. The second man then organised the drawing of lots to decide which piece each man got. The third member of the group had the privilege of collecting the crumbs; these he usually kept in a tin or other receptacle for future use. The duties within the group were changed in rotation, in an attempt to convince ourselves that all was as fair as possible.

The bread issue each day became one of the high spots of an otherwise pointless existence. There was usually some fat to spread on it; this went under the name of margarine. Occasionally there was a jam issue, one spoonful per man. This commodity had the appearance and texture of mashed beetroot. We were once told that it was a by-product of the German chemicals-from-coal industry. On a few occasions we got another luxury, which went under the name of cheese. All distribution was organized daily by the Hut Commander while the rest of us queued down the length of the hut.

The main meal of the day was skilly and potatoes. A large tub of soup and a similar tub of spuds, boiled in their jackets, was brought into the hut each lunch-time. Everybody got a ladle of the soup (or skilly) and a few potatoes. Fair distribution was the responsibility of the Hut Commander who also had the job of seeing that any leftovers were served as seconds in strict rotation. Skilly was an indeterminate recipe. I remember a green skilly which was reported to be turnip tops; sometimes it was a thin watery liquid with a few bits of fatty meat floating about in it. The best-remembered skilly was the infamous millet soup. It was commonly known as boiled birdseed: it was at best filling and tasteless.

The only other items supplied by the Germans were the "hot" drinks. These were a cup of tea in the morning and a cup of coffee in the afternoon. The most noticeable feature of these drinks was that the tea was not made from tea, and the coffee was not made from coffee. Rumour had it that the tea was made from mint; it was tasteless and lukewarm. I couldn't enjoy drinking it, but I did occasionally use it for shaving. It was better than cold water. It was generally understood that the coffee came from roasted acorns. Even when sugar and milk was available, we never wasted it in coffee. It was better using pepper and salt instead: it made the drink taste like beef tea.

After this description of the German rations, it becomes clear that survival depended almost entirely on food received from the Red Cross. The International Committee of the Red Cross decided that an adequate diet could be maintained on one food parcel, per man, per week. When food parcels started to come in, this rate of supply was maintained. Unfortunately, as the war progressed, there were periods when we were on one parcel between two, or even three. There were even long spells when there were no parcels at all. As the war was reaching its end, we got nothing from the Red Cross, and less than our usual rations from the Germans.

Apart from food, Red Cross supplies included soap and cigarettes. The ration was 50 fags per food parcel. The cigarette issue became vital, even to the non-smokers. In a world where money didn't exist, the basic unit of currency for all transactions was the cigarette. Heavy smokers were known to sell food to satisfy their craving for fags, and non-smokers could always supplement their rations with a few purchases. As time went on, and clothing and fag parcels arrived from home, a camp shop was opened.[1]

THE ARRIVAL OF THE ARMY

During the late autumn of 1943, after only a few months of captivity in Stalag IVB, a tremendous change came over the place. After the collapse of the Fascist government in Italy, we became puzzled about the future of the war. None of us however could have guessed what would happen next. There were thousands of British prisoners of war in Italy, who had been captured in Crete, Greece, Tobruk and other places in the North African desert. When the Italian government formally surrendered to the Allies, the Italian guards walked out of the various POW camps. The British authorities sent a message to the newly released British POWs. "Keep cool, keep calm and you will be collected." They were collected, by the Germans! Large numbers of them were brought by train across the Alps into Germany and installed in Stalag IVB.

The arrival of several thousand British army prisoners made a tremendous difference to life in the RAF Compound. They were housed in D Compound next to ours and henceforth known as the Army Compound. The first change was that the gate from the RAF compound to the rest of the camp was no longer closed. This was done to allow all the British prisoners free access to each other, but it also allowed us to move all over the camp, including those compounds occupied by other nationals. The new arrivals accepted W/O Meyers as the Man of Confidence, but their appointment of Hut Commanders illustrated immediately the great difference between the two services. Each Army hut nominated its most senior sergeant major or warrant officer: no question whatever of there being an election.

The biggest change they brought to the camp was their whole attitude to captivity. Most of them had experienced a year or two "in the bag" and it showed. They introduced us to travelling "hut entitlements," a directory of speakers and lecturers, the production of camp newspapers, and the organisation of inter-hut sporting competitions and games. This changed our whole attitude to our captivity. Until the influx from Italy, we had concentrated on existing. From then on, the emphasis was on living life to the full, as far as our circumstances would permit.

Here began rivalry between the two services, and between the two compounds, which at times became quite a serious matter. An example of this difference of philosophy came to the fore in the spring of 1944. A newly-arrived German Commanding Officer ordered a huge parade and march-past along the main road of the camp. A saluting base was arranged at the side of the road and all prisoners had about a week to prepare themselves for the great day. The occupants of the Army compound spent the time ensuring that their boots were polished to perfection, that their uniforms were repaired as far as possible and that their trousers had been slept on sufficiently to produce a smart crease. They even practised marching to produce as smart a turnout as they could. We in the RAF compound objected most strongly to the whole procedure, and no attempt was made to smarten ourselves up. No way were the Royal Air Force prepared to show any honours to the detaining power. On the great day, the Army excelled itself and produced a display worthy of its great traditions. Meanwhile the RAF were the most slovenly, disreputable shower of men that could be envisaged. The Army accused us of letting down our own country. This criticism stung the airmen into an immediate response. Far from being disrespectful to our own nation, we claimed that our disrespect was directed to the Germans alone. To prove our point we decided to repeat the exercise exactly one week later. On the saluting base were the British Man of Confidence, W/O Meyers and his staff, but no Germans. Only the RAF marched past, but I have never seen a smarter parade from any section of HM Forces. Due honour was given to the most senior airman on parade, and the contrast between this and our performance the previous week emphasised our insult to the enemy.

The difference in the attitude to captivity of the two services was never smoothed over, but it was never again allowed to surface to the same extent. Personal friendships developed and cooperation on projects continued.

There were two other groups of men who had arrived in Mühlberg from Italy together with the prisoners I have just been talking about. First, was a whole compound full of Italians. It was difficult to comprehend how a country can actually change sides in the middle of such a bitter war. Since 1940 Italy had been Germany's main ally. I suspect the Germans had some difficulty keeping Mussolini's troops apart from the men in our Army compound, who had until very recently, been captives of the Italians. At one stage the Italians had to be put in tents in the middle of one of the other compounds.

The second group of newcomers was a handful of British Officers. It is difficult to imagine how the many thousands of British and Commonwealth troops had managed to carry on without an officer in sight. The seven officers who arrived made no difference to our organisation at all. Major Whyte was a medical officer, and another, whose name I cannot recall, was a dentist. They were never allowed anywhere near the compounds where we lived. Major Whyte lived and worked in a hospital hut, which I believe was somewhere near the French compound.

The other five officers were all army chaplains; Captain Banks was a Roman Catholic priest, Captain Day and Captain Willis were both Anglicans. Captain Thompson was a Methodist missionary in China, and served in the British army under the sponsorship of the Church in China. He was a remarkable man. The senior padre was a New Zealand Presbyterian Minister, Major McDowall. These five men lived some distance from us m the camp, but they were granted access to our compounds and began their pastoral work immediately.

CAMP ROUTINE

One of the dangers of an existence such as ours was routine, which could so easily degenerate into boredom. There were routines imposed by

7—Doug's Story

the Germans, but for much of the time, our life was governed by what we made of it ourselves. During the day, most men went for a walk; there was always a continuous procession of hundreds of men tramping round the compounds just inside the perimeter wire. Once round the RAF compound measured about 220 yards, which meant eight circuits for the mile. For a longer stroll, a complete circuit of the whole camp was just under two miles.

Throughout our walks we were under constant surveillance from the "Goon-boxes," positioned at intervals all round the outer fence. There were armed guards in all the goon-boxes which were placed at 300 yard intervals. The outer fence, of barbed wire, was 6 feet tall and topped by coiled barbed wire. Every 50 yards along the whole length of fencing were floodlights directed on to the fence itself. A more important fence to us was what became known as the "tripwire." This was a single strand of barbed wire a couple of feet above the ground. It ran parallel to the outer boundary, 20 yards inside the six foot fence. The space between the fence and the tripwire was classified as forbidden territory. Anybody encroaching into this area was liable to be shot on sight, and this was no idle threat.

Small items of useful equipment began to come into the camp, usually from Sweden or Switzerland. Some books arrived, footballs, and other games apparatus, but one of the most welcome arrivals was the large number of packs of cards. Gambling was out of the question as no one had any money. In my hut a weekly bridge tournament became a major event. A knock-out competition of 32 pairs began on each Monday morning, with the Grand Final on the Saturday night. Ronnie and I reached the final once, and it was the only time in my life that I have played cards before a silent crowd of fifty or so spectators, anxiously watching every card from the high vantage point of the upper bunks.

Out-of-doors activities which grew to become major events, included volleyball. It was a game I had never played before, and I very quickly dropped out when I realised that the net was taller than I was. The growth of football, both as an activity and as a spectator sport, was quite surprising. There was no such thing as grass within the camp, so a football pitch was something I could never imagine, but the enthusiasts set about levelling a compound and building up banks for spectators. The stage was soon set for major competitions to begin.

For those who were not sport-orientated, in fact for the whole population after dark, some other form of entertainment was required. A complete range of travelling performers offered their services. It was the responsibility of the Hut Commander and his staff to construct a programme of events for his hut. Lecturers were available covering almost every aspect of life. Even now I can still remember listening to a guardsman telling us what it was like preparing for Trooping the Colour before King George V in Jubilee Year. During lectures most men retired to their beds and spent a pleasant evening learning something about an amazing variety of subjects. Another subject I recall was a most amusing collection of stories from an undertaker's apprentice.

Some of the travelling entertainers brought staging, scenery and costumes with them and presented their own version of the "End of the Fire Show." However, the most popular form of entertainment was the radio show or radio play. This was a most interesting phenomenon. When the team arrived in the hut, the first thing they did was to erect a screen, behind which they sat, with a few candles. All the rest of the lights in the hut were then extinguished and the audience lay on the beds, in the dark, pretending they were at home, listening to the wireless. The combined skills of the actors and the sound effects staff produced some memorable evenings.

At one time I was invited to join a group who were rehearsing a series of radio plays. Padre Willis was preparing a presentation of the Dorothy Sayers plays she had written for the BBC. The series was called *The Man Born to be King*. I enjoyed this experience very much, probably because I rather liked the plays themselves. Following this venture I received an invitation to play Princess Flavia in a radio production of *The Prisoner of Zenda*. It involved using my voice in the highest possible register, but at least I didn't have to wear a frock. This was the start of several months of full-time work in the entertainment business.

Roy Goodhind, who had been a producer in a repertory company before the war, was preparing a new production for the CADS, and was looking for potential actors. He asked me to read female parts, and so began my new career as a female impersonator in the "Empire." I then became a full-time member of the theatre staff, and reported to the theatre every morning as soon after the normal German parade as I could manage.

At one time I was working on three plays at the same time. Each morning I spent reading, plotting and doing first rehearsals for a new production. In the afternoon I was doing full rehearsals, for the play which had been cast, read and plotted two weeks earlier. In the evening I was performing in the play which had begun two weeks before that. This ensured continuity and we could genuinely claim that "we never closed."

The repertoire was very extensive. The first one I took part in, was a romance based on the lives of two Victorian poets. This was *The Barretts of Wimpole Street*, perhaps a strange choice for an all-male cast; it involved an invalid poetess languishing on a chaise longue for a whole scene. The play was remarkably well-received and played to full houses.

The procedure for receiving parcels was of some interest. All people whose names were on that day's list to receive parcels were marched to the

7—Doug's Story

Post Room. We soon learned that it was necessary to take a blanket. After a German soldier had opened your parcel, each article was examined and thrown into your blanket. If it was a cigarette parcel, every packet was opened, so all you got were 200 loose fags. If the parcel contained books, they were retained for censorship. When they were eventually handed over, much of the binding was removed and the hard backs had been cut through with a knife. All this was to prevent the smuggling of documents into Germany in the binding. The chapters on radio in my physics textbooks had all been removed. It was tragic to see such damage to valuable scientific textbooks.

Except for the occasion when we marched past the German Commandant, we never had any sight of the German officers. Official contact was made only by the Man of Confidence. Our contact was with the equivalent of warrant officers, corporals and some soldiers. The man in charge of the RAF Compound was an NCO whose name was believed to be Schmidt, but was well-known throughout the camp as "Blondie." He was never known to smile and, by his bearing and attitude, clearly showed his hatred of each and every one of us. He claimed not to be able to understand English, but I am certain he knew what was going on, particularly when some of our chaps told him, in English, what his fate would be when the war was over.

Blondie used to come into the compound early every morning and again just before curfew, in order to conduct a head count. We paraded in five ranks while his troops counted the occupants of each hut. In bad weather, or when it was particularly cold, we behaved ourselves fairly well, so that we could get back inside as soon as possible. In the summer we managed to extend these parades over a considerable period, by deliberately moving about and making the count inaccurate. If a prisoner was ill, he was allowed to remain in the hut. The call *"Ein Mann krank"* went out and Blondie would enter the hut to check each sick man. He showed no sympathy, and on occasion he was known to insist on the sick men wrapping themselves in blankets and getting on parade.

Blondie made regular tours of the hut during the day, and made himself as big a nuisance as he could. To him, it was justifiable to tip over a man's food as it was cooking on the stove, or trample on somebody's washing as it hung up to dry. Before these incidents he always took his revolver out of its holster to give himself an extra bit of confidence. One man in our hut once put a jacket over a lump of concrete in the middle of the floor. Sure enough Blondie kicked it when he saw it. I don't think he broke his toe but it was a near thing.

On one occasion, near the gate to the compound, a grave was built. The mound was carefully constructed with sand from the compound, and Blondie's name had been neatly painted on to a wooden headstone. When he saw it he went mad and smashed it up with his feet and charged through the nearest hut like the proverbial bull in a china shop.

Blondie's superiors only came into the compound occasionally. Once one came with a group of German soldiers, and organised the painting of a bright red triangle, stencilled on to the back of everyone's jacket, and the knee of all our trousers. There was a rumour that many of the Germans left our compound with red triangles painted on the backs of their uniforms!

In the back corner of the hut, near the washroom, was an old-fashioned boiler or copper. This was used for a communal brew-up. Tea and coffee was collected from Red Cross parcels and stored in the Hut Commander's office. One boiling made by the "Hut Brewmaster" could supply a good hot drink all round.

The only alternative to the communal brew was for each group of muckers to have their own electric water-heaters. These water-heaters proliferated, and were of strange and unusual designs. They were made from pieces of metal cut from empty food tins. If the excess usage of electricity caused the fuses to blow, they were replaced by six-inch nails. We never understood why the whole place didn't burn down. The Germans had regular searches looking for these luxuries, but prior knowledge of the Germans' approach gave ample opportunity for the owners to hide the evidence.

The supply of fuel for brewing-up and cooking was never sufficient for our needs. The only way, therefore, to remedy this situation, was to steal coal from the Germans. The coal was in the form of reconstituted briquettes, and was stored in a fuel store in the north-east corner of the camp. A coal raid was a remarkably well-organised operation involving almost everyone in the hut. Boxes, like tea chests, were saved when bulk food was issued from the Argentine Red Cross. These were fitted with handles, rather like the handles of a sedan chair. The population was then briefed. There were scouts, carriers, loaders, unloaders and various other minor trades. The route to the coal store was chosen to keep as far as possible from the perimeter lights. The scouts' job was to direct the carriers into the shadows, and by a system of signals, warn the whole company if patrolling Germans appeared unexpectedly.

On the night of a raid, the pathfinders would set off first, and arrange for the door of the fuel store to be lifted off its hinges. As each box was filled, it set off for its journey back to the hut, where other people began the job of stacking and covering the heaps of coal. The whole operation was a very dangerous exercise, carried out with great care and skill. The dangers involved came sharply into focus one night, when Sergeant "Taffy" Jones was caught trapped in the coal store, and was shot dead by the indiscriminate firing of a gun into the darkness.[2]

Storage and hiding large quantities of coal presented a good-sized problem. Most of the coal was stacked along the walls, behind shelves carrying Red Cross parcels and other personal belongings. Great care had to be taken because of the frequent and unannounced searches we had to endure. It was during these searches that we discovered another interesting phenomenon. If German soldiers came looking for coal, they didn't seem to notice all the unauthorised lights and water-heaters which happened to be switched on, so obviously, in the hut. Yet on one occasion, while searching for and confiscating electric water-heaters, they walked round a heap of coal in the middle of the floor, covered only by a blanket. Had they only got one-track minds?

Doug Gillam as another of those camp "ladies" — Bella in *The Barretts of Wimpole Street* — at the Empire Theatre, July 1944 (Ray Newell).

The most outrageous prank played on the authorities was to do with hiding coal. Somebody decided to dig up part of the brick floor, excavate a hole and bury the coal inside. The spoil from the hole was not difficult to get rid of, and the bricks were replaced on top. The Hut Commander then complained to the Germans that the floor was dangerously uneven. They then sent a workman in the following day, to relay the section of floor!

Very rarely we used to get visitors into the camp. The Swiss authorities occasionally toured the place, in their capacity as the Protecting Power. We once got some visitors who were far from welcome. A small group of men arrived to begin a recruiting campaign; they were trying to persuade our chaps to change sides, to fight against the communists. The Germans were upset because no-one would speak to them. The one who came into our compound wore German army uniform, with a small Union Jack as a shoulder flash. On his sleeve were words which apparently meant "Free British Corps." He quickly returned to the gate of the compound, glad to get out with his life. There were, however, stories that one of them didn't get out of the camp alive. We saw no more of any of them.

Great debates used to arise about the maximum permissible amount of "goon-baiting." Many believed that all German guards were legitimate targets for practical jokes: it was considered that anything which caused them to think again was in our interests. On the other hand there were those who considered that every time we put one over on the Germans, they had the power to retaliate, and it was only ourselves who suffered. This was only one of many serious discussions which took place. The question which never got a satisfactory answer concerned some of the activities in which I became involved.

EACH MAN TO HIS OWN JOB

In the spring of 1944 my name was called after morning parade, and I was instructed to appear before the German Camp Commandant. I was escorted to the office by the main gate, rather fearful about my fate. I need not have worried. I was told that I had been promoted from Flight Sergeant to Warrant Officer, with effect from the day before I had been shot down. I felt very proud, particularly as my pilot, Robbie, was similarly promoted. The Air Force continued this policy of promotions, and almost all occupants of the RAF compound were warrant officers by the time the war was over. I remember buying a sergeant major's brass badge of rank from a chap in the army compound, and fastening it to my RAF uniform.[3]

As far as the Germans were concerned our compounds were called the "English" compounds. This was a term which included all the British, Australians, New Zealanders, Canadians, South Africans, Rhodesians and Sikhs. There were also a few Americans, but they were still classified as "English" by the Germans. For most of the time the number of Americans was very small, but it grew rapidly in December 1944 and January 1945. With such a mixed body of men, it is hardly surprising that the company included almost every trade and profession you could think of. Such diversity became a valuable asset: if any task needed to be done, there was every chance that a professional could be found to get that job done.

This became very obvious to me, after I got my first clothing parcel from Anne. She realised that provision of footwear could be as much of a problem as providing shirts and jerseys. I was somewhat surprised to get a pair of leather shoe-soles and a bag of little nails in my first parcel. It was one of Anne's brainwaves. All I had to do was to find a cobbler and, for a fee of a few fags, I was able get my shoes repaired. The cobbler was highly delighted to have a job to do. On the other hand, a friend of mine, in his first parcel from his mother, received a pair of boots. Although they were most welcome, they took up almost all the weight allowance for that parcel, and there was very little room for anything else.

Some trades were in greater demand than others. Some of the busiest were carpenters, and even cabinet-makers. It always surprised me how many tools seemed to appear when there was a need for them. Wire-cutters were in great demand, particularly by the Escape Committee. There were hammers of every conceivable size, mostly stolen by the chaps who had jobs to do in the vicinity of the German headquarters. Some tools or equipment were sold by German guards. Older men, who lived locally, were in the habit of bringing anything they could sell into the camp when they were on night duty. Some of them would even sell their soul for a smoke. At one time, when I was sleeping near to the door, I was often wakened during the night by a sentry offering me all manner of goods. I occasionally bought bread from him; tools were no use to me.

Once we started getting materials from the Red Cross, the wooden crates provided a continuous supply of timber for the carpenters. There were some interesting designs of armchair produced from wooden chests. Other tradesmen who were always kept busy were the metalworkers, particularly the tinsmiths. Almost all we had to eat came to us in tin cans, and so we had a continuous supply of sheet metal, in the form of tinplate. Once the top and bottom of a can had been removed, and shears had cut the tin from top to bottom, a sheet of metal could be hammered out flat. This sheet was then ready for manufacture into plates, mugs, and all manner of decorative artefacts. Some of the objects were for immediate use, but there were many people who were more concerned with the workmanship, and produced works of art, rather than utilitarian objects.

Good use was made of butter tins, both English and the larger Canadian Maple Leaf tins. These cans were lined with a brass-coloured metal, which provided a beautiful finish to decorative work. They also were in constant use for the making of drinking vessels, and were fitted with the most cleverly-designed handles.

One of the most amazing pieces of apparatus, which appeared by the hundred, was commonly known as a "blower." This was, in reality, a miniature version of a blacksmith's forge. The hearth of the blower was usually about the size of a small saucer, and was built in a tin and lined with clay. This hearth was fastened to one end of a board to make it stable when the blower was in operation. The base of the hearth was joined by a metal channel to a sort of turbine, at the other end of the board. The turbine was a paddle wheel which was inside a metal casing, and was rotated by a system of belts and pulleys. Operating the blower was hard work. A handle was turned, rotating the paddles as rapidly as possible. This created a draught which was directed to the hearth through the adjoining channel.

Fuelled with a small handful of hot coals, the draught from a small blower could produce enough heat to boil a can of water for a brew, or even to boil a dixie of potatoes. A well-made and designed blower was a real mas-

The blower was an ingenious device used extensively by POWs for heating water and in the preparation of hot food. In this example the indispensable KLIM (milk) tin used in its construction can clearly be seen (Terry Hunt photograph, courtesy RAF Museum, Hendon).

terpiece, and some of them were magnificently efficient. There was an art in making them.

Small amounts of little bits of coal were much easier to obtain than the large quantities required to heat the stove. There were occasional problems getting the blower going at the start. Trying to get the coal to catch was a skilled operation. It was therefore important to listen out for the shout of "embers." This meant that someone had just finished using their blower, and they were then offering their glowing embers to anyone else who was trying to get a blower going.

Cooking arrangements and recipes became more sophisticated as time went on. Once the communal brews from the copper were regularly used, the use of blowers for individual cups of tea became unnecessary and they were then used for other meal preparation. Fried sausages from a British Red Cross parcel, served with a dried egg omelette, required a blower to cook it properly. One drawback to the blower method of cooking, was the amount of smoke generated in the hut. In the winter time particularly, if several blowers were all operating at the same time, the atmosphere was not very pleasant. In the summer, blowers could be banished outside. Blondie, our local "chief goon," hated the sight of our blowers. It gave him intense delight to kick them over, even if there was a pan of Scotch porridge boiling at the time.

THE CHURCH IN STALAG IVB

After some months, there were many other activities in which I felt I should become involved, and I therefore spent less and less time in the theatre. I began to realise the importance of the work being done by the padres. The conducting of services in the huts, in the compounds or even in the theatre, was the most obvious evidence of the work they were doing. But they continuously worked in the camp. Confirmation classes were held on a very regular basis, even though we were aware that there was no bishop in the parish to conduct a confirmation service.

The celebration of the Eucharist was a most remarkable occasion. Padre Willis had been captured at Benghazi, during the desert war, and was still wearing shorts and open-necked shirt. He conducted outdoor services with a blanket thrown over his shoulders in the winter. The Communion vessels were made from cans beaten out by our skilful tinsmiths. The chalice was a Maple Leaf butter tin, stripped of its paint and highly-polished. Bread was a few of the larger crumbs from the collection we stored, and the wine was made by soaking a few raisins or prunes obtained from Canadian parcels.

Those of us who worked with the padres thought that we were well set up for the future of our captivity. It therefore came as an appalling shock to us when the Germans announced that, as officers, they were to be moved to an Oflag, or officers' camp. Protests were made by the Man of Confidence who said he would appeal, and take it up with the Swiss Government. Switzerland was the Protecting Power for the British, Commonwealth and American interests. None of this had any effect, however, and the five padres left Stalag IVB. The German version was that they had been exceeding their permitted brief, by moving about the camp encouraging prisoners to disobey the camp guards.

The responsibility for continuing the work the padres had begun then rested with the rank and file. In true British style, the first thing that was done was to form a committee. This committee was the most unusual parochial church council I have ever come across. The members were a very mixed bag. There was an Anglican ordinand, who had joined up straight from university. Then there was a corporal who had been licensed as a lay preacher in the Methodist Church. Next was a secretary of a Congregational Church somewhere in London. Another was a member of the Plymouth Brethren, and the committee was completed by the Secretary of the YMCA of Tobruk, with myself who acted as Secretary.

Our first task was to decide what we could do. We were intent on keeping a pattern of services going as far as we were able. We hadn't got the expertise to continue all the classes that had been started by the padres, but we continued with prayer groups, bible studies and discussions. We wrote out plenty of notices, headed "The Church in Stalag IVB," in an attempt to let every hut know that we were still in business.

Deliberations in this church committee were not always easy. We Anglicans believed that, without an ordained priest, we could not organise any form of service of Holy Communion. Our Methodist friends held such services, and expressed regret that we wouldn't join them. There was no acrimony in any of the discussions, and I valued the opportunity to argue these important issues, over a number of months. We, from the Anglican Communion, wanted to say our regular offices of Morning and Evening Prayer, better known as Matins and Evensong. These were continued on a daily basis in the school hut. We succeeded, however, in devising an Order of Service for Sunday worship in the theatre, in which all denominations were encouraged to take part. There was a rota of different denominations for reading lessons, another for taking the intercessions and another for giving a sermon.

A shortage of hymn books created a severe problem, but we were able to carry on, using only well-known words to well-known tunes. The choir used to practice regularly, and the shortage of trebles or boy sopranos was never really noticed. I recall some extracts from Stainer's *Crucifixion* being sung on Good Friday 1944. Daily services were sparsely attended, but the theatre was usually well filled each Sunday.

Here was a church which reminded many of us of the very early church, soon after the Ascension. We were ordinary people trying to keep our faith alive but with no active leadership. It was in this church that I attempted to preach my first sermon. I can clearly remember the text I chose. I read from the first verse of Chapter 11 of the Epistle to the Hebrews. "Faith is the substance of things hoped for." These are words which have become almost like a personal motto for me ever since.

It was about this time that Ronnie, my mucker, was rather ill. I cannot recall exactly what was wrong with him, even if I ever knew. I remember he got very pale, listless and depressed. He used to miss morning parade so often, that I gave him the nickname *"Ein Mann Krank."* Eventually he was moved to hospital and for a time was in the Lazarett near the French compound. Fifty years later, he was visiting me at my home and started to cough so I again called him *"Ein Mann Krank."* He nearly exploded with laughter, then recalled the times I visited him in the *Lazarett*, and even what I had preached about at a service I had conducted there.

One of the matters which caused us many hours of discussion when

7—Doug's Story

we were trying to run a church was what we should use to beautify the room we used for services. Many men had worked to make objects for the church; we had an embroidered altar frontal, carved wooden candlesticks and a beautifully-made cross for the altar. These "baubles" were severely criticised by some members of our committee, but a compromise was eventually reached. The candlesticks were to remain on our altar, but should not be lit!

There was one subject where we discovered an insuperable problem. When the committee was set up, we tried to contact everyone, in whatever compound, who accepted that there was a need for a church to be at work in the camp. Hardly anybody refused to join, until we approached the Roman Catholic community. They would have nothing to do with us. What really hurt came after we had issued our first publicity, headed "The Church in Stalag IVB." The following day, notices headed "The Christian Church in Stalag IVB" appeared. This notice announced that a French priest had agreed to conduct services for *all* Catholics in the chapel in the French compound. I like to think that such difficulties would not happen today. I believe that cooperation between denominations is much more realistic today than it was in 1944.

Unknown to us, negotiations were proceeding to try and get our chaplains back to us. Suddenly, we were told that the Germans had relented, and all five padres were on their way back to Mühlberg-on-Elbe. They all looked very well, and had managed to get plenty of equipment while they were at an officers' camp. They had new uniforms, and Padre Willis had managed to acquire a cassock, surplice and stole. The first Sunday after their return happened to be Whitsunday. A Festival Eucharist was organised, and all four Protestant padres assisted with the distribution of Communion to almost 1,000 prisoners.

All types of classes were resumed, together with prayer groups and bible studies. What seemed to have the greatest impact on the camp as a whole was the fact that the padres had free access to all the compounds. They worked unceasingly, going from hut to hut, talking to anybody who wanted to speak to them.

SPORT

Neither the church nor the theatre had universal appeal to the whole population of the camp. One activity which did seem to interest everybody was football. Once the pitch had been levelled and marked out, it seemed to be in constant use. Every hut in both the Army and RAF compounds was given the name of an English league team. Each hut chose its team from amongst its residents, from both amateurs and professionals, if they were available. We were then able to start a full programme of league matches.

A considerable amount of ingenuity was used to provide coloured strip for the various teams. Many of the teams succeeded in purchasing the necessary equipment from the guards.

As in the English Football League, a full programme of matches was played each week. With only one pitch, this meant that the matches were continuous. The first fixture of the week kicked off immediately after roll call on every Monday morning. As soon as that match was over, the next match was ready to start. This went on all day, and started again the following morning. The organisation was such that the last match was completed before Saturday evening, so allowing the publication of the latest league tables on Saturday night.

Loyalty to one's hut became an important principle. Star players were given star treatment, and there were even attempts at poaching, or underhand transfer arrangements. Over and above the League programme there was also a "Cup" competition, culminating in our own Cup Final. I have in my possession a photograph of the players taken before one of the Cup Finals; the teams having been presented to Major White, the British Medical Officer. The photographs were taken by the Germans for publication in their own press. The idea was to prove we were so well-treated that Stalag IVB was really like a holiday camp.

For some of these special matches there were well over 10,000 spectators, so a remarkable atmosphere was created. The cup presented on this occasion was made by one of the metalwork artists, from an Italian dixie. The runner's-up trophy was a sculptured plaque carved out of soap.

Representative matches always managed to bring in the crowds: C compound versus D compound, Army versus RAF and Amateurs versus Professionals. The largest crowds I can remember were for the Internationals. On the morning of January 1st. 1945, there must have been almost 20,000 spectators to watch Scotland play England. Queues for the best places formed as men dashed to the football pitch immediately after morning roll call, a long time before the match was due to start. it was an emotional moment when the Scottish team was led on to the pitch by a Pipe Major of the 51st. Highland Division. He played the same set of pipes he had used when he piped the remnants of his division into captivity at Tobruk. No wonder Scotland won 4-1!

The construction of a cricket wicket is rather more difficult than levelling a football pitch. However, every problem has to have a solution. A clay wicket was prepared in the transit compound and cricket was played. I have no idea where the bats, pads, stumps or ball came from; nor can I recall the details of any of the matches. Once there was a three-day test match organized between England and Australia. The only memorable feature of this match was the wonderful array of comments coming from the

Americans with whom I was sitting. They lost interest at the end of the first day, when they realised that the match wasn't finished, even though the teams had been playing all day. Their disbelief intensified at the end of the second day. When we sauntered back into the hut at the close of play on the third day (having run out of time), they refused to believe that the result could be a draw!

The other team game that was actively played in every compound was volleyball. One competition which I clearly remember was not between huts, or between compounds or even between nationals. There was a volleyball championship between the clubs. The Heather Club were all Scots, the White Rose Club members were all Yorkshiremen, and the men from Birmingham joined the Forward Club. By far the largest was the London Club. Each had its own ideas about what its activities should be. They couldn't get space on the programme for using the football pitch, but volleyball matches were easier to arrange as courts had been made in every compound.

When it comes to individual sports, instead of team games, boxing is the one that comes to mind. It wasn't a sport which interested me very much but there was a large following for some of the professional boxers we had in the camp. One chap I remember was Benny Gray, from Edinburgh, who was a professional champion at the outbreak of war. When I last saw him his face looked as if he had been boxing continuously ever since.

NEWS

With all this sporting activity taking place, it was essential to provide a news service, so that we all knew how things were going. It was for these reasons that the Saturday evening "Sports Specials" were introduced. Newspapers were an integral part of the life of the camp, even though there was no such thing as a printing press.

Drawing paper, pens and Indian ink were all that were required to start in the newspaper business. Those that succeeded had teams of reporters and journalists, artists and handwriting experts. Every page of the paper was handwritten, and there was therefore only a single copy of each edition. Some publications consisted of only a couple of pages, but others went into several sheets. The single copy had first to be submitted to the German officials for censorship. Once it received the censor's stamp, "Gepruft," it could then be displayed on large boards in one of the huts. Every paper was left in place for a reasonable time to allow it to be read by anybody interested. It was then moved into the next hut for a similar period. In this way it went all round the camp, and everybody had a chance to read it, by the time the next issue was ready.

All pictures were hand-drawn and many were coloured. We had colour supplements and full-colour news reports, many years before such things became a regular part of Fleet Street. Many of the publications were directed at a particular clientele, such as those produced by some of the clubs which flourished in camp. Some were not displayed for general readership. These were written in exercise books, and then circulated round the membership of the club or society for which they were intended.

Another newspaper which is worthy of comment is "The Scotsman." This was published for those of us who had a particular interest in Scotland. However, my real interest in this paper is the fact that it was written, edited, illustrated and published by my own pilot, Robbie.[4] After I had said goodbye to him in Rouen, he had spent some considerable time in hospital. When he eventually arrived in Stalag IVB from Dulag Luft, he was allocated space in a different hut from me, but our friendship continued to be as close as it had been at Wittering.

His newspaper was completely a one-man operation. He was of an artistic bent and he did all the presentation. In addition he drew his own illustrations, and only rarely did he use articles written by anybody else. Robbie was a real sportsman. He wrote several articles about boxing and Scottish boxers, but his great interest was football. For some time he was even manager of his hut's soccer team. The Saturday evening Sports Special was his own idea.

On the day of a big representative match or International, Robbie would draw out the whole front page of the newspaper before the match began. He then cheated a little, by deciding which players might do well. He drew the caricature portraits in advance, so that all he had to do on match day, was write the story and compose a headline. He used to try and get to the match fairly early, with his notebook. He had previously arranged to be relieved at about half-time. The relief reporter would then write up the story of the second half, while Robbie returned to his own hut, to get the first-half story transferred to the prepared page of the newspaper. At the end of the match, all he had to do was write up the report of the second half and design a suitable headline. By early evening, the Sports Special was ready for publication. The Full Story of the Match ... Read all about it.

The sequel to this account of Robbie's involvement in the newspaper business, came when the war was over. Just before we were shot down, Robbie was planning to get married. The wedding therefore had to be postponed until we were repatriated, and I was then happy to stand as best man for him in Scone Parish Church in the autumn of 1945. As a gift to remember the occasion, he gave me a set of photostat copies of his newspaper, "The Scotsman." He had succeeded in getting the originals back to Scotland when we were released. He then had copies made for me by the national newspaper, *The Scotsman*, in Glasgow. I count these and the Sports Specials among my valued possessions. After Robbie died in 1988, his son showed me the original handwritten copies, and asked me to explain to him what they were.

Robbie was a remarkably busy man in Stalag IVB, and his mucker, Bert Croney, had to look after him, in the same way that my mucker had to look after me when I was working in the theatre. I saw Robbie's mucker not long before he died, in 1995, and he still commented about what he had to do for him, while Robbie was busy with his pens and brushes. Robbie used his skills for much more than his newspapers. During the whole of our time in Stalag IVB, he was a forger of German documents for the Escape Committee. Unfortunately, I can say very little about this aspect of his life. All such work was strictly secret, and we just didn't talk about it.

Pipe Major M. O'Neill. When Tobruk surrendered on 21 June 1942 the Cameron Highlanders fought on until their ammunition was exhausted. The German General Rommel decreed that they should march out to the sound of their own pipes (Ray Newell).

The dissemination of news in a community such as ours became of the greatest importance. Newspapers could only do so much. What we really needed was BBC news bulletins from home. The German authorities used to send copies of the latest German war communiques into the camp, to be read out to us daily. These were most frustrating, mainly because we didn't believe them. We relied heavily on first-hand reports of the true situation from each load of new RAF prisoners arriving from Dulag Luft. It wasn't long, however, before we managed to get real news from London.

I now know that there were several hidden wireless sets in various parts of the camp. As an example, there was a set propped up alongside the bed I slept on. It was hidden in a brush head with the aerial stretching the whole length of the handle. The odd thing about it is the fact that I never knew it was there until one of the operators told me about it only last year. He slept in the bunk immediately above me, and he just assumed that I knew of its existence. Everybody who was involved with some form of clandestine activity, developed the habit of keeping quiet about everything they were doing.

The most famous example of a camp wireless was constructed in a Canadian Red Cross parcel.[5] This is now kept in the Imperial War Museum; photographs of it appeared at the time of one of our reunions in Edinburgh. It could be dismantled daily, and all parts were normally kept by different men in different parts of the camp. Rumour had it that it was originally built by a radio engineer who was working with a BBC war correspondent, who had been sending despatches back from the siege of Tobruk. There was never any way of checking this type of rumour. The people who really knew, never told anyone.

The system required the holders of the components to meet daily at a prearranged rendezvous. The set was assembled, and the BBC 9 o'clock News was taken down in shorthand. When everyone had dispersed, longhand copies were made for each Hut Commander. It would be about 10 o'clock when a messenger arrived in each hut with a copy of the latest news bulletin. The call went up, "Any strangers?," and as soon as the Hut Commander was satisfied that there were no Germans in the hut, he read the BBC News to us. We were asked not to discuss what we had heard; the idea being that if the Germans didn't know that we had the news, they might not search for wireless sets.

Whenever there was evidence that a news story was about to break, arrangements could be made for somebody to set up a wireless, and get a flash bulletin out to the camp. Throughout early 1944, we were anxiously waiting for news of the invasion of mainland Europe. There were always rumours of one sort or another. On the morning of 6 June, rumours began when a Junkers 52 German transport plane flew westwards near the camp. It probably had no significance at all, but somebody decided to check up. The result was that we knew of the invasion of Normandy by the middle of the morning. This was well before the Germans issued their first reports.

SCHOOL

Quite a number of the men decided that the time spent in a prison camp could be put to good use by studying. The German authorities agreed to requests for premises, and they built a schoolroom for us in the RAF compound. This was a wooden hut, divided internally into three or four classrooms. It was organised by a sergeant from the Army compound, who invited me to do some teaching. I had already been doing a bit of private coaching in mathematics for a chap in the top bunk of my bed block. He had become interested in maths while being trained as a navigator, and he wanted to see if he could ever reach matriculation standard. I wonder if he ever did.

7—Doug's Story

The prospectus for classes held in the school was both varied and extensive. There were quite a number of foreign language classes, covering French and German, with a few students even tackling Russian. One of the French teachers was a Canadian air gunner from Quebec. English literature and history classes were in great demand, but there were not many takers for ecclesiastical Greek, just enough to keep the class going. I taught two groups; one was school certificate algebra, and the other was elementary calculus. Each of these classes met twice a week, and never intruded on any of my other activities.

The school was very active, but it only catered for a minority of the men. It soon began to get very time-consuming. A shortage of textbooks meant that I spent a lot of hours constructing exercises to use as demonstrations, and also for the students as practice. Eventually the school closed in a very dramatic fashion.

The school hut was sited in our compound and it was the nearest building to the perimeter fence. It therefore became the obvious choice for starting the construction of an escape tunnel. We all knew when tunnels were being built, when the appeal went out for bed boards to be used as pit-props. When we arrived at Stalag IVB, every bed had its full complement of boards on which to place the palliasse. During the months we had been there, so many appeals had been made, that all prisoners were sleeping on as many gaps as boards.

Disaster fell late in 1944. The tunnel from the school hut was discovered. Its far end was already outside the wire, but it still had some way to go before an escape could be made. It is fairly certain that there had been a tip-off. Germans arrived one afternoon and cleared the hut of all classes, and it wasn't long before they found what they wanted. Although I was never involved with this project, its discovery cast a shadow over all our activities.[6]

With the end of my teaching career, I tried to refresh my mind with some of my own studies. Using the books I had received from England I began to try and solve the differential equations associated with "the whirling of shafts, and the subsequent distortion of their longitudinal axes." I soon realised that this was completely useless; peace and quiet did not exist in the hut, and in November 1944 it was too cold to sit on the floor outside.

Not all was doom and gloom. In the summer of 1944, a postcard was delivered to me from the International Committee of the Red Cross in Geneva. It told me that Anne had given birth to a baby girl on 10 March. She was to be named Elisabeth Anne, and both she and her mother were reported to be well. I honestly can't remember what my immediate reactions were to this news. I suppose I must have been very excited.[7]

THE BEGINNING OF THE END

Throughout these reminiscences I can only record those events which were memorable. It may seem therefore that we led an exciting and enjoyable existence, almost like a holiday camp. In fact the few memories I have recorded here have to be set against a background of days, weeks and months when nothing happened at all. When anything of interest did occur, everyone talked about it for days on end. An example of this was when the American Eighth Air Force sent their formations of Fortresses into Germany during the summer of 1944. All we could see were the long parallel vapour trails, but we cheered nevertheless.

After the Invasion in June 1944, we took a greater interest in the progress of the war. Maps became valuable, as we were trying to follow the progress of allied forces from the west and the Russians from the east. All we knew for certain was that we were sandwiched in between. As new names were mentioned in the news bulletins, we had to find them on the map. I recall trying to discover the whereabouts of Arnhem. We soon found out however, when men in maroon berets arrived in camp in October.

By this time, our hut was as full as we could imagine. The German organisation classified all airborne forces and parachutists with the RAF. We therefore found army personnel moving into our compound. They were neither fish nor fowl. The army didn't look on them as soldiers, but to us they were still "brown jobs." There had been a constant stream of new residents during 1944, and there were no empty spaces by the end of the year. Little did we know that we had even more to come.

As we approached the end of the year, there was a distinct feeling of uncertainty. After D-Day, there had been an upsurge of optimism. We were all sure we were going to be home for Christmas. As Christmas approached we began to realise that our circumstances were not as good as they had been. Food supplies were reduced by 50% when we went on to one Red Cross parcel between two. December also happened to be frightfully cold and snow started to fall, just to add to our misery. When the news bulletins told us that the Germans were counter-attacking in the Ardennes we began to think we might never get home. As the news improved and the German offensive was held, we received a dreadful shock.

Information reached us that a whole crowd of American Army prisoners were on their way and would be housed in our huts. I don't think they had marched all the way from Belgium, but by the time they reached us they had been on their feet for a considerable time. Apparently many of them were inexperienced troops who had only left England just before Von Runstedt went on to the offensive. We spent a whole day preparing for them, but they didn't arrive until very late at night.

In preparation for the American "invasion," we broke into our stock of fuel which we had built up ready for the winter. We kept the place as warm as we could, right up to the time they arrived. We also kept the boiler going and pulled out some coffee from our Red Cross stock cupboard. A collection was made of socks; these were kept in the oven until the Americans arrived. Warm dry socks were then provided for each man as soon as he got his boots off. We airmen, meanwhile, had arranged to double up in our single beds, in order to provide accommodation for our guests.

I recall Ronnie and me, sitting on the edge of my bunk, massaging an American's cold feet and helping him on with warm socks. Then we curled up with each other in my bunk so that our Yank could get some sleep in Ronnie's bed. It was a night none of us could ever forget. It was much easier for Ronnie and me than it was for a lot of the chaps in our hut, as neither of us was very big.

The following day, most of us did what we could to make the Yanks feel at home. We were all on half rations of Red Cross food at this time, so none of us had much to spare. We helped them sort out their bread ration, and showed them the sort of routines we had got used to.

It wasn't long before alternative permanent accommodation was found for our American guests. Life could return to normal once again, and Ronnie and I returned to our individual bunks. Red Cross food supplies improved once more, and as the Allied armies reached the Rhine, our morale improved considerably. At this stage of the war, the whole atmosphere of the place used to change rapidly, as different news reports came in. By the end of February, food supplies fell once more, and a feeling of depression descended again.

We were in a real need of a piece of good news to lift our flagging spirits. Before the end of the month we got it.

8

The Escape Imperative

To all Prisoners of War!
The escape from prison camps is no longer a sport!
                    (The heading of a German edict in all stalags)

ESCAPE ATTEMPTS

The business of escaping was a controversial one: not because of the increasingly hardening German attitude concerning escapes, nor the threat to shoot on sight those caught near "forbidden zones." Other principles and obligations were involved. In British Commonwealth and allied regimental units it was commonly advocated in the course of training that, if captured, servicemen had a duty to attempt escape and to make their way back to their own lines. Many took this seriously and actively sought opportunities to make a break.

Escape organizations were set up in most large POW camps, with the aim of systematizing the process, to give best chances of success. In Stalag IVB the Escape Committee was run during its first nine months by Warrant Officer Makarewicz, RCAF and, together with some army personnel, initiated the "switch-over" system.[1] After this Sergeant J. Seddon, RA, became head of the organization, with Makarewicz as his assistant. They planned and helped with all "official" escapes, enlisting the talents of artists, draughtsmen, men with skills in lettering, designing, bookbinding, sewing, and other skills the better to equip escapers with maps, passes and other documents, money and clothing for arduous journeys through the hostile world beyond the wire. Requests by coded message were made to London for additional material, and some ingenious ruses were devised to get these past the censor.

SECRET CAMP HISTORIES, **Stalag IVB (WO 208/3274). "The first special parcel was sent from IS 9 on 8th January 1944 and was received on 1st March 1944. This was after a special request for a map of the Swiss frontier and compasses and, if possible, addresses of outside contacts."**[2]

Once it was known that the parcel was arriving, a request was made to the Man of Confidence for special representatives to be stationed at the postal center. He refused, and they had to alert the POWs normally on postal duty to keep careful watch. Though bribery was usually possible with guards it was less successful here because they were under more rigorous official surveillance. All the same the parcel got through with a map concealed beneath the label. The report continues:

SECRET CAMP HISTORIES. "Soap and chocolate were not very satisfactory ways of packing escape material as these were always suspected and were broken into small pieces. The censors always sliced open the covers of books and often broke gramophone records. Clothing was suspected and searched but maps were frequently hidden successfully, especially in battledress. Food parcels were rarely opened and tins of milk always provided good cover.[3]

"Nearly all games equipment came under strong suspicion, though money was often found safely in chess and ludo boards, and compasses in dice shakers. Most musical instruments held good hiding places, though it was essential to know when they were arriving or they might be given to the wrong people."

Key Escape Committee personnel:

Sergeant J. Seddon, RA	Head of committee
Flight Sergeant A.R.G. Warne, RAF	Documents, clothes, photographs
Private D. Bristol, AIF	Contacts with POWs
Warrant Officer J. Rees, RAF	Routes planning
Lance Sergeant A. Thawley, CG	Diversions
Flying Officer J. Hunter, RAF	Interrogating recaptured escapers
Warrant Officer Harris, RAF	Interrogating recaptured escapers
Warrant Officer Makarewicz, RCAF	Welfare of recaptured escapers

This group operated until May 1944, when there were some changes, though Sergeant Seddon continued helping by providing useful escape clothing.

It was always a surprise to allied POWs arriving in the Stalags to find how much greater freedom the French were commonly allowed than others. Parties of largely unsupervised French seemed continually to be moving in and out of the gates, going off to rail depots, farms and villages almost with the same ease as local civilians. It suited the Germans to send these groups out to work, saving on guards in the process, confident of their return. They were trusted principally because, as the French were well aware following the occupation of their country and the establishment of the Vichy regime, the Germans could always arrange reprisals against their families. This had occurred, as they knew, and the Germans had also not hesitated to make scapegoats of some prisoners.

This situation could work both ways. Many loyal Frenchmen detested the occupation and were prepared to take risks in helping with activities which could make life less easy for their captors. At IVB it was usually possible to make deals of various kinds with the French. As regards intended escapes, the swapping of identities and places in their work parties was one such option. It meant taking a good deal on trust, of course, as there was always the possibility of German "plants."

Thorough preparations for escape took time, of course, but inevitably there were those unwilling to wait, who looked for earlier opportunities to leave, who tried, sometimes more than once but, as a rule, failed.

FRED HEATHFIELD. "Four of the group … one of them a Czech, made contact with the French and planned an escape. They got out with a French working party going to the local POW cemetery where they exchanged with four Frenchmen working outside, who wanted to come into the camp. Taffy Harris, our hut leader, knew of the break and we managed to fix the evening parade so that the Germans were satisfied with the count.

"In the early hours of the morning we were awakened by the German guards calling us out to parade on the clear side of the stoves. They counted us. The total was correct and Taffy wondered what all the fuss was about! We were counted again and again.

"More guards were brought in to check the bunk area, and to try to prevent movements between the parade and the bunks. Our identity documents were brought from the Kommandantur, we were called by name and, in the very dim light of the two hut bulbs, checked against our photographs. When all was done there were several men on parade who swore their names had not been called out. And so it went on until, at about 5 a.m., when the Germans were getting very short-tempered, Taffy suggested we should admit there were four men missing and go to bed. The Germans knew there were four men out: a French informer had told them.

"The escapers got to Vienna where they had their hair cut at a barber's shop. Then the Czech offered to show them the sights of the city from a horse-drawn carriage. They moved down to Yugoslavia, but there they found the poverty of the people so bad they could get neither food nor help so they returned into Austria. They were captured on a train heading towards Switzerland."

It's hardly surprising that the escape committee usually considered these "unofficial" attempts half-baked and counterproductive, merely antagonising the Germans and making their own job more difficult. Nevertheless, when possible, some help was also given in these cases.

Some men who'd escaped in Italy, other venturesome spirits as well, were convinced there'd be greater opportunities for getting clear in the smaller camps, the Arbeitskommandos: 50 blokes as a rule, sometimes many more, detailed to work at warehouses, factories, mines, farms. The armed guards were still there, of course, and the two daily roll calls, but it was a chance to be free of some of the petty restrictions, away from the bloody barbed wire fences and watchtowers, and with luck, be better exercised, better fed and fitter for the break.

Warrant officers and noncommissioned officers above the rank of corporal were excluded from joining Arbeitskommandos by the Germans, as were all RAF personnel. The more determined of these therefore had to find ways round the ban, so there was a fairly lively "trade" in the swapping of identities with lower rankers who preferred to stay in the Stammlager, to be with their mates or because they objected to working for the enemy. Correct number counts were of primary importance to the Germans, but switched identities did not please them either, and those prisoners caught doing it usually spent a few days in the cooler.

Joe Seddon, the leader of the escape committee, was a very active fellow in many ways, maintaining liaison with the French, organizing diversions as needed, arranging exchanges of identity, even calling on his medical training to help other men if required (Ray Newell).

To stay in the RAF compound with his brother John, Alex Shand of 22 Battalion 2NZEF, swapped identities with a Canadian named Grant who wanted to get out to an Arbeitskommando. The Germans discovered the switch, Grant was returned to IVB, and Alex was confined to the cooler for six weeks.[4]

PADRE MCDOWALL gives this example of the correct numbers principle as practised in the camp by Russians and others: "Another wagon pulled by only 4 men has gone by. A small man with a black tammy on his head is pulling one side. Ah! A Serb nearby has touched him. He looked round. The guard was behind the cart and out of sight. Quick as lightning this chap slipped from his yoke and the Serb took his place."

The chaplains' rooms were in the recreation hut, under which the tunnel had been started. In this painting by Ray Newell, Major Robert McDowall, senior padre in the camp, is seen at left. The legs belong to an unidentified companion (Ray Newell).

THE TUNNEL

The recreation hut was a building standing alone in the RAF compound close to the tripwire. After being made available by the Germans it was used for education classes, housed a library and the offices of three camp chaplains.

SERGEANT TOM FIELDER (RAAF), 40 Squadron. "Now what we noticed was two paratroopers from our hut laboriously carrying earth and building a bank around the outer wall of this recreation hut. We watched the progress of this wall-building for many days without comment. Then one day I said, 'Roy, why the wall?' Roy replied that it was to keep the football from lodging under the floor and the inconvenience of crawling under to retrieve it, and that they had gained permission from the Germans to do this."

Tom Fielder and his friend Fred (a Geordie coalminer in civvy life) had concluded that something was going on under that hut. After discreet enquiries and probable vetting by the escape committee, they were invited to join the tunnel workforce. They found that the entrance was via a trapdoor in one of the chaplain's offices.[5]

8—The Escape Imperative

The Man of Confidence had serious reservations about the tunnel scheme because, though the library/recreation hut was certainly as close to the wire as any building in the camp, he believed the Germans would shut it down once the tunnel was discovered. Use of its facilities would thus be lost to all prisoners.

Not everyone in the camp retained confidence in Snowshoes. There were complaints about his lack of support for those planning escapes, that he ignored genuine submissions regarding German mistreatment, or simply showed disinterest in the men's welfare.

SECRET CAMP HISTORIES (WO 208/325 P. 10). "Meyers ... rarely took advantage of the escape material at his disposal and took no interest in the recaptured POWs, not even going to visit them while they were in close confinement for punishment, which was his privilege and job."

CYRIL G. JENKINS (late November 1944). "At a meeting of the hut Red Cross representatives a show of 'no confidence' was expressed against WO Meyers, Man of Confidence at Mühlberg: A complete lack of zeal, in not attempting to remedy points of dissatisfaction in this camp [Jacobstahl] and for failing to visit the camp and personally observe the grounds for complaint.

[10 December]: "With 660 votes Sergeant Parker has been elected British Man of Confidence.

[11 December]: "The Germans are refusing to accept Sergeant Parker as the new Man of Confidence."

TOM NELSON. "I particularly remember Snowshoes Meyers being outvoted on it. [He also] pointed out that 50 RAF officers had recently been shot in the escape from Stalag 111B."

But, as FRED HEATHFIELD records, Meyers survived as MOC. "On later elections [he] was always re-elected by massive majorities, despite being outranked by many senior army sergeant majors. When we were liberated he controlled over 16,000 British and American troops.[6] For his magnificent work he received the MBE."

S.G. WOLHUTER. "I quite often accompanied Snowshoes to the Kommandantur, either on individual missions, or collectively with members of all the other nationalities when summoned by the Commandant. Dolmetschers became well-known and more often than not the German personnel spoke to them regarding camp matters instead of to the Vertrauensmänner to save time and trouble. This placed considerable power and responsibility in their hands, which as far as I know was always used with discretion."

Some dissatisfaction had also come from other would-be escapers, who felt that not enough help and encouragement was forthcoming from the MOC. However, his not unreasonable view was that, had he been found by the Germans to be actively involved in escape plans, his position would have been compromised, reducing his capacity to work on behalf of British POWs in other ways. The tunnellers were not deterred by this lack of support.

Tom Fielder. "As our eyes became accustomed to the now-darkened area, someone standing at a hole passed us each a pair of full-length overalls to protect our ordinary clothes. 'Get into these,' he whispered.

"As we did so he began to pass us bundles of earth in pieces of blanket about two feet square. 'Push this earth back against the far wall,' he instructed. We could now see that the 'hole' was a shaft about six feet deep, walled with bed-boards stolen from someone's bed. At the bottom the beginnings of the tunnel had been dug a few feet towards the fence and freedom—or so we hoped."

Eventually, with about 50 men working three shifts daily, the tunnel lengthened and in the process a number of obstacles were encountered. First of these was one of the hut's supporting piles, and dealing with this enabled the provision of some welcome ventilation for the workers. Later an ingenious air-pump was constructed from a stolen garden hose and a kitbag, providing fresh air at the work-face.

Tom Fielder. "The sandy-clay spoil was removed by packing about 10 lbs on a square of blanket and drawing it out along the floor by lengths of rope made from the string from the British Red Cross parcels. This was fairly quick and efficient and the disposal was no problem as there seemed to be ample space under the hut, but it took a number of men to pass it along as the men themselves could not move from the one spot.

"Between the inner single fence and the outer double fence was a German vegetable garden about 50 yards wide under which we had to burrow. The water supply to the garden was by pipe buried deep along the near edge of the garden. To our dismay, we found this pipe to traverse the tunnel at about half the height of the tunnel. The earth above was loose and proved to be a great nuisance as it continued to collapse regardless of how many bed-boards were used to shore it up.

"As the pipe crossed the tunnel at about mid-height, it was an obstacle to those who had to move past it. It was too high to crawl over and rather too low to slide under. So a hole had to be excavated under the pipe to be able to pass by. But the hole tended to fill again as blanket loads of earth were pulled along. So inevitably it was a tight squeeze every time."

Tom goes on to tell how a working light was devised using light fittings swiped from the toilet block in the compound, connecting the cable to the

8—The Escape Imperative 107

power supply in the hut and running it along the boards lining the tunnel. Unfortunately this light flex was not fully insulated and in the dampness of the tunnel, when resting on the water pipe, it became live.

TOM FIELDER. "Most of us at some stage received a few 'tingles' as we slid under the pipe. However when Gil, our carpenter, crawled under and, being a big man, needed more space when the hole had refilled with sand, became stuck with his neck against the live pipe. The current, fortunately only 100 volts, knocked him out. He was removed from the tunnel—'blue' and unconscious—but, luckily for all concerned, revived and was no worse for his experience."

Since the Germans themselves had sited the hut in this position and sanctioned the building of a bank around its base, the possibility of its use for "extramural pursuits" could not have occurred to them. In any case the tunnel was started and during the many weeks it took to remove all the earth, install the supports and reach a point beyond the wire, activities above-ground and subterranean proceeded smoothly.

In the hut on one occasion while Ray Newell was painting the German Obergefreiter (Corporal) Hermann Groh, as he posed for him there, some fellows were on the job below, digging out toward the wire. Ray recalls, "Instead of doing a one-hour stint they were down there for three. Naturally I hadn't been told. However, he [Groh] didn't hear anything."

TOM FIELDER (working under the vegetable garden). "Without warning, a flood of water descended upon me and threatened to collapse a large section of roof. I frantically replaced the bed-boards to prevent total disaster when, to my amazement, down through the roof came a tomato plant with green tomatoes almost two inches in size still tied to a stake. I had to draw the lot down to the floor to continue to repair the damage and, fortunately, the deluge of water ceased."

Tom wondered about the reaction of the gardener, watering a tomato plant, to see it disappear into the ground before him, and later eagerly chatting about the mysterious event with his friends until perhaps it reached the ears of an alert German officer.

In the meantime a different kind of misfortune occurred. Driven by a Russian woman internee, a tractor had worked steadily at harvesting the ripe barley crop in the field beyond the wire. Only a short stubble remained, leaving no cover at all inside the field. It was generally believed among the tunnellers that it was probably too dangerous now to try to use it for escape. Nevertheless, after all their hard work, they were reluctant to give up and continued digging as if all were not lost.

Several inaccurate versions concerning the fate of the tunnel have been recorded, the most popular being this one: The very day the first men were due to take the tunnel route to freedom after dark, disaster struck. When cutting the linseed (actually, barley) in the field outside the wire, a wheel of the tractor broke through and exposed the lightly covered escape hole.

TOM FIELDER. "Two days later, I had just started my shift, had donned the by-now very grubby and soil-caked overalls and was standing in the shaft pumping air, when Dick in the Chaplain's office above gave a warning tap on the floor with his heel to alert me to danger. As I looked up through a crack, I saw a German officer enter the room. I could see his hob-nailed boots and uniform and that he was carrying a long-handled shovel. A few sharp words were exchanged which I could not understand. He then left the office and walked around the other side of the building where, according to observers who reported later, he attempted to force the shovel handle through the wall of earth built by Roy two months before. The handle could not penetrate the wall by now because it had all the contents of the tunnel packed against it. He then came back to the door of the Chaplain's office. Placing the handle between the steps, he easily pushed it through the narrow wall of earth beside the tunnel shaft, narrowly missing my head. He was then seen to walk quickly out of the RAF compound heading for the main guard room. Dick by now knew the game was up. He opened the trapdoor, told me to remove my overalls and warn the others. I gave three sharp tugs on the sand rope and, as casually as possible, walked back to my hut, lay on my bunk and began reading a book."

Obergefreiter Groh, a German corporal who had been a prisoner of the British in World War I, had a son missing on the eastern front and, with his wife and daughter living in Dresden, was unhappy about World War II. Padre McDowall had found him a reasonable man, as did Ray when painting him in the recreation hut. All the same, he could hardly have been expected to ignore a tunnel had he been aware that it was being worked on below him there (Ray Newell).

Within a few minutes the compound was swarming with armed Germans, bayonets fixed to loaded rifles. They surrounded the hut, ordered all out and marched them away for questioning.

8 — The Escape Imperative

During all this TOM FIELDER lay on his bunk, reading. He recalls, "The tunnel caused great excitement. High-ranking German officers from Berlin and other places came for days to look at it and photograph it."

Tom also records that none of those held for interrogation could be proved to have any connection with the tunnel, and neither the tunnel workers nor the escape committee were ever discovered or penalized. The lack of scapegoats notwithstanding, the German response was typically quick and uncompromising and, on their orders, load after load of excrement—as many as 50—from the Scheissenwagens were dumped, over the next few days, into the shaft. It would never be usable again.

There were others who were convinced, in view of the timing and the circumstances that followed, that the Germans had received a tip-off. (See Chapter 7.)

Fred Heathfield recalls this verse from an ode published in one of the camp's wall newspapers over the name of the noted camp poet, Rudyott Klimtin:

> *Gracious me. God bless my soul,*
> *Someone's been and dug a hole.*
> *Burrowed like a cunning fox*
> *Underneath the sentry-box.*

ANDY ANDERSON. "If one of the prisoners from our hut escaped during the night we would attempt to cover it up on the roll call. Someone in the back row ... would be counted and bending down would run down the line to be counted again so the numbers would appear correct. Of course if he were caught it would mean a few days in the cooler."

FLIGHT SERGEANT O.J. DAVIS (429 Squadron, RCAF). "We all knew what was in store for escapers—if they were lucky enough to even get free for a while. One chap tried to climb over the wire and was shot by a sentry in the box. I was luckier, probably because the Germans knew their time was almost up. I was 'awarded' 21 days in the Cooler."

PADRE MCDOWALL (24 July 1944). "Two Russian officers were shot last night trying to escape: 6 shots fired. One died just afterwards, the other while I was at hospital this afternoon."

SECRET CAMP HISTORIES—Stalag IVB (WO 208/3274). "Between May and August 1944 many POWs escaped mainly by disguising RAF personnel as Army and putting them on the wood-gathering parties which worked outside the camp."

The report goes on to mention a dozen U.K. personnel, several Australian NCOs and a Belgian who escaped by this method.[7]

The indefatigable Joe Seddon would have had a hand in these enterprises, one of which involved Doug Denton, the hypnotist. Joe asked whether he and another soldier named Kitcher would swap identities with two air crew personnel planning to escape. Both men were happy to participate in this bit of fun, so Denton became Flight Sergeant Gardiner, and Kitcher Flight Sergeant Stephenson. Only the battledress blouses were exchanged, leaving all four wearing mixtures of khaki and blue.

Away went the escapers and for six weeks Denton and Kitcher appeared on Appell without trouble as Gardiner and Stephenson. Then the latter were marched back into camp under close escort. This seemed an ominous sign to Denton and Kitcher and, sure enough, the next day they were summoned to the German orderly room, where they were ordered to stand in line with the RAF men.

DOUG DENTON. "The Germans now had in front of them two Gardiners and two Stephensons, or two Dentons and two Kitchers. It took the Teutonic minds some while to work this out. At first they got it wrong."

What followed was pure farce. The Germans began by dubbing the army men (Denton and Kitcher) Terrorflieger Schweinhunds and plying the real fliers with chocolate and cigarettes. When they discovered their mistake they reversed the process, at which all four of their victims burst out laughing. The Germans were not amused and each member of the quartet was sentenced to 30 days in the camp jail. As usual, this was full, and the sentenced men were added to a waiting list until called.

DOUG takes up the story: "Your Stalag tag was taken from you and sent to the jailer. This individual was a meticulous Teuton who was thorough in his procedures. The "Kriegie" tags of those waiting to come into the cooler were on one side of his desk, and those serving their sentence on the other side. As a "client" arrived, his tag was removed from the waiting side and placed at the bottom of the pile on the serving side. As the days passed it gradually came to the top of the pile and was handed to the released man as he left the cooler. Having observed this procedure, Kitcher arranged to be included in a ration party serving the inmates of the cooler. He picked (and mixed) up all the Kriegie tags—and pandemonium followed. Whether or not the jailer was sent to the eastern front I am not sure, but none of the four of us served our sentences!"

As in the following examples, other attempts at escape continued.

Tom Fielder's ambitions had not been extinguished by the discovery and filling in of the tunnel and, with help from escape committee members, he was teamed up with two other determined characters to attempt a break from a wood-gathering group. Tom had been out a few times on wood details, had seen the way the system worked, and felt that the chances for this trio were good. Bob was a Scottish RAF Bomber Command pilot with the experience of two previous runs, while Georges was a French soldier who'd made as many as six previous attempts.

Body searches of wood parties were frequent, both departing and returning. On this morning Tom knew he could be in trouble when two guards ordered the 80 men into open ranks and began the careful frisking of clothing and bodies. Tom had traded food with a Russian for a compass and had this round his neck on a chain, as well as a pair of pliers tied inside his sock to his right ankle. From his place in the fifth rank he saw one possible chance and, with heart pounding, stepped across into a blank file in the fourth rank. Very soon the men either side of his original position were being thoroughly searched.

These searches took place between the main entrance and another gate marking the end of the security zone. It was a busy area because of the nearby German administration office, the post office hut, the shower and delousing unit, and this was helpful in enabling a shortfall of numbers in returning groups to be made up after a signal was made to the post office before the German count got under way.

Joe Seddon of the escape committee was with the detail to oversee the exercise and would give the trio its tip to slip away.

Being air crew, Tom had been obliged to borrow an army identity disc to enable him to get out with the wood detail. This would be handed to his stand-in at the return head count, then back to its owner. Regarding Appells, arrangements had been made for Tom's and Bob's absences to be covered for three days. Georges hadn't bothered and was duly posted as missing.

The group got going, heading out past Neuburxdorf into an area of scattered trees where it began gathering bundles of branches. There was little cover here, but on the way back a likelier opportunity occurred when, beyond a plantation of mature trees, they came upon a copse of younger ones, bushier and offering some cover. Joe gave them the word, they dived in and crawled a few yards under the lowest branches, then lay still, expecting shouts, even shots, if their flit had been noticed. Eventually all became quiet as guards and wood party continued on toward the camp.

It was now a case of waiting for dark, when they could make their way to the Neuburxdorf cemetery to collect the haversacks containing food and their water bottles, which the escape committee had arranged to be left there for them by French trustees working at the cemetery.

During the afternoon they were suddenly startled by the screech of shells passing through the air and landing close by. Their hide was close to a firing range where reconditioned artillery pieces were tested. Fortunately the shells were not fitted with warheads so did not explode.

Eventually, hungry and thirsty, they headed for the cemetery, though it was still only twilight. Now in the open, they had the bad luck when rounding a group of trees to meet a German soldier on a bicycle. He recognized them immediately from their British battledress, aimed a pistol at them and gestured for them to get moving towards the Stalag. They moved, and only after hearing some odd clicking sounds did they realize that luck might still be with them. Bob got in first with "His pistol is not loaded — run!" They ran. They took different directions, which may have confused the guard, and found different hiding places, remote from each other.

Tom climbed into a tree, tied himself to a branch and slept for a couple of hours, after which he made his way in the dark to the cemetery where the sound of snoring led him to Georges asleep on a form. Finding no sign of their provisions they moved off to a grove of pine trees where, in the morning, some food and water was delivered to them by a French friend of Georges working at the memorial.

At about midnight they located their own haversacks and were rejoined by Bob who was in poor shape after spending the day in a barley field unsheltered from the hot sun, and drinking contaminated water from a large drum on a construction site. They all walked toward Falkenburg, with Bob supported by the others, and near the railyard took cover in an old quarry building. Their hope had been to board a train for Switzerland, but such trains went only monthly and, urged by Georges, they opted for one bound for Hannover. A Free French worker at the railyard broke the seal of an enclosed wagon, resealing it with a special tool after they had climbed in.

Some further tense incidents followed. In the vicinity of Hannover, while the train was stopped briefly, they climbed out through a ventilator and hid in the grass, afterward spending the day alternatively walking and hiding. Always trying to move westerly towards Holland, they had to cross a busy road before entering a forest, from which they emerged suddenly onto a street running between tall apartment houses. After passing a number of people they came upon a German military post with iron gates, well lit, with swastika flags and soldiers in uniform. All they could do here was march past boldly, and succeeded in doing this without challenge. Soon they reached open country and traversed this only to arrive at a waterway which crossed their route. This proved to be the Mittellandkanal, running from north to south round Hannover before turning west toward Holland.

During the following four nights they walked along the canal towpath, hiding by day and eventually reaching an aqueduct which carried the canal across the Weser river near Minden. As they stepped onto the bridge at about 2 a.m., one of two guards at the entrance wished them "Good night" in German, and George immediately repeated this. It was a lengthy aqueduct, and more sentries were encountered in the middle of the bridge and at the end. Georges spoke the greeting each time and they passed unchallenged, also much relieved, onto rising ground beyond the valley.

Tom and his friends were now moving fairly confidently up a hillside on which a crop had recently been partially mown, and here their luck ran out. They had stumbled upon an emplacement area for anti-aircraft guns used in the defence of the aqueduct against RAF bombing. They were seen as silhouettes against the clear night sky and immediately ordered by armed guards at close range to halt. It was a fair cop.

Returned by train to Neuburxdorf, they were marched to Stalag IVB and locked in the cooler in separate cells. Next day, as Tom has recorded, there were searches and lengthy individual interrogations. His sentence of seven days solitary confinement could not be served in the cooler because of the long waiting list for such punishment. Instead he had to spend it squeezed among 250 men of various nationalities in the Strafebaracke.[8] Confined inside this except for a half-hour morning and afternoon when they were allowed out into a small exercise yard, they all suffered severe discomfort from the cramped conditions and the chronic foul stench.

Warrant Officer Geoff Taylor, an Australian pilot, of 207 Squadron, was brought to IVB in October 1943 after being shot down over Hannover. His ideas for escape—more elevated than through the wire or under it— led to one of the more original and daring attempts made from Stalag IVB. Not many miles from the camp, at Lonnewitz, was a Luftwaffe air base from which it was known Ju88 fighter-bombers operated. The scheme Geoff and his bomb aimer "Smithy" (Canadian Sergeant C.R. Smith) hatched involved appropriating one of these aircraft and flying it to freedom. Getting away from the Stalag and across to the air base without discovery was one thing; taking over an unfamiliar enemy plane and getting it airborne was another, and the scheme stalled as little more than fantasy for more than a year. Early on Geoff had realized that the controls in a German aircraft could be markedly different from those of British planes and that it would be essential for him to secure a diagram showing the layout of a Ju88 cockpit. This was where the freer-ranging French might come in.

Taylor's original idea had been to fly north to neutral Sweden but, after a year had passed and with the Russians now much closer, he opted for the alternative eastward flight to put down behind the Russian lines.

In due course the French secured some diagrams for the Ju88, in which he noted some variations of layout—something which would have to be sorted out on the spot. The next stage was to get out of IVB without arousing suspicion. Again the French escape committee supplied the solution, by means of one of the easy-come, easy-go work parties for which they were able to wangle the personnel and numbers; and on the morning of 13 March 1945 Geoff and Smithy walked out dressed as French prisoners. A diversion to mask their absence would be staged when the group returned. Earlier, back in their hut, arrangements had been made to cover for them on Appell for a few days.

Well, having spent a good part of the day with the work party, the two doughty lads took the nod to hide themselves until the coast was clear. They then followed along the railway line running south to Dresden. After several miles they'd reached a small wood on the airfield's perimeter and, covering themselves with leafy foliage, settled there for the night.

They woke to the sound of exploding bombs, heard the roar of many powerful aero engines overhead and, from the nearby airfield, the racket of Ju88s and Ju188s taking off along the flare path. It was the night of the first of the massive raids on Dresden.

Hardly a promising omen. What chance for their plan now? The Germans conceivably would be more vigilant. Yet might the confusion caused by the raids work to their advantage? Having got this far anyhow, Geoff and Smithy weren't ready to give up.

Slipping back into their role of French time-servers, lifting an end each of their "prop"—a long trimmed log—they tramped in workmanlike fashion along the inside of the airfield boundary. Apparently unnoticed, they began cautiously attempting entry to several aircraft, but all proved out of order or locked. When Mustang fighters roared across the airfield, signalling the start of the daylight raid on Dresden, they encountered a few Germans taking cover, but were ignored.

Their one chance of success came late in the day when they got into an unlocked Ju188 which they knew had been checked and refuelled. Geoff was trying to make sense of the controls when interrupted by a German sentry who objected to the presence of French workers in a Luftwaffe aeroplane and brusquely ordered them, in the Deutsch equivalent, to push off.

Other aircraft they tried were all locked and finally, at dusk, cold and hungry, they climbed into an out-of-service trainer plane in which they could shelter for the night: a sleepless night because of the continuous roar of aircraft engines and bombing raids to the south.

They had given the scheme their best shot, but reluctantly concluded now that it wasn't going to work. They headed for "home," trudging wearily back through the countryside to IVB, where their trumped-up explanation was readily accepted at the gates. The boys in the hut were agog over their experiences but accepted their urgent need of hot drinks, grub and sleep.

There were at least 200 escape attempts from the Stalag, but only four are documented as successful:[9]

Two men known to have made it back to Britain by way of Holland are Warrant Officer James Branford, 149 Squadron, RAF (subsequently decorated with the MBE), and Army Sergeant J.L. Warren (awarded the BEM). They were debriefed in London.[10]

8—The Escape Imperative

Greater detail is available concerning two others who succeeded after heading west and north. Private Alfred M. Kuhn, 1st Brigade, South African Defence Force, had been captured at El Adem in Libya on 23 November, 1941. Transported to Italy, he escaped and was recaptured once there and later twice in Germany.

Flight Sergeant Stanley K. Gordon-Powell, 35 Squadron, RAF, was shot down over Cologne the night of 28–29 June, 1943 and subsequently made five escape attempts, the fifth in company with Private Kuhn.

Back in Stalag IVB, after serving their sentences of 21 days in separate punishment areas and threatened with being shot if caught escaping again, Gordon-Powell and Kuhn immediately began planning their next attempt. According to Gordon-Powell, the Man of Confidence refused to give them any help but new sets of papers were supplied by Sergeant Joe Seddon of the escape committee and their battledress was exchanged for civilian clothing acquired from two Polish internees from Warsaw. They then joined a Dutch work group sent outside the camp. The date was 21 March, 1945.

Leipzig via Riesa was chosen as the route, since Dresden had been severely bombed. At Bitterfeld near Leipzig they were able to spend the night at a French Arbeitslager and received chocolate, raisins and cigarettes from some British prisoners also working there. With help from the French and some good luck they were able to reach a hospital at Berlin where friendly Dutch doctors found both accommodation and Berlin police passes for them.

Colonel R. SUTTON-PRATT, then British Military Attaché in Stockholm, recorded their stories for the official records: "These passes did not suffice to get them out of Berlin, however, and before being allowed to buy a ticket for Flensburg, a special pass from the railway police was necessary. After getting to the head of the long queue they were refused, but in the next queue they were successful, although outside there were hundreds of bombed-out people who had been refused and were trying to force their way into the office.

"They bought a ticket direct to Flensburg and travelled via Hamburg-Neumünster. When they arrived in Flensburg they hoped to make a good contact and found a German Catholic railway worker, who put them up in his house and said he would help them. After trying for two days to board a goods train they left him to find help elsewhere."

Now without food coupons, having eaten nothing for two days and suffering from malnutrition, Kuhn and Gordon-Powell tried their luck first with a German Catholic priest and later with other German people, but all were too afraid to help. They had no option now but to try to cross the frontier with Denmark. Near Niehus they found this and four other places too heavily guarded, but eventually came to a marshy area, through which after a long struggle they reached a river. They were able to wade this, though it was dark and the water was up to their shoulders. They hoped their wet clothes would not prove a disadvantage next day. They continued walking and by 6 a.m. knew they were in Denmark. Seeing several farms and, tired, wet and hungry as they were, they decided to seek help at the nearest.

COLONEL SUTTON-PRATT. "As they were about to enter the first farm they met the milkman, who looked rather surprised to see them. Kuhn told him they were English, and he pulled them away and told them that all the farms but one were owned by Nazis (Volksdeutscher).

"He showed them the Danish farm, and there they were received with the three words: 'Wash—Eat—Sleep!'" They were given such a breakfast as they had not seen for years, and then went to bed.

"Later in the day a doctor arrived and told them to get ready to leave. They were given Danish identity cards (they had passport photos taken in Berlin) and that night they left on bicycles to Renkeness, where they spent six days on a farm and were received with the greatest kindness. Their 'rations' consisted of 10 eggs a day and as much meat, butter, milk and cream as they wanted."

A difficult and dangerous part of the journey for Gordon-Powell and Kuhn, and no less for their helpers, was about to begin. Another doctor called to inform them that arrangements were under way to get them to Copenhagen. Their guides now were two Danes who had apparently escaped

Ausweis. This forged pass was collected in Sweden by Colonel R. Sutton-Pratt from one of the escapers at the end of a successful run (courtesy Jeremy Sutton-Pratt).

from a concentration camp. They had to cross Fyn and take two ferries, on the second of which, between Fyn and Zealand, they passed successfully through a German control check.

COLONEL SUTTON-PRATT. "In Copenhagen they were told that the underground were making preparations to get them into Sweden. At 6 a.m. on 17 April they went to the harbour and were taken aboard a small craft. They were hidden, together with six Danes, between a double partition in front of the engine.

"Just before they left, some Germans came on board to search with dogs. Luckily the skipper had washed the decks with ammonia to spoil their sense of smell. The search lasted three-quarters of an hour and they even lifted the floorboards, but even then did not find the escapers.

"One hour after they left a German patrol boat signalled to them to stop, and a naval officer came on board, had a look round and left. They were then met by a fast motorboat flying the Swedish flag, but manned by Danes, off the Swedish coast near the port of Landskrona. From there they continued their journey in the motorboat along the coast in a northerly direction to Hälsingborg, where they landed and shortly afterwards were met by the British Consul, who came to the police station where they were interrogated."

STANLEY GORDON-POWELL. "The whole success of the trip is due to Private Kuhn whose five languages made this trip possible. He employed French, German, Dutch and Italian, all without accent. His fluent German pulled us out of many a tight corner."

It has not been possible to check escapes from the Arbeitskommandos but it is known that many attempts were made and that almost certainly several of them were successful in reaching Switzerland or other places outside Germany.

Neutral Switzerland, though too mountainous from some directions for practical access, bordered four European countries, and there were long stretches of frontier which could be crossed — as long as the German guard posts could be avoided and the patrols eluded. Many succeeded, and acknowledgment of this and of Swiss sympathy is given in an article published in *Prisoners of War Bulletin*, Vol. 3, No. 2, by the American National Red Cross, in February 1945: "This small country is sheltering over 100,000 refugees, military internees and military escapees, who have poured into Switzerland from all over Europe."[11]

What this burden meant for the Swiss can be put in perspective when it's realized that the country's own total population then was c. 4,200,000.

Escaping may not always have been merely a matter of getting clear of the Stalag. For example, how about escaping within the camp? Or even escaping *into* the camp?[12]

9

Discipline/Punishment/ War Crimes

> *On the whole, punishment hardens people and diminishes their sensibilities; it concentrates; it intensifies the sense of alienation; it toughens the power of resistance.*
> (Nietzsche, *The Genealogy of Morals*, Essay 2, 1887)

Discipline for the German armed forces was a linchpin of its efficient functioning. Only the Japanese would approach that degree of martial severity, which in the allied services was regarded as a kind of paranoia. All the same, it's a matter of history that this discipline, together with obsessive dedication to the service of the fatherland, unswerving loyalty to the Führer and consummate planning, enabled the German forces to sweep all before them in the first three years of World War II.

In the Wehrmacht it was a requirement of every serviceman, from gemeiner Soldat, to salute anyone of higher rank. The Germans confidently expected this ingrained and inflexible ritual, along with others, to be observed by their prisoners.

SERGEANT S.G. ("WALLY") WOLHUTER. "Our first serious dispute with the Germans was over saluting. They wanted us to salute them all from the rank of corporal upwards, as was customary in their army as well as those of [some] other nationalities. We refused and stated that we were prepared to salute only their officers as required by the Geneva Convention. They responded by arresting many of our chaps, but no amount of threatening or punishment ever helped and they eventually gave up."

SERGEANT FRED HEATHFIELD. "The Commandant, a very mild gentleman, Colonel Stossier, occasionally stumped along the Main Street. There was a rumour he had tin legs but I do not know if this is true. One story is that, one fine morning in the very early days, he stopped an RAF sergeant and asked why he had not saluted. The sergeant replied that he *had* saluted the Colonel. The Colonel had not seen a salute. The sergeant explained that, as he was not wearing a hat, he had saluted in the acknowledged British Forces manner by doing an "eyes right!" He had to demonstrate that he simply put both hands by his sides and swung his head to the right for a number of paces.

"'Ah!' said the Colonel, 'and how do I acknowledge your salute?'

"'By saluting with the hand in the usual way, sir.'

"'Ah! So *I* appear to be saluting *you*. I think not. In future you will salute in the normal way, with or without a hat!'"

Sergeant NORMAN PAGE received less tolerant treatment from a member of the commandant's staff:

"At about midday on 19 January 1944 I was walking along the main central road through the camp when along came a German officer on a bicycle. As he passed me he stopped and jumped off, shouted at me to come to him and gave me a proper rollicking although I couldn't understand a word he said. It appeared this was all because I had not saluted him.

"He called to a Feldwebel who was nearby and told him to put me under arrest. I had to go with him to the guardroom just inside the main gate where they recorded my name and number and then put me in Cell No. 5 in the cooler. This was ... about 8 feet × 5 feet, had a small barred window set high, the door was strengthened and had a small aperture, and the only furniture was a bed and stool, and a bucket in the corner.

"I remained there until 6 pm when the officer arrived and proceeded to yell at me through an interpreter for a few minutes, telling everyone what he thought of the English. When he had finished he told me I could go, and I returned to my hut much to the amusement of my pals."

QMS FREDERICK HEDGES. "Flap on at roll call this morning, when 46 of our hut, who were late getting out, were marched at revolver point, to stand on the wire for 2 hours. Not very pleasant these cold mornings."

Another day a group was on its way back from Jacobstahl (304H) to IVB, under the control of a Feldwebel.

CSM Richard Hall recalls "The Brits were singing as they marched through a German village and he shouted to us all to stop; then, losing his temper and turning suddenly, he punched one soldier in the mouth."

Though this incident was reported to the man of confidence, no more was heard of it.

QMS FREDERICK HEDGES. "The Russians cause Jerry quite a lot of trouble by roaming about the English compound in search of food, and are continually being rounded up. Occasionally one gets shot, but it doesn't seem to deter the others."

FRED HEATHFIELD. "They hung round our cookhouse waiting for the great iron buckets of soup to be handed out over the counter which was open to the path or track outside. Soup splashed into the mud, to be pounced on by these poor devils who would scrape it up with a spoon, including the dirt, and eat it immediately.

"On one occasion when this happened a German officer ran out of the cookhouse and kicked one of these crouching Russians to send him sprawling in the mud. He followed up with repeated kicks as the man cowered on the ground, and proceeded to kick him to death, jumping on his body with both feet. We could hear the bones crack. From the other side of a high wire fence a crowd of aircrew, unable to get round to the other side, shouted at the German but to no effect.

"An RAF sergeant came round the corner and saw what was happening and tried to pull the German off. The officer drew out his revolver but a German Posten had also run up and he restrained the sergeant who was taken off to the cells. The dying Russian was carried away by his friends. No action would be taken against the German, but he would not appear inside the camp again."

SERGEANT ROBERT JAMIESON, 421/157 Field Regt, RA (Repatriation Report, 29 May, 1944): "Oberfeldwebel Folk was guilty of brutal treatment of POWs and did all he could to make things unpleasant. At Christmas 1943 he came to the barrack when a card game was in progress and hit one POW over the ear, pushed the table against the wall and pinned another POW. The latter pushed the table back onto him and Folk drew his revolver. The barrack commander rushed up and Folk kicked him in the crotch."[1]

WALLY WOLHUTER witnessed an incident in 1944 which had the British prisoners seething with rage and nearly ended in tragedy for many. "Immediately after roll call on 21 June, the second anniversary of our capture at Tobruk, a chap named Brown from a neighbouring hut, instead of leaving the parade ground, crawled under a wire fence surrounding the Arbeitschule (work school) to pick some strawberries that were growing there for the benefit of the Germans. The Arbeitschule, where legless and crippled Russian prisoners were employed to make toys for an outside factory, was situated inside the camp, but nevertheless surrounded by wire to separate it from our compound. As Brown reached forward to pick some strawberries a German, Nordmann, drew his pistol and shot him between the eyes from a nearby window of the Arbeitschule. When we reached poor Brown there was already a death-rattle in his throat and he died soon afterwards.[2]

9—Discipline/Punishment/War Crimes

"Within a few moments a great crowd had gathered at the spot, hooting, booing and shouting at Nordmann as he made his way out of the Arbeitschule enclosure away from us. The situation looked very ugly and soon Oberleutnant Hölzel, with drawn pistol and supported by armed guards, had taken up a position opposite the crowd on the other side of the fence.

"Hölzel shouted to us above the din to command our men to disperse or else they would start shooting at us, indicating also that machine-guns in the guard-towers were trained on us. The crowd was extremely excited and angry and in no mood to listen to anyone, so it seemed that the only way to defuse the situation was to set an example. Several of us, therefore, believing that discretion is the better part of valour, started walking away advising everyone around us to follow. It saved the day and slowly but reluctantly the crowd walked back to their huts, muttering threats and swearing revenge."

FLIGHT SERGEANT JACK DAVIS. "One day seeing two soldiers carrying the bucket of 'skilly' [soup like water] from the cookhouse to our hut. They were pretty weak and stumbling a bit, and the German guard gave one of them a prod with his bayonet. Sergeant Major Turner [our hut commander] was outside and witnessed this incident. With a rush and a roar he sprang forward, grabbed the guard by the back of his uniform, shook him and shouted 'You do that again to one of my men and I'll kill you.' He was a very brave man."

TOM NELSON. "I did see brutal attacks by German guards against other nationalities, mainly Russian. I recall particularly Russians who had been caught stealing potatoes being stood at the back gate of the camp in the middle of winter. They were forced to take their hands out of their pockets and face into the biting cold east wind."

The men collapsed unconscious onto the ground, where they were left for a long period. It's believed they were dead.

PRIVATE TOM BARKER, 1st Bn, Argyll & Sutherland Highlanders, tells a tale about a German guard known as "Blondie," in charge of the Russian work parties.

"He would have to be the meanest bastard in any army. He would hit a POW for no reason; he usually carried a pick handle and would lay into anyone who got in his way.

"He was about six foot tall and heavy built with blond hair, blue eyes and a permanent scowl, and looked what he was in his grey uniform with all the relevant badges to show he had been in the Hitler Youth, a typical SS bully boy.

"And we knew for certain he had killed eight blokes in this camp, blokes who could not fight back.

"One day a cart with rubbish and potato peelings from the guards' barracks was on its way to the rubbish pit to be burned when some hungry Russian POWs grabbed some of the peelings off the cart.

"Blondie saw them and put his pistol to the back of one bloke's head and shot him; beat the other senseless with his pick handle and broke his arm, and lashed out at others who came too close to him.

"He then made the rest pick up the dead man and put him on the rubbish cart ... and the dead man was taken to the pit and burnt along with the rubbish."

The German attitude to POWs generally was often hostile and always unpredictable. When it came to the Russians—a less than human species to them—it was uniformly callous, and they were frequently shot out of hand for the slightest lapse.

Private First Class Russell Kuehn recalls such an incident when the daily wagon, pulled by a pair of oxen, was bringing rations into the camp. As was often the case, Russians were there trying to steal turnips, intended for the POWs' skilly, from it.

RUSSELL KUEHN. "On that day the guard 'lost his cool' and shot a Russian through the head. It was a terrible price to pay for stealing a turnip.[3]

As the war news improved PADRE MCDOWALL noted on 22 February 1945 how the starving Russian prisoners had become even bolder in their attempts to obtain food: "Ulbricht had his revolver out and was shoving the Russians about. They are driven by hunger and are a bit overbearing owing to the proximity of their forces. They were diving after the carts and one German was laying into them with a stick; and Ulbricht was bashing round with his revolver. I saw him knock one down on his face."

JOE TOMBLING (27 March 1945). "German shot a Russian for stealing potatoes off the wagon as it went up the main road.... Bullet went right through the Russian from back to front and through an English chap's shoulder who was pushing the cart."

Padre McDowall recorded an incident at the sugar beet factory. "A South African had come in tired and wet through, and a German NCO ordered him out to work again. The chap demurred and was knocked down. When his brother, who happened to be there, remonstrated, the NCO seized a rifle from a guard and shot him. The bullet wounded another man in the wrist and a third in the leg."[4]

FRED HEATHFIELD. "Next to the Revier compound was the Straflager, where prisoners awaited an empty cell in the cooler for their period of solitary confinement. One man had found a way out via the Revier compound into the main camp and he had been in the habit of getting through late at

9—Discipline/Punishment/War Crimes

Carts of various sizes were a common sight, hauled by prisoners collecting rations or on other errands. Two men can be seen with this one, under the eye of a guard near Main Gate (Terry Hunt photograph, courtesy Joe Tombling).

night, to visit his hut mates and have a meal with them. In the early hours of one morning there was a rifle shot and a bullet passed through the wall of our hut. Our orderlies ran in to check us, then went outside where they found the Straflager inmate hanging dead on the wire. A sentry in the Straflager had shot him at point blank range as he tried to return to his hut."

During an expedition to "liberate" coal from the fuel bunker one dark night, Taffy Jones was shot while inside. He was hit in the back and died two days later in hospital.[5]

WARRANT OFFICER ANDY ANDERSON. "The usual volley of shots were not fired over his coffin because they [the Germans] considered that he had been killed during a criminal act against the German state."

EUGENE WOPATA (Private First Class, Company G, 242 Regiment, 42nd U.S. "Rainbow" Infantry Division). "One day I was sent to another compound and I was in the pool for a work detail. A German guard was at the gate that separated the two compounds. I was not selected to go on the work detail, so I passed through the gate to return to my hut with no problem.

"The next day I decided to go back to this compound to pick up [collect] something. This time the guard didn't say a thing, but hit me under the chin with his rifle butt. This sent me crashing into a fence post and to my knees. He then took another swing at me, missed my head, hit my shoulder and knocked me down. I also hit my head on a metal post on the way down. I was now lying on the ground and he started to kick me.

Because "Taffy" Jones had been shot in the commission of a crime (stealing coal), the Germans would not provide a firing party of guards at his graveside, as in the case of Corporal Brown. Padre McDowall, at right, conducted the service, while Corporal Mickey Read, with bugle, sounded the Last Post (Terry Hunt photograph, courtesy Dr. Mary A. Tagg).

"After I rolled over I managed to absorb a few kicks with my hands. After one of his kicks I managed to grab his foot, nearly knocking him down. Next thing I knew I was looking into the business end of his rifle. Half crawling and running I rapidly left the scene, bleeding, bruised and thankful that I hadn't been shot."[6]

Padre McDowall describes what occurred after French had killed a German guard: "50 French were taken haphazard to be shot, one a father with six children. A lad of 18 offered to take the place of the father. He was included in the 50, but the father was shot dead just the same, 51 instead of 50."

The POWs also exercised discipline among themselves. Severe punishment was applied for certain transgressions. Stealing food from a fellow POW was considered one of the worst crimes, and punishment could take many forms.

JOE TOMBLING. "Two Yanks found pinching in 16A. They were given a hell of a beating-up. Sent to sick quarters and MO said don't turn them over to Jerry because the cooler is a better and warmer place ... than our billets. Everyone knows them as they are now covered in bandages."

KURT VONNEGUT. "The car thief from Cicero, Illinois ... had been caught stealing cigarettes from under the pillow of an Englishman. The Englishman, half asleep, had broken Lazzaro's right arm and knocked him unconscious."

Other examples of such summary punishment include being treated as outcasts and totally ignored for days or weeks; flogging; even being thrown into the latrine pit and immersed there in the foul excrement before being allowed to climb out.

10

Bartering and Bribery

I will buy with you, sell with you, talk with you ...
(Shakespeare, *The Merchant of Venice*, I.iii)

THE SWAP SHOP

The canteen established at the outset by the Germans had run out of goods and become inoperative during 1941; thus, for the increasing numbers of men later being brought into the camp, the need and opportunity for alternatives was clear. The exchanging of items between POWs was a natural by-product of their environment, but it wasn't until the swap shop was established that a value ratio could begin to be formulated.

Eventually the swap shop became both the central valuing authority and also for a time the main outlet at which commodities of great variety were bought and sold. Money generally counted for nothing. The German Lagergeld (camp money) was considered valueless, while the pound, the dollar and other tenders—for those who had them — might sometimes be used with special deals. The cigarette was the real standard of currency. Red Cross parcels provided items of food or clothing to be traded, while bread acquired from the Jerries—officially a strong verboten practice — in exchange for tea, coffee, cocoa or other beverages was often available.

A camp finance committee met every Monday morning to fix prices, taking into consideration the supply of food parcels, cigarette parcels and personal clothing parcels received during the previous week. All goods offered for sale had been sold to the shop for cigarettes, and then appeared in the shop with a price tag marked in cigarettes. This was supposed to eliminate profiteering, but inevitably, as the war went on, it proved an unsustainable ideal.

SERGEANT FRED HEATHFIELD. "Despite the official prices of food there were always the entrepreneurs or 'wide boys' who bypassed the official

Lagergeld: The German issue of camp money was generally regarded as valueless, especially once the supply of goods in their canteen had dried up (courtesy Norman Page).

exchange. They would go round the barrack huts calling out 'food for sale' but at a slightly higher price than the market, such as bully-beef for thirty-two cigarettes. There was always someone too lazy to walk across to the trading area and these fellows soon made fortunes in cigarettes. The richest of all was a cockney soldier known as "Mo" who operated with a partner, "Half-a-Mo." I think they had been East End bookies.

"They inaugurated the Stalag IVB race meetings, advertised for days in advance. A track was prepared in AD North compound, with six lanes marked off in squares. Mo and Half-a-Mo had obtained two tea-chests and on the sides of one of these they had painted the numbers 1 to 6 just like on a dice. The second cube had colours or patterns. Six jockeys had army vests dyed or painted to match the six colours or patterns. Bets were taken in cigarettes and the race started. The coloured dice rolled, and a colour was called out. The second dice was rolled and the number told the first jockey how many squares to advance, and so on until the race was won. In The Grand National, squares on the track were named as famous jumps, and a jockey landing on one of these was deemed to have fallen. When Mo and Half-a-Mo were posted away from IVB they each had to employ people to carry their two suitcases, each filled with cigarettes!"

QMS FREDERICK HEDGES. "In a POW camp, whenever there is a shortage of anything, there will arise a racket. And so a terrific racket exists for coal. If your hut is fortunate enough to get inside the racket your cooking and heating facilities are assured. If not, well just too bad."

PADRE MCDOWALL (mid-December, 1944). "There is a tremendous lot of trickery going on in the camp.

"Some of our chaps have been selling off their overcoats to other nationals. One sells the coat, the other goes and gets it back again, and the two split the cigarettes. The thievery and knavery passes belief."

New enterprises were being always being initiated and, while the German rations tended to diminish, the supply of goods from various sources inside and outside the camp increased.

WARRANT OFFICER "ANDY" ANDERSON. "The French were allowed to work in Mühlberg ... in many of the German civilian houses, which gave them access to many of the things denied to the 'Brits' (and the opportunity for profit!).

"For example, the French would buy chocolate from the British for twenty-five cigarettes (trading was always in cigarettes, this was our currency) and trade them with the Germans for a loaf of bread, which they would then sell to us for eighty cigarettes."

SERGEANT SAM GILLETTE. "Local women would bring stuff to the fence to sell. I bought vitamins, DDT powder etc. from them. I had a fountain pen, a non-working watch and a silver dollar I had hidden, to trade."

Eventually the bartering process generated such popularity that it spilled over into what became known as the International Market, a hectic beehive of activity on Main Street. There, for much of the day, representatives of many nations could be seen haggling and bargaining over an extraordinary range of items, in an atmosphere basically commercial but also functioning at a social level and not least as a form of entertainment.

CORPORAL JOE TOMBLING. "John Bushell got a large packet of oats and 3/4 lb of salami for his white sweater (from Danish police). One of them wanted an RAF badge so I obliged for 2 slices of bread and 2 ozs of butter."

QMS FREDERICK HEDGES. "I've seen English pound notes sold here for 1 cigarette, during the last week. Also a 17-jewelled watch, 18 carat gold—worth, I suppose, all of £25—it went for a loaf of bread. I saw a Russian receive from a Yank, a gold ring which must have cost £10, for 5 packets of pepper. The Yank thought they were soup powders, but by the time he'd found out his mistake, the Russian had vanished."

Sometimes bartering for particular commodities wasn't the answer and in such cases, a different approach might be needed.

FRED HEATHFIELD. "Prior to the coal operations[1] Sergeant Jock McVittie came to me, just before our first Christmas, and asked me to help him. He had an idea it would be very nice if we could provide every member of the hut with an aluminium bowl for Christmas.

"He knew there were hundreds of them stacked up in the work hut in the Russian work compound, wired off from AD North. After dark we went

10—Bartering and Bribery

The International Market: Ray had originally intended this as a mural for the Empire Theatre, but it never got that far. However, those depicted near the front are, from left, an American, two Russians, a Dutchman, a Belgian, a Dutch trader, a Bulgarian, a little Russian, a British army man, a Serb, a Danish policeman, a Russian and a Polish rebel (in tricorn hat). One of the ubiquitous Scheissenwagens can be seen at upper right (Ray Newell).

through the wire dividing us from AD North, dodging the searchlights, and reached the single wire into the work area. Suddenly, from behind one of the huts appeared a German corporal who challenged us. McVittie, in carefully rehearsed German, quickly asked him if he had brought the bread and held out a handful of cigarettes.

"The German was a bit surprised and asked something we did not understand, but we persisted in asking for the bread. Finally the guard ordered us into a nearby barrack of South Africans where an Afrikaner sergeant major interpreted and told him we had arranged to meet a German and buy bread from him. A cup of real coffee was produced for the German. Then the Afrikaner said, I've persuaded him to let you go, as it's Christmas, and you don't want to spend it in the cooler. Give him the cigarettes and he will take you back to your hut. We were lucky."

SERGEANT S.G. ('WALLY') WOLHUTER, a Dolmetscher in the British compounds, describes some of his experiences of trading with the Germans: "Each half-barrack had its own stove fuelled by briquettes, under the supervision of two stokers—a popular job because of the pleasant warmth it provided. We could brew and cook on the stove, the only problem being the inadequate coal supply. As the compound office—a small area surrounded by Hessian—

was situated in our hut, and as I had daily contact with the Germans, it was expected of me to procure more than our normal issue of coal for our stove. I did so very successfully through Feldwebel Sonntag and Gefreiter Teichgräber who were our Blockführer. Sonntag, a mild-mannered little man, was a carpenter in civilian life and Teichgräber was a farmer. They both loved smoking and while Sonntag eagerly accepted English cigarettes, Teichgräber preferred the dark French variety which were easily procured by swapping. Sonntag also had grandchildren and would do a great deal for one or two bars of chocolate to take home to them in Leipzig when he got weekend leave.

"It was not only extra coal that was procured in this way, but extra bread as well—delicious rye bread from Teichgräber's farm which not only added to our supplies, but was a pleasant change from the camp Schwarzbrot with its complement of added sawdust."

On occasions, when special commodities were required for use in the camp, a levy of cigarettes was made on all the men. An example of this, noted by Wally Wolhuter, occurred late in 1943 when it was decided to acquire the instruments for an orchestra. Ten cigarettes collected from each man produced a total of 100,000, a virtual gold mine in German eyes. A fully equipped orchestra was duly established.

WALLY WOLHUTER goes on: "Another of our guards, a private soldier, supplied me with one loaf of bread each week for which I had to give him either 10 cigarettes or a bar of chocolate. He also required a few Marks in cash and three bread coupons for the favour, but both these items were easily procurable as Marks had little value and coupons could be faked. According to the guards bread coupons were in any event dropped over Germany by the RAF and were therefore plentiful.

"The soldier, whose name was Müller, had a girlfriend in a nearby village whom he kept happy as her husband was away on the Russian front. She worked in a bakery and every Saturday evening Müller cycled to spend part of the night with her. He gave her the cigarettes or chocolate and with the bread coupons and the Marks she was able to produce three loaves for him to take back to camp. The guard on the gate got one, Müller kept one and I was given the third which was dumped on my bunk between 3 and 5 o'clock on a Sunday morning.

"It says a great deal for both hunger and sex for a man to venture out at night in sub-zero weather in order to sleep with his girlfriend and at the same time procure some bread!"

Two months into 1945, when the German rations had suffered cuts and the delivery of Red Cross food parcels had become irregular, Joe Tombling noted: "Prices of bread and biscuits have rocketed to 60 cigs per loaf and three French biscuits for 5 cigs."

10—Bartering and Bribery 131

Even so, PADRE MCDOWALL observed at the time that the international market still seemed to be flourishing, with the following articles for sale: "Thread, soap, pocket books, hair brushes, clothes brushes, scents, boxes, basins, pots, thermos, pipes, spurs, belts, iodine—not obtainable in the hospital—antiseptics, badges, cigarette holders, boot-soles, boots, white collars, bottles, food of all kinds, coins, clothes-pegs, laces, slippers, pliers, tin openers, razors, boats, hair oil, pincers, hair-cutters, biscuits camp-made, rings, watches, pens, clothes of all kinds, suitcases and whatnots besides."[2]

11

Stranger Than Fiction

'Tis strange — but true; for truth is always strange;
Stranger than fiction.
(Lord Byron, *Don Juan*, Canto xiv, 101)

DEATH BY DIVE-BOMBING

Over two or three weeks from early April 1944, no doubt with the aim of impressing the RAF personnel, two Ju88s from nearby Lonnewitz airfield flew over the camp, sometimes three times in the day, zooming in from every angle and performing skilful but dangerous aerobatics at heights estimated at 20 to 30 feet above the ground. On one occasion a big football match was being watched by some 7,000 prisoners.

QMS Frederick Hedges. "After the match had been in progress for a quarter-hour an 88 made its appearance and cocked its wings in readiness for his usual swoop over the camp, in the course of which he must have spotted the match in progress and right away transferred his efforts to the football pitch in a dive which just enabled him to clear the heads of the prisoners on the touchline down to within inches of the ground and pulling out just in time to clear the prisoners on the opposite touchline.

"This surpassed anything that he had done so far. The slightest misjudgement would have resulted in the deaths of hundreds."

Following this incident a protest was lodged with the German authorities through the chief man of confidence. It's not known whether this was passed on to the Luftwaffe but, on a sunny afternoon in the following week, one of the Ju88s appeared again, zooming to within inches of the rooftops. In recalling this event QMS Hedges refers to the two barbed-wire fences some thirty feet apart, running the length of the southern side of the camp, inside of which was no-man's-land. A sentry tower stood just beyond the outer fence, while about ten feet from the inner one was the POW's chapel.

Hedges recalls: "The 88 comes in with one of its dives, approaching from due west and immediately above the lane formed by the two belts of wire ... he suddenly sees, looming up in front of him, the chapel on one wing and the sentry box on the other. He seems to have instantly pulled back on his controls ... and, being so low, the sudden drop of his tail catches the wire, but unfortunately the tail planes also caught two prisoners who were walking along the wire, instantly killing one and seriously injuring the other."[1]

The two luckless prisoners who were victims of this madness were Canadians, Sergeant Herb Mallory of 434 Squadron, who was decapitated, and Sergeant Wally Massie, of No. 24 OTU, who suffered a severely fractured leg after being thrown violently in the plane's slipstream.[2]

This portrait of Wally Massie was made in November 1944, several months after Wally had been injured when struck by a low-flying Ju-88 performing stunts over the camp (Ray Newell).

SERGEANT NORMAN F. PAGE. "Sgt. Mallory's funeral was on 4 May 1944. On this occasion ... the Germans agreed to allow a funeral party to be formed and approx 20 from my hut (45A) including me, were escorted to Burxdorf cemetery for a ceremony with some military honours. We had pulled a handcart from the camp carrying the coffin."

DAVE MCINTOSH, in an article in the *Canadian Legion Magazine*: "In May 1944 the Swedish ship Gripsholm repatriated some Allied POWs to Britain. Among them was a group from Stalag IVB who related that dive-bombing practice had been incessant over the camp.... A few days later a German Posten, a guard who lives in the area, reports that the German Warrant Officer pilot who was flying the JU-88 has been stripped of his rank and wings and sent to gaol for damaging his aircraft and certain camp structures. On completion of his stretch in the Luftwaffe cooler he will be posted, as a private soldier, to an infantry battalion on the Russian front."

This was not the only aircraft shoot-up that resulted in death for POWs. Tragically, very close to the end of the war, two American Mustang fighters dived on a wood-gathering party just outside the camp, strafing and killing five men, among them the German guard, and wounding a dozen. Bullets also sprayed huts within the camp, causing further casualties.³

A familiar sight around the camp were the Scheissenwagens, usually given as wide a berth as possible, though their function was acknowledged to be essential. Each of these strange vehicles consisted of a large tank, three feet or so in diameter, mounted on four wheels. Hitched either side of a long wooden shaft at the front was an old horse or mule, sometimes an ox or cow. The function of these contraptions was to carry away the excrement emptied from the latrines in all the compounds, an operation unavoidably carried out near the huts. The men kept well clear while this went on because of the awful stench invariably stirred up — at its most pungent in warm weather.

Permanently saddled with this delightful job, the unfortunate Russians were obliged to hand-pump the excrement from the latrines to the tanks. When full, each wagon was hauled to a farmer's land outside the camp. There the bung was removed and the sludgy, malodorous contents spread around as a fertilizer.

CSM Richard Hall, in *With the 4th Battalion, the Green Howards*, recalls an occasion when Russians were emptying one of the latrines:

"There was great consternation; something was blocking the business end of the suction pipe. Engineers were called…. It turned out to be the body of a German soldier."

We may speculate about how this unfortunate fellow had met such a fate.

Nor was he the only German who came to a sticky end. Henri, Richard Hall's French friend, told of work on a building site under the eagle eye of a Feldwebel who was leaning over watching concrete being poured into a large wooden mould. (*Mais, quel hasard!*)

A sudden shove with a foot from behind and, with impeccable timing, as the Feldwebel fell head-first into the mix, the next load was poured in on top. He'd vanished without a sound.

(*Ein Feldwebel weg!*)

Many Irishmen had joined the British forces and, while sometimes their commonwealth comrades-in-arms found their vagaries irksome, the Germans had no hope at all of understanding them.

SERGEANT FRED HEATHFIELD explains: "In 1944 all the Irish prisoners, North and South, were taken away to another camp. About ten days later they came back and we got the story in our hut from our friend Sam (Paddy) Muldoon. They had been taken to a special camp where they were given single bunks with blankets and sheets. The dining room had tablecloths, crockery, and knives, forks and spoons. The food was very good and they lived well.

11—Stranger Than Fiction

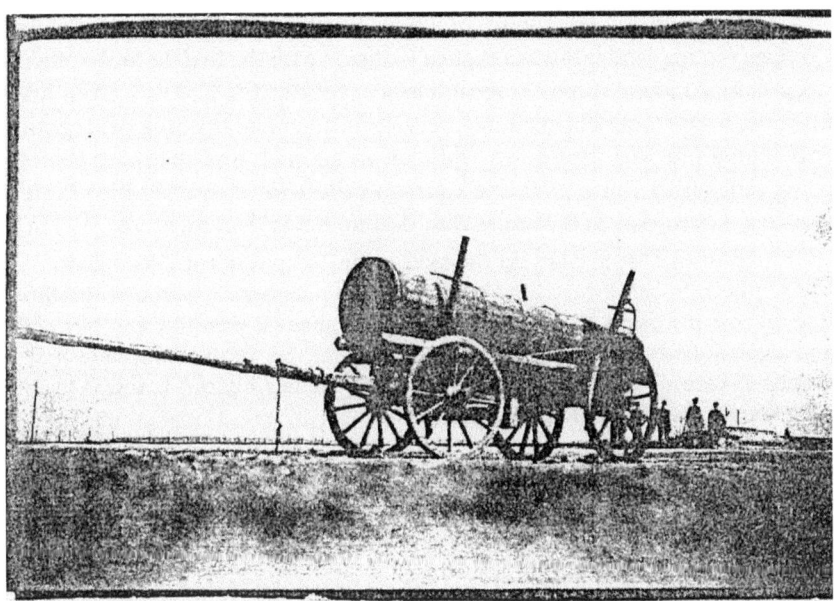

Silhouetted against the sky, waiting for two animals to be hitched to its shaft and a Russian crew to drive it, here is an example of one of the best-remembered sights about the *Stalag*, the Scheissenwagen (E.J. McGregor photograph, courtesy Norman Page).

"They were told these were the conditions they could enjoy if they enlisted in a special Irish Force to fight against the Russians. They would not be expected to fight the British unless they particularly wanted to. (The Southern Irish were all volunteers for the British Forces.) The Irish dallied and thought it over, spinning out the luxury as long as possible before telling the Germans where to put their Irish Force. They immediately lost their sheets and good living and were told they were going back to IVB.

"In the next compound was a large group of Dutch who had volunteered to fight for the Germans so, before leaving, the Irish climbed into the next compound and showed the Dutchmen what fighting was really like. 'We had a whale of a time,' said Paddy."

WILF SUTTON contributes an anecdote about New Year's Eve 1944/45: "Dressed and made up as a gorgeous gypsy girl and partnered by a South African ballroom dance champion, who was dressed as a gaucho, 'she' [Wilf] danced a tango to 'La Cumparsita.'

"The audience had got a bit 'high' on a special strong brew concocted in the camp and, affected by the music and the exotic dance, made some advances to Wilf of a kind which persuaded him to grow a moustache afterwards!"

Terry Hunt was a cameraman who worked for the Gainsborough Film Company in England but was assigned to flights with the RAF to make official newsreels. To prevent his being shot as a spy if captured he was given RAF uniform, a short induction course, service number and the rank of sergeant. Sure enough he was shot down while on an air raid. At Dulag Luft, before being sent on to Stalag IVB, the German officer interrogating him hinted that they knew who Terry really was, despite his RAF credentials.

ANDY ANDERSON takes up the story after Terry reached IVB: "Terry had not been in camp very long before he built a camera, which was installed into a book, the pages having been cut out. He made a viewfinder in one end and carried the book around with him everywhere he went, taking photographs of various things in the camp. He was taking a big risk and had he been caught would probably have been shot."

Terry's book was actually a Bible. Some of his Stalag photographs are reproduced in this book.

It's clear that among some POWs in Stalag IVB — British and French POWs particularly — a considerable talent for hoodwinking the Jerries/Les Boches had developed. The radios in the camp remained undetected, though they were known by the Germans to be there. Coal stocks melted away despite their best efforts; and numerous diversions were successfully mounted to cover other activities. One of the most extraordinary examples of this was the incident which has come to be known as "The Disappearance of Private Ward."

New Zealand Military Forces records show that when he enlisted at Ngaruawahia Camp, near Hamilton, in 1939 soon after New Zealand entered the war, Frederick William Ward's date of birth was recorded as 3 February 1912. A 'Missing, believed prisoner-of-war 14–7-42' notice based on a cable issued from North Africa on 22 July 1942 gives the birth date as 3 February 1913. A German document dated 24 March 1944 quotes 3 February 1911.

Whichever is correct, it's clear that Ward was relatively old at a time when men of 20 or younger were putting their ages on to enlist. For Ward, at the time serving as a policeman in Ngaruawahia, his age was no kind of handicap. He was an active man, known as a useful boxer, and was very independent of spirit.

Captured in North Africa at the time of the Battle of El Alamein, Ward was eventually transhipped to Italy, where he seized an opportunity to abscond from a POW camp in September 1943, going on to join a group of partisans in the hills. After being involved in the ambushing and slaying of a high-ranking German officer and some of his staff, Ward had subsequently been captured when the Germans mounted a surprise retaliatory action against the partisans, from which he was the only survivor. In August,

11—Stranger Than Fiction

Left: Terry Hunt with camera, close to a hut. Despite its being disguised as a book, Terry had to take great care to prevent its discovery by Germans, since at least one sharp-eyed fellow POW was not deceived. Tom Fielder recalls: "One day while walking around the compound, I saw Terry holding a book in front of his face in a most peculiar manner. When I asked him the reason, he opened the book, which happened to be a Bible, to reveal that it was hollowed out to conceal a small movie camera" (probably E.J. McGregor photograph, courtesy Tom Fielder). *Right:* Paddy: the Germans went to considerable lengths in trying to turn the Irish captured in British army or RAF units. The Germans seemed baffled when their efforts failed entirely (Ray Newell).

1944 he was held in the Straflager (prison) in IVB, pending court-martial at Leipzig.

FRED WARD himself continues: "On arrival I was put in a cell, later tied to a chair and interrogated by Gestapo officers one of whom bashed my face to pieces.[4] "Somehow the International Red Cross were notified that I was to be taken to Leipzig for trial. A message was got through to the camp Escape Committee who decided to help."

The escape plan was for Ward to demand to be deloused and showered before being taken for court-martialling. The shower room window had been cut out and lightly tacked back into place. A distraction in the French compound was organized, Ward climbed out the window, evaded the sentry and ran first toward the main street, then dodged in and out of barracks, to reach his prearranged hiding place in a hut at the far end of the camp.

FRED HEATHFIELD gives this account of what followed: "I was in the barrack hut one morning when there was a shout at the hut door...."

(COPY)

DIVISIONAL COURT NO. 404

St.L. III K No.99/44.

4 Fabrice Strasse,
DRESDEN N.15

24th March, 1944.

COMMUNICATION

1. Judicial proceedings have been instituted against the British prisoner of war:

   Pte. FREDERICK WARD, identification No. 279823 IV B, Stalag IV B, born on 3.2.1911 at Herne Bay, New Zealand, in civil life waiter, single.

   The accused is sufficiently suspected of having, without being recognisable as a member of the armed enemy power by the outward marks prescribed by international law, carried weapons and committed acts which, according to the rules of war, may only be carried out by uniformed member of an armed power.

   Offence, insurgence under paragraphs - of the War Penal Decree and 158 of the Military Penal Code.

   The accused was taken prisoner on 15.7.1942 near El Alamein by the Italians. After the revolt in Italy he escaped from the prisoners of war camp at Carpi in North Italy. He got rid of his uniform, which was marked with red patches showing him to be a prisoner of war, wandered about the hills of Northern Italy and got in touch with bandits whose endeavour it was to injure the German army. Among other things he participated with a group of bandits in the vicinity of the locality Ostra in a raid on a store. At the end of January he was captured in a house in Ostra. On 28.1.1944 a German special leader named Schartel had been shot dead by bandits. During the search of the property used as a hiding place by the bandits, the accused was caught with a bandit leader and another bandit cleaning two revolvers. In the room in which the accused was arrested there were also found at least 12 Italian hand egg bombs and 53,000 Lire in cash. The accused disputes having render himself guilty of insurgence.

Above and opposite page: The German indictment of Fred Ward: This version in English was issued at Dresden and was never implemented following Ward's "escape" (copy held at Base Records, New Zealand).

He states that on his march through Italy he merely came in touch with the bandits by chance and he only took part by compulsion in the raid and robbery of the store as admitted by him. Through his presence with the bandit leader and his exact knowledge of the composition of the individual gangs and their activities, the accused will however be incriminated of insurgence and his participation therein.

Remand arrest was imposed because a crime forms the subject of the examination and in view of the punishment expected, the danger of escape is given.

2. The "Gerichtsherr" preferred the charge on 24th March, 1944.
3. The accused has been in custody since 29th October, 1943, at the Burg Hohenstein.
4. The main hearing has been fixed for 10 a.m. on 24th May, 1944, at 4 Fabrice Strasse, Dresden.
5. The accused has been informed that he has the right to select a lawyer to defend him.

p.p.
(signature)
"Kriegsgerichtsrat"

Fred Ward, left, with two companions at Ngaruawahia military training camp, New Zealand, before being posted to join 2NZEF in North Africa (courtesy Sharon Haslam).

'There's an emergency. We need everyone out now and walking a left-hand circuit of the French compound. Quick as you can, everyone!' I jumped off my bunk and went with the crowd across the road to join hundreds of men swarming from other huts to walk in an anticlockwise circuit of the French compound.

"Soon there was activity among the guards and sections of German troops came trotting into camp. The word was passed round to return to our own compounds or huts, which we did. Everyone was talking and wondering

11—Stranger Than Fiction

Florence Barrington at the Stalag IVB reunion in Edinburgh in 1996, listening to a camp radio, still functioning and operated by Harry Watson, right, one of several experts who made receivers there. In the center is Florence's son, Winston. Others are Jim Middleton, left, and Alex McKeeman (British IVB Committee photograph, courtesy Alex Franks).

what was going on when the Germans appeared at hut doors with 'Raus! Raus! Appell! Schnell!' which meant outside quickly and on parade. We lined up, the guards counted us. The barrack leaders were being bombarded with questions. The parades were kept waiting, then troops appeared outside the wire and set up machine guns, pointing into the camp.

"A message was passed round that there had been an escape ... and the Germans wanted this man badly. He was still in the camp and being hidden by his friends. He was to be handed over and a deadline was set. We dismissed until the time had expired when we were ordered out again and a fresh ultimatum was delivered. Still no details of who the man was nor why he was so important.

"All day we moved on and off parade, with new deadlines being given, until evening came and nothing had happened. The Germans apparently gave up."

FRED WARD. "I had to live up in the rafters of one of the huts for 18 months or so—no picnic, I can tell you. The Gestapo and dogs came through the hut regularly for the first month."

Eventually the frequency of the searches was scaled down, and Ward was able to leave his cramped hiding place, to break the monotony and stretch his limbs.

Ray Newell noted that the process was helped by Ward's appointment as resident caretaker in his hut in D South compound. Joe Seddon of the Escape Committee had collected shaving soap so that at morning Appell or when guards checked the hut Ward could cover his face with soap and not be recognized.

The Germans never fully accepted that Ward had got clear of the camp and still made surprise raids with the Alsatian search dogs through the huts in the hope of discovering him. On one such occasion he just had time to get back into the roof as guards with a dog burst through the door. Keeping as still as possible he looked down between ceiling boards. The dog had stopped and seemed to be staring directly up at him. It was a tense few seconds before guards and dog moved on.

For German ears it was later leaked out that Ward had got clear away from the camp altogether. Part of that may have been the report, attributed to the man of confidence, that he'd got out of IVB concealed under a load of hay ... a load of "bull," in fact, as Ward actually remained hidden in the camp until its relief by the Russian forces.

Florence Barrington, a widow with a (then) 13-year-old son, had married a German photographer when he was working before the war in Britain, and they had gone to live in Vienna in 1938. When war broke out the husband was called up in the Luftwaffe. The son (Winston) joined the RAF. He was shot down and became a POW at Mühlberg. Florence somehow heard about this, moved into Germany and began to smuggle food and clothing to him in the camp through a contact, even arranging to visit him with her husband on one occasion. But this wasn't enough for Florence, and her story takes a more bizarre turn.

The Escape Committee arranged a "reverse escape"—*into* the camp and, swapping clothes with a prisoner from IVB who was outside the camp on a working party, she was smuggled in.[5] With her breasts strapped up tightly, her hair cut off and dressed in this old army uniform, she lived in the camp as a male POW, to be near her son. From then until the end of the war, Florence was kept in secret sleeping quarters, always had an escort when taking exercise, and even went to rehearsals for some of the shows put on at the Empire.[6] Most other prisoners in the camp never saw Florence, and to those who knew she was there she was a sort of legend. After the Stalag was liberated by the Russians, Florence, disguised now in RAF uniform, was among the earliest to be moved westward.[7]

12

The Satellite Camps

Arbeit macht frei[1]
  (Slogan at German concentration and forced work camps)

Stalag IVB developed a sort of corporate self-sufficiency within its perimeters, but it had other obligations. Among these were the so-called transit camp of Jacobstahl (H304) near Zeithain, a few miles to the south, and a network of many hundreds of *Arbeitskommandos* (work camps) radiating throughout Saxony and beyond into Czechoslovakia.

JACOBSTAHL[2]

Jacobstahl (Jacob's Valley) Stalag no. IVH/304 — a punishment camp and death camp (sometimes ambiguously also known as "Zeithain"): The grapevine version claimed that it was set up before the war as a concentration camp and that many Jews were buried there, though the Germans have subsequently denied this.[3] Of the vast numbers of Russian deaths, there can be no doubt.

DRIVER ALEX FRANKS. "My first sight of the Stalag 304 (IVH) had a very depressing effect on me. Immediately on entering the gate and on my left I saw a mass of human misery, skeleton figures: my first sight of our Russian allies!"

FRED HILL (on arriving at Jacobstahl, October 1943). "Suddenly a weird sound started up. Through the barbed wire we could see the inmates, emaciated and poorly clad Russian prisoners, doing their best to give us a welcome. Three prisoners were 'playing us in' with battered cornet, trombone and drum.

"We felt deeply touched. But a German officer near us seized a rifle and roared at them as they fled for their lives."

For British POWs Jacobstahl was a transit camp, though sometimes they were sent there as a punishment. For the Russians it was the end of the line.

SERGEANT CYRIL G. JENKINS. "A Russian tells us that 32,000 lie buried in this camp, having died of malnutrition ... in the winter of 1941/42."

FRED HILL. "According to Russian and English doctors we were to meet later, 70,000 died in one year."

Some Russian women prisoners—internees or, in some cases, the pilots of planes shot down—were also held at Jacobstahl, where they were compelled to work as nurses in the camp hospital.

The Russian compound was separated from the British by a no-man's land some 20 yards or so across. The guard towers were manned day and night by Germans armed with automatic weapons and searchlights, which seemed to be in continuous use at night. Yet Russians somehow managed the hazardous journey across.

CSM RICHARD HALL. "I heard the whispered words "Kamerad, brot" and realised we had been 'invaded.' Several Russians were in the hut and the washroom, most looking like bundles of rags. All had their hands out, begging for bread. Some food was given."

In another compound stood a single hut, a mystery building, removed from any others. Russian prisoners carrying stretchers with human shapes to the hut and coming away empty were a common sight. The hut covered a Kalkgrube (lime pit) into which these bodies had been dropped (Russians, obviously enough), dispensing with a need for formal burials. Kalkgrabe (lime grave) seemed a more suitable name for it.

One of these apparently wasn't enough to cope with the Russian dead.

Alex Franks also mentions noticing in the Russian compound a massive hole with sloping sides, looking rather like a miniature football stadium, but lacking the green pitch.

ALEX FRANKS. "The following morning I was shocked to see the Russians as stretcher bearers, shuffling along the top of that hole and without ceremony tipping their dead down the slopes of the hole, where they plopped into the lime pit ('Is this where I shall end up when the Germans have starved me to death?')."

CSM RICHARD HALL. "At night we could hear rats scratching the zinc baths outside the hut door.... Never during our stay at Zeithain was any action taken by the Germans against the ever-increasing rat population." And at Christmas there, when the men had made streamers as decorations, using coloured paper from Red Cross parcels, he notes, "We watched the rats using these garlands to cross from one side of the hut to the other."

FRED HILL (leaving H304). "The day arrived when I took one last look at Jacobstahl camp. The phantom-like figures of the Russians and Jews, despair written on their features, watched us go. It seemed that for some of them emotion of any kind had died."

ARBEITSKOMMANDOS

Little publicized and largely overlooked by historians, the Arbeitskommandos (work camps) were supplied with POW manpower, either directly from the Stalag, or via other Wehrkreis IV establishments, such as IVC Wistritz, IVF Hartmannsdorf or IVG Oschatz. They employed groups ranging from a dozen to some thousands of men on work of almost every type and in conditions also of extreme variety. The nature of the lives led by these men would be in the hands of German army commandants (often noncommissioned officers) whose power in their camps was absolute. While many groups were detailed to work in or near Dresden and Leipzig, hundreds of other Arbeitskommandos were scattered throughout Saxony and across into Czechoslovakia.

Dresden was a flower among German cities, Saxony's pride. It had grown up round the medieval town known as the Altstadt, which lay at the southern end of the Augustus Bridge across the Elbe. In the eighteenth century Dresden became one of the great show cities of the world through the construction of a number of magnificent public buildings, all of which were erected in the Altstadt district.

Beyond the Brühl Terraces along the left bank of the Elbe and within a radius of half a mile from the southern end of the Augustus Bridge was built a unique group of palaces, art galleries, museums and churches: the towered Schloss, containing the famous Grunes Gewolbe with its priceless art treasures; the great Zwinger Museum housing one of the world's finest collection of paintings; the Frauenkirche with its famous statue of Martin Luther; the beautiful Catholic Hofkirche with its frieze of statues; in the Ringstrasse stood the Protestant Kreuzkirche and the Rathaus (town hall), also with a fine tower.

For prisoners of war, seeing all this for the first time, it was a revelation.

GEORGE K. ZAK passed through Dresden on his way to a work camp about thirty-five miles to the east. He recalls, "I had looked out in awe at a huge, beautiful, rather majestic old city."

KURT VONNEGUT. "The Americans arrived in Dresden at five in the afternoon. The boxcar doors were opened, and the doorways framed the loveliest city that most of the Americans had ever seen. The skyline was intricate and voluptuous and enchanted and absurd."

ROBERT LEE (72nd Field Regiment, 150 Brigade, British 50th Division). "We were taken by train to Dresden and then had to march all the way, about 6 miles, to our working accommodation at the unused gymnasium Schillerschule, not in use for the duration, at Freital, a suburb of Dresden.

"The very next morning, after arrival, we were on parade and had to volunteer for the firms who sent someone to collect us. Two millers each took six, the soap factory four, most others just took two. There were ninety in the Arbeitslager; any left over went to work for the council, road work, refuse, parks etc."

With Richard Green, a draughtsman from London, Robert was employed at *Börners*, which collected usable waste: rag, paper, bones, scrap material of all kinds.

ROBERT LEE continues: "The rag warehouse at *Börners* was large; there two Poles worked baling rags and different textile materials, and stacking them some 30 feet or so, the height of the building. There was also in the yard a large bay of bones, principally of horses, including their hooves. A link rail line ran into this yard, as it did for many other Freital firms, and the Polish POWs loaded the wagon with rags and paper. Another firm came to collect the bones for processing."

Air-raid warnings around Saxony became increasingly frequent during the summer of 1944. Robert Lee was working at the Siemens factory in Freital when, on 24 August, the sirens sounded. He moved quickly away from the buildings into a large storage area where he took shelter in a huge concrete pipe with a French prisoner.

ROBERT LEE. "Quite soon two flights of nine Fortresses came over us from the south. They were over us when we heard that all-too-familiar rushing sound and knew we were not the target. In seconds we knew the Fortresses' bomb loads had fallen on the Dresden end of town and I was anxious about *Börners*.

"There was no anti-aircraft fire, the guns had been sent off to the Russian front. No fighter aircraft defence. The air was filled with smoke, dust and debris in seconds. On return to the Lager that evening I found that it was Henschells and its twin firm that had been the target. They were both multi-industry firms, both had engineering workshops and were reputed to be making V-weapon components."

The bombing was not selective and, though the factories were hit and burned for some days, the housing estate between them suffered equally in the raid and at least 200 civilians, mostly women and children, were killed.

The POWs were ordered by the brownshirts to be responsible for the burial of these Germans. It was a ghastly job and Robert Lee was thankful to be a gravedigger rather than among those detailed to recover bodies, or body parts, and load the coffins. The smell would haunt him for weeks; some of the sights would never leave him.[4]

Identities and ranks were frequently exchanged between the services, and even between nationalities in the Stalag, in order to escape or remain together. Sometimes this involved self-promotion, but Paul Brokensha, a South African sergeant, opted to drop that rank to go out with his brother David, a lance corporal, to an Arbeitskommando. They managed to avoid being detailed to the Silesian mines, despite the inducement of double rations. Instead they went to Gorbitz, another Dresden suburb about 10 miles west of the city. This was No. 1169, made up of about 200 British and South African POWs, and being a new Lager it lacked the lice and other parasites which were the curse of most camps. There they were employed at the Bahnhof (railway station) loading and unloading railway trucks. Nicknames soon applied to their German gaffers included Big Fritz, Donald Duck, the Polecat (who looked as bad as he smelled), Dopey, Happy, Wooden Legs and the Missing Link.

Gunner Harry Muse (81st Anti-tank Regiment, RA) had escape in mind when he and a couple of friends volunteered to go on a working party. They were among a group of 32 sent to Annaberg, a small camp about 15 miles southeast of Zwickau and quite close to the Czech border.

HARRY MUSE. "After a month there four guys did a runner during one night. One of them was a South African who the Krauts said could speak perfect German; however, three of them were recaptured and returned. We then learned that the so-called South African was a deserter from the Afrika Korps but

Robert Lee's image "The Burden of Dreams" (102.8 × 50.3 × 6.4 cm) is described thus: "Case and objects in ramin and other hard and soft woods, with drawing and photocollage" (courtesy Robert Lee and Smith Settle Ltd.).

had changed his uniform from a dead South African and surrendered to his own troops to masquerade as a prisoner.

"He was never caught after his escape, and this information was given to us when the others were returned after serving punishment in a Straflager."

ALEX FRANKS recalls moving out to an *Arbeitskommando*. "The 18 of us were put onto a train ... to a small hamlet, Bülzig, five miles east of Wittenberg-on-Elbe. We all realised how lucky we were compared to our comrades in the Stalags." The work of this small group involved digging clay from a pit for shaping as bricks and firing in a kiln.

"Our accommodation was superb by previous standards; warm and cosy beds, tables and chairs, more food, mostly potatoes, Sauerkraut, bread, hot water, warm fire, plenty of coal....

"Next morning 5 am: the usual 'Raus! Raus!'"

PRIVATE WILF RAPSON, 2NZEF (on Mumsdorf, north of Leipzig). "Z71 was a real rough one, 12-hour shifts in a coal mine (open cast) seven days a week. Unfortunately we were on the bombing run (day and night) for the synthetic oil factory at nearby Leuna.... Hair-raising to say the least."

In Leipzig a group of 75 men designated Lager 39 was lodged in a new building, their work being in the rail yards. The city became a frequent target for British bombers. During one raid the building was burnt to the ground and not only were most of the men's possessions lost but one of their number was hit and had to be carried off on the latrine door for medical attention. He lost a leg just below the knee.

An earlier raid by 400 bombers had left Leipzig burning for five days. Nearby a larger camp (Lager 41) was manned by 150 mainly British servicemen whose work was under the control of a particularly harsh Unteroffizier (a corporal).

Some of the Lager 39 men sheltering there learned that during that big raid the corporal had asked for volunteers to help next door at a former pub in which two German mothers, each with two young children, had taken shelter. Volunteers were at his side immediately, but when they reached the pub the corporal was amazed to find four other POWs already there — one boiling water, two comforting the distressed women, and the fourth bottle-feeding a baby. That episode changed the corporal's opinion of British POWs.

GEORGE K. ZAK recalls his time: "Our train started heading east, and after a relatively short ride, we arrived at our new home, the quaint little town of Lobau. We knew we were now in the easternmost end of Germany, about thirty-five miles east of Dresden. [A group of 35, all strangers.]

12—The Satellite Camps

"A German Hauptmann (captain) announced ... that we were going to be put to work at the local blanket factory ... and told us we would be shot if we fraternised with any German women."

The group worked mostly weaving army blankets on mechanical looms, loading small packets of spun wool into a narrow wooden box, pointed at both ends, called a shuttlecock. The wool trailed out of a hole in the box and wooden paddles on the left and right propelled the box back and forth, weaving the wool with strong threads to form blanket material, which ended up on a six-foot-wide roll under the table. "We were hungry most of the time and were treated as nameless laboring robots."

WESLEY ECKBLAD (U.S. Army). "In Gleina, near Zeitz [about 45 miles due west of Dresden], we worked clearing rubble in a nearby refinery. From January 17th to liberation on April 13th ten of the hundred men interned there died. It was quite brutal.... In fact I couldn't talk about it for 40 years."

TONY VERCOE (22 Battalion, 2NZEF was at IVG/682, Meissen).[5] "Our workplace was supposed to turn out pre-moulded blocks for building. Our method of sabotaging these, which involved decreasing the allocated proportion of cement—already rationed to an essential minimum—and adding sawdust and more gravel, was soon being applied. Carted away on diesel-burning trucks, the blocks probably didn't survive the bumping about to reach their destination intact, and it wasn't long before the Jerries had rumbled it."

ALEX FRANKS (on Bülzig). "We were marching down the lane to the brickworks when a civilian shouted loudly "Heil Hitler!" One of our boys replied "Heil Churchill!" and the eighteen of us burst out laughing.

"Our guard had to protect us from this maniac. If he could have got the guard's rifle he would have shot us all."

WILF RAPSON (on Mumsdorf). "The main way of amusing ourselves was Jerry-baiting—a dangerous occupation at times, as they had very little sense of humour.

"In the winter, with temperatures at minus 20°, sometimes we found it hard to smile but developed a weird sense of humour, such as my pal Jim coming up to me with a big grin and saying: "I just played a dirty trick on a flea—I lifted up my shirt, let him jump out into the snow and walked off and left him!'"

At Borna, halfway between Leipzig and Altenburg in the south, the job of Sam Gillette's work group was repairing railway tracks. He reports about the last weeks of the war: "The bunch of us were taken directly to the head of the food line and given the same thin turnip soup we had in IVB. The 'line' was comprised of German civilians—old folk and young children."

DAVE BROKENSHA (at Gorbitz, quoting his friend Jake). "Our war effort included pilfering out of parcels, swapping labels on parcels and on trucks ... Parcels from Fritz to his Frau in Berlin and from the Frau to Fritz were intercepted.... Socks were removed and replaced by our old worn-out ones, to say nothing of the sausages which we consumed.... Sometimes we sent the latest Paris fashion hats on to Fritz, sitting in the snow-drifts of the Eastern Front."

TONY VERCOE (on Meissen). "We were shunted out of the factory, up the track and isolated from the others in the quarry above, there to dig out gravel. This was mostly rock and quite heavy going but we'd cope with that in our own way. Our being there also meant extra duties for the guards, another plus in our book.

"Out in the open here we could look up the hillside at the agreeable sight of two Polish girl internees working maybe two hundred yards away in the sugar beet field below the farmhouse. Fraternal signals were exchanged."

KURT VONNEGUT recalls: "Every other big city in Germany has been bombed and burned ferociously. Dresden had not suffered so much as a cracked windowpane." As Arbeitskommando 557, his group of 100 U.S. servicemen was led to the Dresden slaughterhouse.

"The Americans were taken to the fifth building inside the gate. It was a one-storey cement-block cube with sliding doors in front and back. It had been built as a shelter for pigs about to be butchered." They were to be quartered there in Schlachthof-fünf—Slaughterhouse No. 5—which right then may not have struck them as too promising.

"Their only English-speaking guard told them to memorize their simple address, in case they got lost in the big city."

George K. Zak tells of a group of GIs who had been identified as Jewish and segregated from all the rest. Only long afterward did he learn of the fate of such men, transferred to Stalag IXB, Berga-am-Elster, a notorious death camp.

GEORGE K. ZAK. "With only starvation rations, these American soldiers were worked to death digging a tunnel into the side of a hill with primitive tools under the supervision of merciless, brutal guards."

ALEX FRANKS (on Bülzig). "During one of the many air raids we were locked up in our dormitory. One bucket for 18 men for the whole night was definitely insufficient! So as 'Fritz' paced back and forth beneath our window Eric Murrell decided to fill a Klim tin with urine, push it through the steel bar window and at the precise moment drop his bomb!"

12—The Satellite Camps

The reaction from below suggested that Eric would have been valued by the RAF as a bomb-aimer. More buckets were duly supplied!

WILF RAPSON (on Mumsdorf). "A few things hard to forget. One is the memory of a South African boy hearing via the Red Cross of the death of his wife, and then seeing him grieve for months as letters from her held up in transit continued to arrive. Another is seeing a boy struck by lightning and killed a week before the war ended."

From Stalag IVB Fred Hill had been sent to IVF Hartmannsdorf where his "parish" embraced 80 fairly widely scattered Arbeitskommandos. For a 23-year-old Salvation Army officer it probably seemed a tough prospect, but Fred also saw it as a challenge. He was there to visit the men and bring them whatever spiritual help he could. He got cracking. One of his first calls was to a lead mine at Freiburg, accompanied by a guard/interpreter.

FRED HILL. "With a haversack of hymn-books across my shoulder and my accordion in my left hand, I left my sleeping comrades and was soon walking briskly towards Hartmannsdorf railway station with my compulsory companion. At Freiburg ... we turned towards the slag heaps and the winding gear of the mine.

'Two hundred prisoners worked there in appalling conditions—one wash-tap between them. All day they worked in wet conditions in the mine, only to return to damp huts where they slept. Seeing me looking at the line of washing strung across the hut, the corporal commented: 'That's been there for two weeks, and it's still not dry.'"

Fred was not surprised to find that most of these men suffered from rheumatism; he also learned that, while the guards seemed reasonable, there were civilian bosses, fanatical Nazis armed with rifles, who did not hesitate to use the butts on any fellows who protested. Fred determined that at Hartmannsdorf he would protest on their behalf about their conditions and treatment.

After some months Fred was joined by a colleague of the same surname, Richard Hill, an Anglican chaplain, and they shared the work, of which there was never any shortage. Fred tells of a visit to a camp near Chemnitz:

FRED HILL. "I met the South African camp leader, nicknamed 'Zulu' Brown. There was a spirit of caring in his camp. He looked after his men, buried them, conducted services, and even managed to get some dying American prisoners transferred to his camp, so saving their lives.'"

Later, at another camp where some Americans were housed in a former beer house under appalling conditions and a number of them had recently died, he saw listless groups of men who seemed past caring. Moans came from the three-tier bunks.

FRED HILL. "As no preparation had been made for the service, I placed my bag of hymn-books and accordion on the floor and grasped the nearest form. 'Come on, you fellows! You're dying like flies. Get to this service!' shouted a fellow who introduced himself as the camp leader. Gradually those not too ill shuffled towards us and took their places.

"'Choose your own hymns,' I said, handing out the hymn-books. A former student sat at a grand piano, left behind by the landlord of the beer house. If only I could describe the unique atmosphere of that occasion! A sprinkling of negroes looked at me from the congregation. I thought that black faces looked even more sad than the white ones. Their thin faces, eyes appearing larger than usual, looked wistfully for some comfort and hope.

"The piano began the tune 'Toplady.' Then the prisoners lifted their hearts as they sang:

Rock of ages, cleft for me,
Let me hide myself in thee.

"The pianist played as one inspired. It seemed that I had never heard such music. God came very near as sadness and exquisite beauty blended. Like Christ on the cross, here was suffering and victory, defeat and triumph."

KURT VONNEGUT (in Dresden) saw the public hanging of a Pole: "Walking to work with some others shortly after sunrise ... came to a gallows and a small crowd in front of a soccer stadium. The Pole was a farm laborer who was being hanged for having had sexual intercourse with a German woman."

Sebastianus ("Bas") van der Laan was one of a group of 1,200 Dutch POWs, sent in September 1943 via Stalag IVC to Brüx, inside the Czech border (the Czech name is Most) to work at a vast factory (die Sudetenlandische Treibstaff Werke AG) producing synthetic petrol from open-cast coal. The hours of work were long, the food even poorer than at IVB, and the conditions generally deplorable. Sixty-three Dutch POWs are known to have died in that camp from malnutrition or allied bombing.

BAS VAN DER LAAN. "We had to work from 6 a.m. to 6 p.m. Sometimes we had Sunday off. No energy left for recreation or socialising. All we wanted to do was sleep."

After the first air raid on 12 May 1944 the factory area was subjected to frequent bombing, day or night. A booklet published by the Dutch Wapenbroeders in February 1999 records 18,591 bombs dropped there. Bas says, "Mind you, I did not count them. I was too scared when it was raining bombs!" The Germans had built large effective bomb shelters in the factory complex, but these were not for POWs.

BAS VAN DER LAAN. "The bomb shelters provided in our camp were very flimsy, more like rat traps, and we preferred to be above ground. As the bombing started the camp commandant opened the gates and we could run for our lives, usually in the direction of open cast brown coal mines, for shelter." And pollution from the brown coal dust was terrible. "In our camp no tree could grow. Any open wounds would not heal. I had an open knee wound for nearly all the time I was in Brüx."[6]

Dresden was massively bombed the night of 13–14 February 1945 by at least 770 RAF Lancasters in two waves, and the next morning by about 530 Fortresses of the USAAF, all delivering huge bomb loads. There has been considerable and continuing criticism of this operation as being barbarous and unnecessary, but it is worthwhile recording the following first-hand account by one who, while not applauding the bombings, was close by during the critical period and was able to have his observations endorsed by German residents.

This sketch of a black U.S. soldier from Alabama, was made on the coldest day Ray Newell could remember as a prisoner, in what was an extremely severe winter (Ray Newell).

ROBERT LEE. "On Christmas Day and Boxing Day, 1944, Fortresses came over dropping vast quantities of multicoloured cellophane to block the German radar, along with thousands of leaflets and NO BOMBS. The leaflets bore the American and British Coats of Arms. They stated that unless the Germans ceased to fire V-weapons on Western Europe and England the Kultur Städte of Germany would be bombed. Dresden, Munich and Nuremberg were named. The leaflets were signed by the Supreme Allied Commanders, Eisenhower and Montgomery.

"Over the next ten weeks there were a further many thousands of casualties, killed and wounded, civilian and military, both in Europe and southern England. In mid-January '45 leaflets were again dropped, demanding that Dresden be declared an Open City (like Rome). There was increased military personnel and it was claimed by the Russians to be the main supply centre for the Eastern Front. This warning was also disregarded. These leaflets can now be seen in the War Museum in Dresden."

Dutch group at Brüx soon after arrival in 1943. Bas van der Laan is at left in the front row, in hat. After two years of extremely harsh conditions, working long hours on substandard rations and subjected to frequent bombing, they would hardly have looked as vigorous or cheerful (courtesy Bas van der Laan).

Jim Bard and Wally Martin (of the U.S. 106th Infantry Division) were in a group of 30 U.S. servicemen at Brand Erbisdorf, about 20 miles from Dresden, a woodmill work camp.

WALLY MARTIN. "We both had frost-bitten feet. Most of all we remembered being hungry all the time. The night Dresden was bombed, although the city was some 20 miles away, the bombing lit up the sky at the woodmill. We scampered to our air raid shelter and could hear the bombers and bombing."

FRED HILL (at Hartmannsdorf). "At night we witnessed the bombing of Chemnitz and Dresden. The sound overhead made it difficult to carry on a conversation. The sky was ablaze with light and the two towns shook. So many beautiful buildings were destroyed in Dresden, including the cathedral, and the scarred statue of Martin Luther lay face down in the rubble, blasted 20 yards from its pedestal."

DAVE BROKENSHA (in Gorbitz). "Being on the outskirts of the city, we were in no immediate danger, but we saw and heard the raids and it had an

12—The Satellite Camps

impact on the remaining two months of our stay in Dresden: I thought I would never get rid of the stench of burnt and rotting flesh that pervaded the city."

During the raids the American S5 work group in Dresden itself took shelter with their guards in the meat locker below the slaughterhouse, reached via an iron staircase with iron doors at top and bottom. Some cattle, sheep, pigs and horses were hanging from metal hooks there.

KURT VONNEGUT. "There were sounds like giant footsteps above. Those were sticks of high-explosive bombs....

"The meat locker was a very safe shelter. All that happened down there was an occasional shower of calcimine. The Americans and four of their guards and a few dressed carcasses were down there, and nobody else. The rest of the guards had, before the raid began, gone to the comforts of their own homes in Dresden. They were all being killed with their families.

"There was a firestorm out there. Dresden was one big flame. The one flame ate everything organic, everything that would burn.

"It wasn't safe to come out of the shelter until noon the next day. When the Americans and their guards did come out, the sky was black with smoke. The sun was an angry little pinhead. Dresden was like the moon now, noth-

The American "Slaughterhouse 5" work group took refuge in the S5 cellar during the bombing of Dresden, one of the few safe places well below ground level (Szpek and Idzikowski photograph, courtesy Ervin Szpek Jr. and Frank Idzikowski).

ing but minerals. The stones were hot. Everybody else in the neighborhood was dead."

Two days after the bombing of Dresden the Germans had assembled prisoners of many nationalities to recover bodies buried under the desolate moonscape of the city, fused to a hard crust by the intense heat. The men were instructed to dig through the rough surface. Among them was a New Zealand Maori who had been captured at Tobruk. He had traditional tattooed whorls on forehead and cheeks.

KURT VONNEGUT. "They made a hole in the membrane. There was darkness and space under there.
"A German soldier with a flashlight went down into the darkness, was gone a long time. When he finally came back he told a superior on the rim of the hole that there were dozens of bodies down there. They were sitting on benches. They were unmarked."

The men were ordered to enlarge the hole enough to take a ladder, so that the bodies could be brought up, beginning what Vonnegut has called "the first corpse mine in Dresden." After a time, with many such mines in operation, the smell, which was not too bad at first, became overpowering, as the bodies rotted and liquefied.

KURT VONNEGUT. "The Maori ... died of the dry heaves, after having been ordered to go down in that stink and work. He tore himself to pieces, throwing up and throwing up.
"So a new technique was devised. Bodies weren't brought up any more. They were cremated by soldiers with flame-throwers right where they were. The soldiers stood outside the shelters, simply sent the fire in."

GEORGE K. ZAK, transported back from the Lobau *Arbeitskommando*, remembered Dresden as he'd seen it just 11 weeks previously: "But now! Our train came into what had been the center of the city on a newly repaired elevated track, and stopped outside the ruins of the Central Station.
"Everywhere I looked there was utter devastation. Block after block, mile after mile, there was nothing but rubble.... This once thriving city was now a giant, ghastly, silent graveyard."

FRED HILL recalls, "To aid identification more than 10,000 wedding rings were cut from bodies. German custom required the initials of the wearer to be engraved on the inside of the ring."

Thirty miles away at Stalag IVB, TOM NELSON noted after the bombing: "Many of them [the guards] came from Dresden and were on a few days leave. When they returned we thought there might be some reprisals especially against the RAF, but the men were in a state of shock. In addition to the knowledge that they had lost the war, many of them had also lost their families."

At the end, when disorder and chaos reigned across Germany, the scale of the task of locating, identifying and repatriating the enormous numbers of displaced persons, men, women and children, throughout the country was vast. Prisoners of war, whether in the main camps or in the scattered Arbeitskommandos, represented one aspect of this task. Those who eventually made it home often did so after experiences of considerable hardship and hazard.[7]

13

In Limbo

Here! creep,
Wretch, under a comfort serves in a whirlwind: all
Life death does end and each day dies with sleep.
   (Gerald Manley Hopkins, "No Worst, there is None," 1885)

By September 1944 the war had been going for five years and, though the news seemed to be good, still no clear end to it was perceivable. High in the skies increasing numbers of Allied aircraft were being seen, but for the men inside the barbed wire enclosure on the ground, initially heartened by the appearances of these flights, their connection came to seem tenuous at best. The German rations were subject to cuts, Red Cross food parcel deliveries were becoming uncertain, and another long winter was looming. The longed-for mail from home was rarely more than a pipe dream. In these conditions the POWs were finding it an increasing struggle to keep clean and active and, above all, to maintain hope. Sleep often seemed to offer the best comfort.

AFTER ARNHEM

There was a diverting, if not specially cheering occurrence after the battle for Arnhem in September 1944, when about 500 British paratroopers captured were brought into the Stalag.

As LEW PARSONS noted, they looked dirty and scruffy but wholly unbowed: "They had fought a hard fight and justifiably carried themselves with pride. Very soon after they came to IVB, when they were gathered round getting their mugs of skilly one day, a number of cars came into the camp and a tall German general in his full-length leather coat and accompanied by his entourage got out of his car and walked among them. He spoke to several of them and told them they had fought well."

Lew felt that a sense of chivalry was being displayed when recognition was being shown to a foe.

13—In Limbo

PADRE MCDOWALL also talked to the paratroopers and learned about another aspect of the Arnhem story: "One boy saw the Germans shoot a whole Dutch family because they had sheltered a British soldier—children and all. He saw it too, I could tell by the horror on his face."

Out in the Arbeitskommandos during this unsettled period the men were contending with problems enough while trying to make sense of events occurring around them. The Germans had met with a brick wall in their attempt to "turn" Allied personnel in the Stalag and now unwisely switched their lobbying to some of the work camps.

DAVE BROKENSHA (in Gorbitz) recalls that "A Britisher in German uniform [who] joined a volunteer force in 1940 to fight the Russians in Finland had been captured by the Germans and accepted the offer to join a special unit ('the Free British') to continue the fight against communism."

Some of the POWs were enraged and moved toward him menacingly, until he reached the locked camp gate, shouting for the guards to let him out.

KURT VONNEGUT describes an American turncoat who visited his work group in Dresden, Howard W. Campbell Jr., former playwright, a traitor who worked for the German propaganda ministry. "Campbell offered the Americans food now, steaks and mashed potatoes and gravy and mince pie, if they would join the Free American Corps. 'Once the Russians are defeated,' he went on, 'you will be repatriated through Switzerland.'"[1]

Though most of the Americans remained staring stonily ahead, one of the older men got to his feet and, along with some threatening gestures, called Campbell first "a snake," then revised this in the snake's favor, since the snake could not help being a snake.

CSM RICHARD HALL. "Dresden had been declared an open city[2] by the Germans, but Henri (who was there just prior to the bombing) told me that the station was full of troops and supplies for the eastern front and the sidings stocked with tanks, artillery and ammunition."

GEORGE K. ZAK. "Late in the evening on February 13, some of our guards came into the lager and rousted us out. We were led across to the basement of the nearby bakery and told to stay there. An air raid was expected. No bombs fell on Lobau, but after some time, we could see from the window a great fire lighting the sky off to the west. We knew some place was taking a terrible pounding.

"The next morning one of the guards came in and said, 'Dresden *kaput!*'"

Meanwhile the Polish women captured during the Warsaw uprising had all been moved to work-places of great variety in the Reich, or onto farms, or into factories producing munitions and other war materials, or given jobs like sweeping snow. Yvonn Lucyna Kozakiewicz's story is typical of their experiences. While in a factory that made caterpillar tracks for tanks, she was able to initiate some sabotage by milling her piece 1 millimeter too small or 1 millimeter too large.

She escaped several times from her work-places—once with a friend for as long as two months—but was always recaptured. The one example of kindness shown by any German was during that two-month period, when Yvonn and her friend Wanda were standing one night in a town and saw two German women talking. One of them was looking their way, and she was sure the woman must have known who or what they were. However, they were too tired and hungry to care. To a question from the German woman about what they were looking for, Yvonn replied "Somewhere to sleep." To their astonishment, instead of turning them in, the woman took them home, fed them, allowed them to bathe, gave them fresh clothes and the next night showed them on a map where to go and advised them how to avoid the Gestapo and patrols on leaving the town.

Later their freedom came to an end when they were picked up by a German truck. Yvonn's explanation that they had been left behind by a working party was accepted and they were delivered to a camp at which the guard again did not question their story of being left behind.

Back in Stalag IVB PADRE McDOWALL observed the various attitudes in the camp: "French, Dutch, Indians, Russians and all the races of Empire ... uniforms of bits and pieces, of many nations and many services are here, but the most cheerful men in spite of their years of prison life, are the prisoners. The Germans, it seems to us, look drawn and haggard."

At about this time JOE TOMBLING noted an improvement to their accommodation: "RAF personnel moved from compound C North to A & B North. There is more room. Only 160 per small billet instead of 186. Other advantages were that A & B were not wired off from the rest of the camp and running water from the washroom sprays was available almost all day."

Meanwhile Ray Newell had continued working steadily, adding to his collection of portraits of fellow POWs and contributing to other camp enterprises. Occasionally, if left with time on his hands, he'd have a crack at a self-portrait, less easy than it may seem.

During Ray's sessions of three hours or so with subjects of various nationalities, the men would often talk, revealing something of their backgrounds, attitudes and experiences.

Most parts of Germany had become increasingly the targets of bomb-

13—In Limbo

ing during 1944, as the Allies moved forward from the west and the Russians from the east. By 1945 great cities in Saxony, such as Leipzig and Dresden, were no longer immune from large formations of bombers carrying out day and night raids.

PADRE MCDOWALL (2 March 1945) recalls one incident: "Heavy flights of bombers were to be heard and at times seen through gaps in the rainy clouds. Suddenly there was shooting up above us and shortly after, down through the clouds, swaying like the pendulums of clocks, came six parachutes."

Soon after this a big bomber came swinging down and crashed in a cloud of smoke near Altenau, a village a couple of miles away. Meanwhile, all but one of the parachutists had been carried well past the camp by the strong wind. This one landed not far outside the perimeter of the camp. According to the padre he was a tall American.

PADRE MCDOWALL. "He might have made a job of it and landed inside! He was dragged about a hundred yards before a civilian got his 'chute and he clambered to his feet. The officer from here went out on his motorbike and brought him in. I heard afterwards two sentries talking: 'He is English.' 'No he isn't, he is American.' 'He is English.' 'He is American.' 'He is English.' 'How do you know?' 'He speaks English!'"

That bomber may have been a victim of a new type of interceptor that appeared during March 1945, one of two remarkable German technical developments which, had they been available in quantity earlier, would almost certainly have greatly affected the course of the war. They were the rocket and jet planes pioneered by Willi Messerschmitt, who had earlier produced the effective ME 109 and ME 110 machines. Anticipating that superior fighter aircraft were going to be needed to defeat the vast Allied bomber formations which he believed would increasingly dominate the skies over Germany, he engaged the best engineers and aeronautical designers available and by 1941 had produced a working prototype for a rocket plane. This was the ME 163 Komet, which in a test flew at 625 miles per hour.

Both Heinkel and Messerschmitt were by now also working on jet propulsion. Heinkel's HE 178 remained undeveloped, but the ME 262 was completed for testing in March 1942, when it achieved over 540 miles per hour, a good deal faster than any Allied fighter of the time. Initially it had some defects and had to spend more time on the ground than in the air. These would be largely rectified and, if put into production then, the ME 262 would undoubtedly have realized Messerschmitt's aims of destroying the Allied bomber fleets. However, Hitler intervened, as he was to do so often, insisting that the new technology be applied to the production of bombers rather than fighters, so that he could resume a major bombing

Top left: One of a few self-portraits which Ray Newell occasionally found time to attempt — not so easy because of the need to use mirrors. As no brushes were available, this was done in oils using an army jackknife. He'd made the hat from part of a greatcoat (Ray Newell). *Top right:* "Adamovitch — Son of Adam." Following an exhibition of paintings by Ray Newell in the United Kingdom, some people of Serbian extraction requested a copy of this portrait, asserting its subject to be their uncle (Ray Newell). *Bottom left:* Following the D-Day landings in Normandy, many members of the assault forces were captured by the Germans, including this British paratrooper (Ray Newell). *Bottom right:* Josef Pokotny, a Czech gendarme captured by the Germans as the Russians approached from the east, suffered severe malnutrition and told Ray his uniform had previously been too tight for him.

13—In Limbo

offensive of Britain. The delays that resulted for both types of plane proved critical.

In the meantime Messerschmitt had not entirely abandoned the Komet, even though for its propulsion it depended on a dangerously volatile mixture of methanol and hydrogen peroxide, could remain airborne for only short periods and was difficult to land.

S.G. WOLHUTER. "As I stood talking to Oberleutnant Hölzel one day, we heard a loud whistling noise which quickly developed into a thunderous 'swoosh' directly overhead. Like everyone else around, I instinctively ducked and, rather shaken, asked: 'What was that?'

"'That,' replied the oberleutnant, 'is our latest fighter plane. It has no propellers and can reach a speed of 1000 kilometres an hour.'

"I am sure he could see the disbelief in my eyes, but I prudently said nothing, as he was known for his violent temper and strong Nazi leanings."

SERGEANT SAM GILLETTE. "Remember the banshee howl out of the German airfield towards Torgau? The rocket planes as they flew up through the flights of bombers headed for Dresden and Chemnitz were something!"

Sam is referring to the Me163B Komet, a late German wartime development. Too late to affect the course of the war, this short-range rocket plane could rise at great speed to 30,000 feet or so, shoot down bombers and glide back to base.

SERGEANT SAM GILLETTE. "They would run out of fuel, wing over and fly back to the field. One had three P51 Mustangs on its tail, the 51s firing all the way, and 50 calibre bullets kicked up the sand in the compound. Everybody ran for cover, diving under huts etc."

JOE TOMBLING. "Fighters ... opened up on him when he was over the camp. Empty shell cases fell on D North compound. Thought they were shooting up sentry box as shells were exploding all round it. Wizard show. Bullet holes in several huts including theatre."

EUGENE WOPATA reports on the reaction in the Stalag to the news that President Franklin D. Roosevelt had died on April 12, 1945. "The Camp took it quite hard. Everyone was depressed more than usual. The Camp held memorial services for the late President on April 15. About 2,500 Americans attended the services along with English, Russian, Polish, French, Dutch, Italian, and Danish POWs."

In IVB the German authorities were by now starting to initiate some actions indicating a differing view of their responsibilities. At lunchtime on 13 April it was announced that Hauptmann König, the Lageroffizier, had "surrendered" control of the camp to Lieutenant Jessop. The signed order read as follows:

SPECIAL NOTICE
Hauptmann Koenig has asked all Men of Confidence (the leaders of all nationalities) to be responsible for the discipline of their own men in the camp. All have agreed.
Lieutenant Jessop is in Supreme Command of the camp and has issued the following orders:—

1. Keep the main thoroughfare clean and do not loiter.
2. Do not gather in large numbers in the compounds as Germans outside the camp are not conversant with internal conditions and are liable to think a mass breakout is contemplated.
3. If anything happens outside, keep away from the wire.
4. Germans are still in control, inside and out.
5. We are responsible for our own discipline.

Signed:
Camp RSM (for the Army)— RSM Samuels
A & B Compound (for the RAF)— W/O Harding
Senior RAF Officer— F/Lt J. Hunter, RAAF

Naturally this development caused considerable speculation throughout the camp. What did it really mean? The actual Senior British Officer was Major Whyte, the principal medical officer, but Lieutenant Jessop, though camp dentist, had been a serving army man. The Germans were still in control, but preparing to decamp, make a last stand here, or what?

A week later a partial answer was forthcoming, when Hauptmann König called all the camp leaders to a meeting and asked if they wished to move their nationals westward, to the other side of the River Elbe. Lieutenant Jessop, as supreme camp leader, replied that under no circumstances would the British or Americans move. All the other nationals agreed, with the exception of a majority of the Poles who, afraid of what might happen to them on arrival of the Russian troops, moved out at about midnight. The remaining Poles apparently preferred to take their chances.

WARRANT OFFICER DOUGLAS GILLAM. "We were all losing weight by that time and yet we were told to try and keep up as much exercise as possible. Football and other organised activities had already stopped, but we were encouraged to go for a walk every day. A warning was given to remember, that if you went for a walk, you had to have enough energy to get back. Yet despite these warnings, I went back to the theatre and began rehearsals for what we were pleased to call the Victory Show. This was to be the Aldwych farce, *Tons of Money*, in which Ralph Lynn and Tom Walls had starred in the thirties.

"On the North side of the camp, there was an east-west railway line. We hadn't seen much of interest on the line, but gradually the amount of traffic seemed to be increasing. There was a lot of goods traffic, which we assumed to be military trains. Early one evening in mid-April there was a tremendous

Alliierte Kriegsgefangene

WARNUNG AN JEDEN, DER FÜR IHRE BEHANDLUNG VERANTWORTLICH IST

DIE Regierung von Grossbritannien, die Regierung der Vereinigten Staaten und die Regierung der Sowjet-Union richten hiermit zugleich im Namen aller Vereinten Nationen, die sich im Kriege mit Deutschland befinden, eine feierliche Warnung an alle Kommandanten und Bewachungsmannschaften, die Befehlsgewalt über alliierte Kriegsgefangene in Deutschland oder im deutsch-besetzten Gebiet haben, sowie an alle Angehörigen der Geheimen Staatspolizei und an alle anderen Personen, gleichgültig welchen Dienstzweiges und welchen Ranges, die alliierte Kriegsgefangene in Händen haben, sei es im Kampfgebiet, auf den Verbindungswegen oder im rückwärtigen Gebiet. Sie erklären hiermit, dass sie alle diese Personen ebenso wie das deutsche Oberkommando und die zuständigen deutschen Heeres-, Kriegsmarine- und Luftwaffe- Behörden für die Sicherheit und Wohlfahrt der ihnen anvertrauten alliierten Kriegsgefangenen persönlich verantwortlich machen.

Jedermann, der alliierte Kriegsgefangene misshandelt oder solche Misshandlung zulässt, gleichgültig ob im Kampfgebiet, auf den Verbindungswegen, im Lager, Lazarett, Gefängnis oder wo auch immer, wird rücksichtslos verfolgt und seiner Bestrafung zugeführt werden.

Sie weisen darauf hin, dass sie diese Verantwortung unter allen Umständen als bindend betrachten; auch kann diese Verantwortung nicht auf irgendwelche anderen Behörden oder Einzelpersonen abgeschoben werden.

Winston Churchill   *Harry S. Truman*   *Josef Stalin*

UNG 1

Warning leaflet: In dropping vast numbers of this notice over Germany near the end of the war, the Allies were clearly taking no chances concerning the safety of their personnel in the prisoner-of-war camps (courtesy Norman Page).

racket as we watched a train being attacked from end to end by American fighter aircraft.

"I was on stage, in the middle of a dress rehearsal for the Victory Show, when the attack started. We ran to the windows in time to see the train begin to blow up. It must have been an ammunition train, because explosions started along its whole length. One truck blew up so violently that an axle with two wheels attached, flew though the air and landed near the transit compound. The rehearsal was abandoned."

TOM FIELDER. "One by one the wagons exploded in a mighty fireball, scattering artillery shells far and wide, making a very dangerous mess for someone to clean up.

"'Won't be using that line again for a while,' remarked a bystander.

"'No, and our Red Cross parcels won't be coming that way either,' said a worried voice."

FLIGHT SERGEANT JACK DAVIS. "I was in a small hut next to the Cooler, waiting to go into that to serve time for escaping, when a fighter aircraft (I think it was a Mustang) strafed the compound and a Russian sleeping in the bunk above me was killed. It was thought they were aiming for the German HQ next door."

JOE TOMBLING (17 April). "At 11.45 two Mustangs shot up the camp and killed one Englishman and one Russian. Chap in next hut 14A had a bullet in his neck. Our hut and wash-house hit but no-one hurt. 9A hit the worst. Moe and Johnny were buried beneath a pile of Russians when the firing was heard."

SERGEANT S.G. WOLHUTER. "After this ... as a precaution, we painted the letters 'POW' on all the corner huts in the camp, as well as on the French football ground in letters 70 feet long."

Leon Colbert and Lester McCafferty were two black GIs from the U.S. 2nd Army Infantry Division in Stalag IVB, where they were assigned to burial details.

ERV. SZPEK JR.[3] recalls: "Leon whispered to me that all of the guys don't know what it is like to really have it tough. He noted that being black made them subject to all kinds of prejudice and unfair treatment by their own army. The Germans were no different. He did not elaborate but I assume that the guards took every opportunity to single out these two and assign them the worst of duties as well as verbal abuse. It was probably also a source of propaganda, kindling for their idea of superior race and superior soldiers."

Hitler's mighty Third Reich was now crumbling about him, and the vaunted German superiority was being proved a myth. The Russians were advancing steadily in the east, the British and American spearheads had crossed the Rhine and the Allied air forces ruled the German skies. Fortunately unknown to those in Stalag IVB and the other camps, the Führer, unpredictable in his increasing paranoia, had drafted a directive that all prisoners of war were to be eliminated.

Opposition to this diabolical plan among those closest to Hitler is reputed to have been led by Himmler. In any case the Allies had either anticipated such a possibility or had been alerted to it by their intelligence sources and, soon after Truman's accession to the U.S. presidency, they had dropped millions of leaflets from the air over Germany, warning trenchantly against the ill treatment of prisoners.

SERGEANT TOM FIELDER (mid-April 1945). "All the week tensions increased. Apprehension became fear as the world around us exploded into smoke and flames. For a long while, the confines of the camp had seemed to be our whole world. Looking through the wire, we were in the midst of farmland and pine forests. To the north-east we could see the low grey roofs of the small village of Neuburxdorf about a half-mile away. To the north-west a little further away the same grey walls and roofs of Burxdorf merging into the farmland. Neither of these villages seemed to be under attack. But towards the east, along the horizon, there was a constant rumble of explosions and great billowing clouds of black smoke rising violently skywards.

"We just hoped the camp was not to be overwhelmed with the same spectacular destructive forces."[4]

QMS FREDERICK HEDGES. "Lots of chaps are giving way under the strain lately. Keep a tight grip, is the motto these days. Hang on and see it through."

FRED HEATHFIELD describes how, during that terribly cold winter with its bitter east winds blowing across from Siberia, the nights were often so cold that they could not sleep and were compelled simply to lie and shiver.

"If we did not move the blanket froze stiff. Snow blew in through the ever-open apertures we called windows, and covered our boots which we used as pillows. Sheets of cardboard as barriers were too small to be effective and blew in when fixed in the window openings. The water in the wash house froze and we had to wait for the lukewarm brew of ersatz coffee or mint tea, then hope there was enough heat in the stove to warm up our mugs.

"To keep the stove going we gradually took the barrack to pieces. The planks of the ceiling went first, then self-appointed experts decided which of the roof trusses could be cut out without bringing the roof down. Even the exterior planking was robbed from the outer walls of the in-hut cess-pit. The Germans said they had no coal but we could sweep up the dust from the coal bunkers, wet it and mould it into balls, which might give some heat. This supply lasted only a day or two."

The waiting went on. This was the doldrums, where sometimes the rock bottom of POW existence seemed close. The news was good, but inside the wire, under the guard towers, life went on unchanged. Hopes rose and fell: rose with each nearby bombing raid; fell with diminishing rations and weakness; climbed again with each BBC bulletin; and dropped again. Yet, through all the highs and lows a small flame remained constant, inextinguishable.

A French POW wrote the following later in a book as a dedication to a fellow prisoner and friend:

> *Grey was the colour of Mühlberg*
> *Black our thoughts at nightfall*
> *Red our trousers when we got acquainted*
> *With the Strafkompanie ...*
> *But nevertheless*
> *The colour of our sublime hope was radiant.*[5]

14

Deliverance

Je suis né pour te connaître
Pour te nommer
Liberté.

(Paul Eluard, *Poésie et Vérité*, Liberté, 1942)

THE END

Out in the Arbeitskommandos, news about progress of the war was often either unavailable or unreliable, and the end, when it came, was sometimes sudden and dramatic, sometimes a slow winding down toward stalemate. Through those seemingly interminable final weeks, from the less rigorous of these camps to the truly harsh ones, the men had generally hung on to their convictions of eventual Allied victory, of release and return to their homes. For some the passage to liberation would prove a relatively smooth one.

SIGNALMAN ROBERT H. LEE, RA (at Freital, a few miles from Dresden). "When in April we were ordered to pack and be ready to move out next day, we were hardly surprised. We could hear the gunfire faintly to the east. For the first time the paper had a defeatist headline."

PRIVATE FIRST CLASS RUSSELL KUEHN (at Leipzig). "During the night, we were aware of a gentle rumbling sound in the east—the allies had started a final drive deep into Germany. At daybreak the morning of 15 April we were awakened and ordered to prepare to march. We were also told that President Roosevelt had died the day before ... and so we started to march eastward for 7 days when we heard Russian artillery in the distance, so we reversed our direction and headed west for 7 days.

"Our 4 guards [nice old men who meant well] found some Schnaps, got very drunk and gave us their weapons with a handshake and 'Auf Wiedersehen.' We were free!"

The 50 men at the Meissen Arbeitskommando (682) were assembled among a group of 1,000 or so and for a start were marched westward along the concrete Autobahnen. As these became increasingly congested with military traffic of all sorts—and travelling both ways—they were later diverted to secondary roads and country lanes.

After 10 days or so the march had degenerated to a struggle as the blokes became progressively footsore and dog-weary. Guards with rifles or submachine guns stolidly kept pace along both sides of the column, and a few of the older ones seemed in as poor shape as some of their charges. It was early April and still cold, particularly at night.

TONY VERCOE. "Most of us had been able to bring some foodstuffs with us, which was just as well. Any Jerry rations were forthcoming only about every second day, and pretty sparse they were. Inevitably some foraging took place along the route.

"We slept fully clothed, all of us for warmth, Peter and I because we were keeping our options open. We hadn't given up the idea of escape. As long as we kept moving west though, we'd stay with the mob, always ready to improvise in the event of any unpromising change in the routine. We didn't really trust the bloody Jerries.

"Eventually we noticed smoke ahead and the following day identified what could only be gunfire. Some of the guards were beginning to act uncharacteristically, discernible first as a restlessness, an effect which spread to others, until most of them seemed nervous and twitchy.

"It wasn't long before the reasons for this odd behaviour became apparent. We were on a rough country road, potholes full of muddy water, long empty fields either side. There was a shout and about a hundred and fifty yards away, at the far end of the field on our right Peter and I spotted the movement of a singularly unrustic shape pushing its way through a low hedge there.

"A tank. It halted briefly, then backtracked out of sight. We hadn't imagined it, had we? No. The whole column had come to a standstill and the boys were all chattering, speculating.

"We had reached the outskirts of Weimar. Soon we had the answer. Several tanks now broke through the hedge and began to crawl down the field towards us. Sherman tanks with a white star. Yanks.

"Yelling and cheering—some chaps almost mustering a bit of a dance—we left the road, the guards forgotten, and hopped over the ditch, to stream across the field. Soon the tanks were surrounded, and those of the crews riding on top were tossing us chocolate, cigarettes, any K-rations they had with them.

"Now we found that all the Jerries, as though by magic, had somehow got rid of their weapons. They were standing around apprehensively, hands tentatively in the air. The boot was on the other foot."

14—Deliverance

After being taken prisoner during the Warsaw uprising, her subsequent attachment at various work camps, her periods of escape and recapture, Yvonn Lucyna Kozakiewicz had been moved steadily westward. Liberation for her took place at Oberlangen, not far from the Dutch border, which surrendered on 5 May to Polish troops. One of these men would become her husband and they would subsequently live in England.

For others the route to freedom would prove a less simple process.

At Bülzig Alex Franks and his companions were awakened early on the morning of Friday 13 April, told to pack up and be ready to move out. Their guard led them across the railway line and they headed south. Their long march provided a variety of experiences, including sleeping on the floor for several nights in a hospital packed with chronically sick prisoners and at which a steady stream of pitiful figures continued to arrive from the East. At this point their guard disappeared, never to be seen again. On the morning of 23 April the remaining Germans also left, heading west. The British declined an offer to go with them, believing it safer to keep clear of German troops at that stage.

They felt themselves free at last, when surrounded by Russian soldiers the next morning. Without food and unable to speak Russian they set off foraging, coming soon upon a big boarded-up house which had been broken into. They went in, looked around what seemed to be a doctor's surgery, moved along a corridor and came to a sitting room.

ALEX FRANKS. "We had quite a shock when we opened the door, for we found that it was occupied by a whole German family; grandma, granddad, mother, father, and four children. They were lolling back on comfortable easy chairs and a sofa. But they didn't mind us barging in. They were all dead!

"There was no evidence of any sort of violence, no blood, no bullet or knife wounds, but on the floor was a discarded hypodermic syringe."

Freedom was yet to prove more of a mirage than a reality for this group. After marching 25 miles to Falkenburg, a major railway junction which showed clear evidence of effective RAF bombing, they encountered in succession some rather suspicious Russian troops, a slow-moving column of British POWs and, a few miles from Mühlberg, a number of German soldiers who had been shot.[1] Near Kossdorf a drunken Russian gave them a lift in a lorry, driving erratically and at great speed to the vicinity of Torgau where he dropped them off, shook hands all round and roared away.

ALEX FRANKS. "The first thing we saw at Torgau was the old girder bridge lying half in and half out of the water. It was still littered with dead Germans, quite a number of them floating in the river."

They could now see a pontoon bridge built by the Americans, but the Russians—probably under orders—were unwilling to let them cross. They took refuge in an old fortress overlooking the bridge, found some food there and stayed for two days.

ALEX FRANKS. "The next morning, May 3rd, we were aroused by a terrific commotion outside. Through the window we saw a great procession of ex-prisoners and displaced persons making their way across towards us. They were all on their way home to all points east.

"From our vantage point in the fort we could see the never-ending tide of impoverished, emaciated but liberated humanity as it continued to flow over that American pontoon bridge.

"Many of the travellers were limping, some struggling along on home-made crutches; most had just what they stood up in, others had great packs on their backs, pulled overloaded wooden trollies or pushed 'liberated' bicycles piled high with their goods, chattels and loot. All had happier faces than I had seen for a long time.

"Both sexes were represented in the surge of released prisoners who were making it quite clear that their priority ... was to get as far away from Germany as possible."

When toward dusk the procession began to thin out, Alex and his friends in the fortress saw three American officers walking over the bridge toward them. At a prearranged signal they cupped their hands round their mouths and shouted in unison: 'Sir! We are British prisoners. The Russians won't let us cross the bridge.' The officers stopped, beckoned to them and waited while they grabbed what kit they could and ran quickly across to join the Americans.

ALEX FRANKS. "'Come on buddies. From now on you are one of us. We'll walk you over. I reckon you've had enough to put up with. It's time you were on your way home.'"

At last the "Dear Old Blighty" they'd dreamed of for so long seemed accessible and, together with their confident, well-armed escorts, they crossed the final barrier, the Elbe, to freedom.

FRED HILL (at Hartmannsdorf). "A group of Jewish women being evacuated from a concentration camp in the east passed through our village. Many were without shoes and looked a pitiful sight. The police escort carried whips, and one woman had the side of her face slashed and bruised because she could not keep up."

They had suffered so much. Could they hang on to reach freedom?

WALLY MARTIN and JIM BARD of the U.S. Army recalled their journey south after leaving Brand Erbisdorf: "The days on the crowded roads in

14—Deliverance

Czechoslovakia. Along with the POWs, there were German troops and refugees. Overhead, Russian planes strafed anything that moved. Two members of our work party were killed.

"The Russians moved in and liberated us. A few weeks later, we were at Camp Lucky Strike in France and on the way home."

For Dave Brokensha the journey to freedom was wearisome, frustrating and at times terrifying, ultimately being rounded off with a touch of comedy. Dave and his brother Paul plus the rest of their group from the Arbeitskommando a few miles west of Dresden were ordered to march south toward Czechoslovakia and the alleged safety of the mountains. After two days they reached the village of Hellendorf, where they spent three weeks in a barn waiting for the expected liberation. On 8 May, which happened to be VE-Day, they took to the roads again heading west, a column of some 700 POWs, only to have the same experience as Martin and Bard, being bombed and machine-gunned in three sorties by Russian dive bombers and fighters.

Dave received a head wound which caused a lot of bleeding but proved not to be serious. Five of them set off together and Dave describes walking through a desolate landscape, littered with corpses and dead horses, until eventually being given a ride by some Russians in trucks. More walking followed, sleep in another barn, and more walking. A young Russian soldier gave them a lift on a tractor he was driving. Soon the narrow road became crowded with refugees and the South Africans were horrified when, with complete indifference, the Russian drove his tractor over the body of an old woman who had not heard him coming or did not move aside in time.

In the vicinity of Freiberg, Dave, Paul and two of the others "relieved" some Germans— soldiers and civilians— of their bicycles and pedalled westward. They stopped overnight in an abandoned house, celebrating with champagne and gin found there. Dave has vivid memories of their meeting with the Yanks next day.

DAVE BROKENSHA. "I was in front of our gang of four, cycling along. Once again—as I had been when captured at Tobruk—I was clad only in a pair of shorts and must have 'looked German.' I was quite sunburnt; it had been a warm spring.

"An American soldier stood in the road and said: 'Hey! You can't come through here, you're a Kraut.' 'Indeed I'm not,' I replied, 'I am a South African. I've been a POW.' The guard called out to an unseen figure in a tent by the roadside: 'Hey Sarge, there's a guy here says he's a South African; whose side are they on? Can I let him through?' The sergeant emerged from the tent and said to the GI: 'Why, you dummy, haven't you heard of Jan Christian Smuts? Sure he's on our side. Let them through.'"

At the huge synthetic petrol factory at Brüx the Dutch were kept at work until the very day the German capitulation was received at Rheims.

The German commandant then opened the gates, and the men, most of whom by then were in very poor shape, were free to go or to stay until either the Americans or the Russians arrived.

BAS VAN DER LAAN and some others had no trouble making a decision. "It was the 8th May, my birthday," he says. "As most of us were not too keen to wait for the Russians we started to walk west towards the Americans about 60 kms away. We were in small groups of about six and progress was difficult because we had no food and the roads were chock-a-block with German vehicles of various types going both ways and refugees also heading west. There was still some shooting round about.

"At last, after two gruelling days we reached American forces in the western part of Czechoslovakia. Three weeks after liberation we arrived back in the Netherlands on 31 May."

KURT VONNEGUT and his Slaughterhouse 5 work group were part of a straggling westward migration to the vicinity of a river. He recalls: "The end, where all the lines stopped, was a beetfield.... The rain was coming down. The war in Europe had been over for a couple of weeks. We were formed in ranks, with Russian soldiers guarding us—Englishmen, Americans, Dutchmen, Belgians, Frenchmen, Canadians, South Africans, New Zealanders, Australians, thousands of us about to stop being prisoners of war.

"And on the other side of the field were thousands of Russians and Poles and Yugoslavians and so on guarded by American soldiers. An exchange was made there in the rain—one for one."

BACK IN STALAG IVB

Early in the new year clear confirmation that the Russian offensive in the east was making progress had come when refugees were seen passing the camp, heading west. It began as a trickle but grew day by day over the weeks, until it had become a continuous torrent.

JOE TOMBLING (24 January 1945). "Rumours of evacuated civvies coming in. Dresden overcrowded and people still arriving by train. Berlin stations absolutely packed tight with stranded people. They had to travel in open cattle trucks and many women and children froze to death. Many dying from lack of food."

Joe also recorded that a line of refugees 2 kilometres long straggled past during the afternoon on 3 February 1945, but at the bridges across the Elbe they'd had to take second place to German military movement.

QMS FREDERICK HEDGES. "Mingled amongst them one can see German soldiers who evidently consider discretion to be the better part of val-

14—Deliverance

our. The sound of gunfire can be heard all round. Fires can be seen on the horizon."

At the same time tanks, trucks and troops were moving east. The Russian advance was within 20 kilometres of the camp.

Also being moved west were POWs from camps nearer the advancing Russians. Some of those brought into IVB reported that many of their guards had disappeared along the way, dressed as civilians.

By 22 April chaos loomed as hundreds of prisoners of many nationalities were being brought into the Stalag, and the now seemingly endless procession of refugees with their pathetic possessions, some of the luckier ones with handcarts, streamed past, some heading west, others now east.

W/O DOUGLAS GILLAM. "There was an eerie calm about the hut throughout Sunday 22nd April. News from the BBC told us nothing about the situation in our area. Everyone just waited for something to happen. Very few people went out, but we could see the stream of refugees getting bigger. Gunfire from the east got louder as the day progressed. Even roll call was conducted quickly, nobody had the energy or inclination to tease Blondie any more.

"It was almost dark by the time our potato ration arrived in the hut, by which time most men were lying down. There was nothing else to do. Again, I don't think anyone slept that night. All was very quiet, but we could just hear the odd whispered voice. A few chaps got up periodically and went to the window, and then went quietly back to bed. The gunfire continued well into the night, and just before dawn, small arms fire was occasionally heard. It was a peculiar feeling when we realised that it was all coming to an end, but we still didn't know how it would end.

"As dawn broke, and the first signs of daylight appeared, more people began moving about the hut. The compounds all seemed to be as quiet as ours. At about the time when we should be getting ready for morning roll call, someone shouted, 'The Goon-box is empty.' Immediately others dashed to the window. It was all over."

During the night the Germans had exercised discretion in the face of the advancing Red Army—by then very close—and departed from the camp. Before leaving, the commandant had destroyed all important documents.

CPL. REG. ("MICKEY") READ. "It was April 23rd 1945. I got up to blow Reveille as usual and roll call, and some of the men noticed that the German guards were all gone. They had fled to try to get to the American zone."

Now, from near the main gate, came the sound of a great cheer and then, as the news spread through the camp, a mighty roar rose from compound after compound. It was the sound of freedom.

FLIGHT SERGEANT O.J. DAVIS, 429 Squadron, RCAF. "I was in the cooler when the camp was liberated by the Cossacks. We woke around 6 am and heard all the gunfire etc. Then we found that the locks were all open and the guards nowhere to be seen. We could see the Cossacks riding across the plains. By the time they arrived all the Germans, except for a few who were hiding, had fled. The Cossacks then released all the Russian POWs."

Early that morning Russian cavalry arrived outside the camp. Four of them entered through the eastern gateway and rode through the camp, spending little time there before galloping out the main gate. Freedom of a kind had come to Stalag IVB, and soon a riot of flags (carefully stored out of sight over the months) fluttered outside the gate at the front of the camp.

DOUG GILLAM. "There was nearly a fresh outbreak of war when the Italians put their flag above all the others. The British who had once been prisoners in Italy ... objected most strongly."

FRED HEATHFIELD noted that at 10 a.m. all the Russian prisoners had marched out through the east gate. "Russian huts and the corpses remaining inside were burned down to avoid the spread of Typhus which had been killing them off at thirty a day. For some time the Russians had been taking out the newly dead to prop them up on parade in order to draw their meagre rations. The Germans had dared not approach too close when counting."

GEORGE DUNCAN, an Australian war researcher. "On April 25, 1945, patrols of the U.S. 273rd Infantry Regiment first made contact with Soviet Forces in the village of Leckwitz on the Elbe river. Torgau has been incorrectly reported as the first meeting place and as such is mentioned in nearly all history books." (In fact, Torgau was the second such meeting place.)

Despite an announcement by Winston Churchill, heard in a BBC broadcast, that the historical linkup between the Allied and Russian armies had occurred at Torgau, this almost certainly took place at Strehla (i.e., Leckwitz), on the Elbe, quite near Stalag IVB. Several lads from the camp happened to be there and saw the meeting between U.S. and Russian troops.

ROUGH JUSTICE

A very few German guards had been left behind in the camp after the administration staff had departed during the night of 22 April. They feared the Russians, and with good reason.

14—Deliverance

As the news of liberation swept through the camp Tom Barker had watched as a Russian woman soldier on a shaggy horse galloped between the huts. She had a rifle slung over her back, a pistol at her belt, wore crossed bandoliers of ammunition and wielded a sabre. On the way back to his hut Tom had spotted a bit of paper nailed to a post. It read: YOU ARE ADVISED TO STAY IN YOUR CAMP BECAUSE RUSSIAN SOLDIERS WILL SHOOT AT ANYONE NOT IN RUSSIAN UNIFORM. Tom was glad to sit on his bunk for a while and think about what to do next.

Tom Barker. "I noticed it had suddenly gone very quiet. Outside ... I saw everyone was watching something happening over in the Russian compound. I joined the crowd to see what was so interesting and I wished I had not. It was grisly and haunting.

"The Russian POWs, now freed ... had been busy raiding the small allotment garden to get anything edible, and that was where they found 'Blondie' the German guard hiding in one of the tool sheds ... asleep in a drunken stupor and now struggling to keep his feet while a group of very determined Russian POWs steered him to a lamppost in the camp. A large group had gathered and two or three Russians had hold of Blondie by the arms.

"Blondie was struggling and shouting and screaming but to no avail. The woman on the horse just sat there and watched as a skinny Russian POW threw a rope over the lamppost nearby and fastened it round Blondie's ankles."

Now a couple of the Russians pulled Blondie off his feet while three or four more hauled on the rope. Blondie was left grabbing at tufts of grass in a vain attempt to avoid being hoisted upside down. The Russians kept pulling until his head was two or three feet clear of the ground, and for a short while Blondie was swaying back and forth trying to reach up to untie the rope round his ankles.

Tom Barker. "I shed no tears for Blondie, but to see a bloke die like this was like being in a nightmare."

Going on to describe, in graphic detail, the horrific execution of Blondie there, Tom acknowledges that, for the Russian POWs, it was justice. For him though, it has always exemplified the ultimate savagery of war. Suffice here to record that a knife was used to cut off first the hands and then the head which was spat upon and defiled in other ways.

Russell Kuehn (of the U.S. 28th Infantry Division) has reported confirmation of this incident from comrades still in IVB at liberation.

Harry McLean. "A couple of former German guards who had exchanged their uniforms for rags, to pass themselves off as Russians, were discovered and hanged from the saddles of the horsemen."

Nor was this the end — not for the Germans, not for the POWs, not for the camp itself.

Most of the guards had headed west, aiming to get across the Elbe and put some distance between themselves and the Russians. Most of them got no farther than the river.

MICKEY READ. "I joined a party of six and we decided to walk to the American zone. On the way we saw some terrible sights. Some of our guards had been murdered; even civilian families had committed suicide rather than being taken prisoner by the Russians."[1]

S.G. WOLHUTER. "It was not a pleasant sight watching the Russian conquerors invading Eastern Germany and it reminded me of what I had read of the barbarous raids centuries ago by Attila and Genghis Khan.... Chaos reigned and terror stalked the land."

ALEX SHAND and his brother JOHN had decided to go across to the farming area outside the camp to try to find a couple of hens or a sheep. "While walking around we noticed a number of the local Germans—at least a dozen—had been strung up in the trees ... high up, swinging on ropes. We assumed the Russians from the camp had done this."

There were many brief foraging sorties of this kind made outside the camp but, given the volatile situation all around, and on the advice of Russian officers, most of the men elected to await formal departure arrangements. A first move came almost a fortnight later when, on 6 May, they were assembled for the 25 kilometer hike to Riesa, not exactly a doddle in their condition.

QMS FREDERICK HEDGES describes the start of the journey. "We marched off at 11.30 in the rear of D North. Following us at 2.00 was Transit and RAF. It was raining when we started but by 2.00 the sun was shining. The column stretched itself out and must at the finish have been 5 miles long. A halt every hour for 10 minutes, then on again. At the end of 5 miles kit was strewn all along the road as men discarded, bit by bit, stuff they found they could not carry."

JOE TOMBLING recorded some observations along their route. "Crossed river Elbe at Lorenzkirch, through Strehla. Russian tanks and lorries cramming the roads. Russians travel with their women....

"Lorenzkirch was a shambles. The Germans must have made a stand there. Guns, lorries, carts, tanks and civilians' belongings strewn everywhere."

FREDERICK HEDGES. "I found myself getting along fairly well, due to the fact, I suppose, that every day I had a habit of walking five or six times round the compound, thus keeping the legs and feet in good order; but many were showing signs of wear and tear, and at the end of 10 miles, and after that, it was every man for himself. That is, get there somehow or other. Some got a lift on Russian Panzers, but we three finished on our feet, without having thrown away any of our kit; but by God, my feet were burning!

"We eventually found ourselves in a side street in Riesa, sitting on the kerb and being refreshed with hot coffee by the civilian women. My goodness, were they glad to see us! The Russians had looted and raped all over the town, and the women and young girls were terror-stricken. With 8,000 British and American troops in the town they felt a little more secure."

The billets designated for this mass of men were German barracks far too limited in size to accommodate all of them, and many had spread into workshops and warehouses nearby.

FREDERICK HEDGES. "We three were determined to get a decent billet if possible, so we trekked back into the centre of the town and asked a lady if we could sleep on the floor."

"The place we had chosen was a large block of flats, and when the inhabitants realised what we wanted they nearly fell over themselves getting us inside, and that night, after a good meal and two glasses of Schnaps, I slept in a feather bed, the first time for nearly 6 years."

It was now 11 May, three days after VE-Day, but here at Riesa, as Sergeant Harry McLean, of 427 Squadron, RCAF realized, a no-man's-land situation existed, between the Western Allies on the one hand and the Russians on the other. Like some others, Harry opted to take his chances by walking toward the west and the lure of home. After staying with a German family overnight he set off for Wurzen, on the river Mulde, believing American forces to be there.

He passed a group of Russian officers on the way to Oschatz, and reaching there called at a house to ask for water. The householder requested Harry to take a letter for his son, a prisoner of war in Britain. The word got round and he left there with several such letters, which he posted after reaching home.

HARRY MCLEAN. "At Wurzen I met an American soldier riding around on a white horse, and he directed me to a corner premises where the owner was putting up some refugees. There were about fifteen of us.

"The next morning after passing the dock gates of the local wharf we crossed some ground towards the river Mulde and climbed up the wreckage of a railway bridge, which I suppose the Germans had blown, walked along the footway at the top and down a flight of steps the other side of the river, where two Americans with rifles were sitting. They directed us to a small light industry factory where we were given K-rations and later transported to the old Luftwaffe 'drome of Merseberg Halle."

Two days later Harry was on his way home, via Rheims, landing in

England at the Wing air base near Leighton Buzzard, where he had trained three years earlier.

For the men still at Riesa it would be a long wait. The Russians seemed uninterested in moving them and there was no sign of the British or Americans. Effectively, they were still hostages as the politicians in the East and the West wrangled.[2]

WARRANT OFFICER ROBERT HARDING, 70 Squadron, RAF gives this account of what followed.

"At 1 am on 23 May, there was another meeting of compound leaders. Here I and the others met a Russian colonel—the most sober, or least drunk, officer that we had met during the last few weeks. He informed us that we would be leaving shortly. We then toured the barracks, waking up the men and giving them the good news.

"Then again later the same morning, we attended yet another gathering. This time we met a real, live general.[3] He was a large, florid man in a formal uniform, bedecked with row upon row of colourful medals, and attended by several junior officers.

"Through his interpreter, this new arrival gave us a short speech on the glorious victory of the mighty Russian army. Because of this we were now free to return to our own country and to our families. He did not stay long but did spend a minute or so with a senior army NCO who had fought in WWI and was the only one of us with medal ribbons. Like the Americans, the Russians were into medals in a big way.

"The tension in the barracks was now electric and no one ventured far in case they missed whatever was about to happen. But the day passed without incident. Then, just as we were giving up hope as the evening set in, a very long convoy of lorries arrived driven by black GIs.

"Lieutenant Jessop, RSM Samuels and I were responsible for making sure that no one was left behind. When, at last, we were satisfied that no one was left, we too climbed aboard the last lorry in the convoy, less full than the others. About 11 pm we drove out of Riesa and headed west towards the Allied lines and home."

At this time, back in the Stalag there were still others who, for various reasons, had been unable to leave earlier. Most of these men, among them Tom Swallow, would have to remain in the camp for a further six or seven weeks in steadily deteriorating conditions.

Possibly the worst ordeal for former British Commonwealth and American POWs was reserved for those repatriated by way of Odessa. The very limited and sporadic supplies of food were inadequate to sustain them on their journeys, which lasted several weeks and sometimes months, and which were frequently marred by long, frustrating delays. Many men subjected to this bitter trial at the end of their captivity did not survive it.

As for the Russians who somehow had survived the inhumanities of their years in the prison camps, many would not be given the opportunity to enjoy liberation.

Despite the fact that Stalin's own son was a prisoner of the Germans, the Kremlin's official line was that Russian soldiers who had allowed themselves to be taken prisoner were traitors.

In the Epilogue to his book *Soldier Boy*, George K. Zak reports eyewitness accounts of the Russian prisoners held at Riesa near the end of May 1945 being marched by Russian soldiers to a nearby quarry where they were all executed by machine gun fire.[4]

GEORGE DUNCAN. "In Germany's war against Russia, the Germans captured a total of 5,754,000 Russian soldiers. Of these prisoners, 3,700,000 died while in captivity."

The story of the camp itself did not end there either. Under the USSR occupation forces it was maintained from 1945 to 1948 as Special Camp No. 1 of the NKVD/MVD. German citizens labelled as Nazi activists, "fellow travellers" or alleged to pose some threat to the Soviet authority were arrested and incarcerated there without warrant or trial in appalling conditions. Almost 22,000 detainees—men, women and young people—were involved, and as many as one-third of these did not survive. Among those who did was Achim Kilian, whose history of the camp was published as *Mühlberg 1939–1948* (Böhlau Verlag, Köln-Weimar 2001).

> A camp with dark wooden huts, with watchtowers rising high as on stilts, with high barbed-wire fences and lampposts all around.... A sinister camp filled with uncertainty.
>
> Achim Kilian

We will all remember that.

Glossary

Afrika Korps— German forces in North Africa
Afrikaner — South African (usually white) national
Anzio— Allied bridgehead area on west coast of Italy
Appell/s— Roll call/s
Arbeitschule — Work school
Arbeitskommando/s— Work detachment/s
Arbeitslager — Work camp
Ardennes— Forested region of Belgium and Luxembourg, site of the Battle of the Bulge
Arnhem — A major objective in Holland of Operation Market Garden in 1944
"Auf Wiedersehen"— Farewell
"Aus machen!"— Move out!
Aussie — Colloquial for Australian
Autobahnen — Concrete highways in Germany
Babbelfest, ein — A feast of chatter
Bahnhof— Railway station
Balalaikas— Russian stringed musical instruments
Bassin des Chasses— Beach on west coast of France
Bastogne—Monschau — Line at which German advance was held in Belgium during the Battle of the Bulge
BBC — British Broadcasting Corporation
Benghazi — Port and Axis POW camp in Libya
"Blitz"— POW jargon for lightning raid on hut
Blockführer — Block leader
Boches, les— French POW slang for Germans
Bombardier — Artillery equivalent of corporal in British army
"Bombay Belle"— POW slang for the Scheissenwagen
Brownshirts— Members of a harsh German militia group
Campo 70, Fermo— A POW camp in Italy
Canuck — Colloquial for Canadian

Glossary

Comité International (de la Croix Rouge) — International Red Cross Committee, Geneva, Switzerland

Cooler, the — POW jargon for prison within the camp

Cossacks — Skilled horsemen in Russian army

Daily Mail — A British national newspaper

DDT powder — Poison used as an insecticide

Deutsch — German (language)

Dixie — A metal food dish (military)

Dolmetscher — Interpreter

Dulag Luft — Interrogation camp for captured airmen

"Ein Feldwebel weg!" — "One sergeant-major gone!"

"Ein Mann krank" — "One man sick"

El Alamein — Site of Rommel's defeat in Egyptian desert by British forces

Ersatz — Substitute

Feldwebel — Sergeant major

Flak — Anti-aircraft fire

Fritz — Common nickname for Germans

Führer — Leader

Fünf, zehn, fünfzehn, zwanzig — Five, ten, fifteen, twenty

Fusslappen — Foot rags

Gedenkstätte Ehrenhain Zeithain — Memorial site Ehrenhain Zeithain (Saxony)

Gefreiter — Lance corporal

Gemeiner Soldat — Common soldier, private

Geordie — A native of Tyneside, northeast England

Gepruft — Censored

Gestapo — German (Nazi) secret police

Goons — POW slang for German guards

Gunner — Artillery equivalent of private in British army

Gurkhas — Nepalese soldiers highly regarded in the British army

"Heil!" — "Hail!"

Hessian — A woven textile

Hürtgen Forest — An extensive area along the German-Belgian border, the scene of a bloody and protracted battle between American and German forces. The Americans attacked on 19 September 1944 but, in difficult terrain and against stubborn German resistance, it was February 1945 before they prevailed. Both sides sustained appalling losses in the action.

Jerry (plural: Jerries) — British POW slang for German/s

Kalkgrabe — Lime grave

Kalkgrube — Lime pit

"Kamerad, Brot" — "Comrade, bread"

Glossary

Kaput — Dead, finished
Kiwi — Colloquial for New Zealander
Kohlrabi — A turnip-rooted cabbage
Kommandantur — German administrative camp HQ
Kriegie — Abbreviation for *Kriegsgefangene*
Kriegsgefangene — Prisoner of war
Kultur Städte — Cultural cities (of Germany)
Lager/s — Camp/s
Lagergeld — Camp money
Lazarett — Military hospital
Luftwaffe — German air force
M. [Mannschafts] Stammlager — Group muster or transit camp
"Mais, quel hasard!" — "But what a danger!" (French)
Malmédy — In a wood near this town in east Belgium 85 American POWs were executed by the SS
Mark — German currency
MI 5, MI 6, MI 9, IS 9, BIA — British wartime intelligence units
MIS-X — U.S. wartime intelligence unit
Oberfeldwebel — Senior sergeant major
Obergefreiter — Corporal
Oberleutnant — Senior lieutenant
Oflag — Camp for officer POWs
Panzers — Tanks
PFC — Private first class (U.S. army)
Posten — Sentry, guard
Radar — System of high-frequency radio waves developed for the tracking of moving objects
RASC — Royal Army Service Corps
'Raus! (abbreviation of "heraus!") — "Out! Come out!"
Reveille — Wake-up bugle call
Revier — Convalescent hospital, sick bay
RSM — Regimental sergeant major
RTR — Royal Tank Regiment
S5 — Nickname for American POW work group based at Schlachthof-fünf, Dresden
Sauerkraut — Pickled cabbage
Schwarzbrot — black bread
Scheissenwagen — Shit wagon
Schlachthof-fünf — Slaughterhouse No. 5, Dresden
Schnaps — Strong ginlike spirits

"Schnell!" — "Quick! Quickly!"
Sehr nahrhaft — Very nourishing
Sidi Rezegh — Much fought-over desert area in Libya
Springbok — Colloquial for South African
SS — Ruthless German police and security force
Stalag (abbreviation of Stammlager) — Prisoner of war camp
Stalag Luft — POW camp for airmen
Strafebaracke — Punishment barrack
Strafkompanie — Disciplinary group
Straflager — Punishment compound
Streng verboten — Strictly forbidden
Sudetenland — Northwest region of Czechoslovakia on border with Germany
Sudetenlandische Treibstaff Werke AG — Vast German synthetic petrol factory in Czechoslovakia using forced POW workers
Swastika — Ancient eastern symbol adopted by Nazis
Terrorflieger Schweinhunds — (Literally) Terror flyer filthy pigs
Third Reich — German Nazi regime, 1933–1945
Tobruk — Port town in Libya, fiercely contested by British and German forces
Untermenschen — Subhuman beings
Unteroffizier — Corporal
Verboten — Forbidden
Vertrauensmann — Man of confidence
Vichy regime — Puppet government set up under Pétain by Germans to administer unoccupied France
Volksdeutscher — German nationals
Vorlager — Holding compound
Wapenbroeders — Weapon Brothers (a Dutch veterans' organization)
Wehrkreis — War Area Command
Wehrmacht — the German army

Chapter Notes

Chapter 1

1. Stalags IVA (Hohnstein), IVB (Mühlberg), IVC (Wistritz), IVD (Torgau), IVF (Hartmannsdorf), IVG (Oschatz) and the "auxiliaries" IVD/Z (Annaburg) and IVH/304 (Jacobstahl).
2. Russian prisoners.
3. See Chapter 13.
4. This was routine until late 1944, when, because of the increasing numbers of prisoners being admitted, the procedure was discontinued.
5. "Shades of the gas chambers," said CSM Richard Hall, of the 4th Battalion, the Green Howards, thinking back on Hitler's extermination methods. "The only difference between Stalag IVB's ablution block and the abominations at Auschwitz and Belsen was, thankfully, hot water came down from our ceiling nozzles rather than cyanide gas" (from Gordon Stooke, RAAF, in *Flak and Barbed Wire*).
6. A few weeks later the X-ray machine was destroyed in a spectacular fire and was not replaced. Some believe this incident was "arranged" by RAF men who needed certain parts of the equipment.
7. See Chapter 13.
8. The main road was approximately half a mile long.
9. "After curfew, this was in constant use, as we were not allowed to leave the hut and walk across the compound. I can still recollect the dreadful smell permeating through the hut, causing considerable distress to those whose beds were nearest the door" (Sergeant Douglas J. Gillam, RAF 141 Squadron).
10. A disadvantage of the top bunk in winter was that the roofs always leaked because of heavy snow and that condensed vapour dripped from the ceiling. It was difficult to keep beds dry, and tins had to be used to collect the water.
11. Tom Nelson was unique in viewing POW life from three different aspects: Army, then as a RAF sergeant navigator. Commissioned while in Stalag IVB, he was moved in late February 1945 as a flight lieutenant to Oflag VIIA.
12. Brylcreem Boys is army jargon for RAF; brown jobs is RAF slang for army.
13. From British War Office report WO 208/3274, "Secret Camp Histories" (declassified), Appendix D.
14. See Chapter 8.

Chapter 2

1. Major ("Padre") McDowall was a New Zealand Presbyterian who had graduated with an MA in Philosophy at Otago University, Dunedin, in 1924 before spending most of 1925 studying at New College, Edinburgh. As a chaplain with 2nd New Zealand Expeditionary Force in North Africa, he was captured with others at Wadi Carmoset, Sidi Rezegh, on 28 November 1941 when No. 4 Main Dressing Station was overrun by a squadron of German armored cars. He subsequently served as a chaplain in Italian prison camps before being transported to Germany, reaching Stalag IVB on 24 September 1943. McDowall kept diaries throughout, and these were edited and pub-

lished in three manuscript volumes by his daughter, Dr. Mary A. Tagg, in 1996.

2. The Stalag Luft was a prisoner of war camp for air force personnel. Unlike their diligent advance planning for the confinement of army servicemen, the Germans had only one Stalag Luft at the start of hostilities and, though they much preferred to keep the two services separate, they were obliged as the war went on to allocate compounds in some army Stalags to house RAF air crew.

3. Ray Newell contributed artwork to several camp enterprises, including the wall newspaper (the New Times), the Empire Theatre and the Mühlberg Motor Club, also setting up and supervising a sketch club. To continue his work and avoid being sent to an Arbeitskommando he promoted himself from gunner to bombardier. His most remarkable achievement was the more than 100 paintings effected in the camp, most of them depicting, in colour, the many different nationals in their uniforms. Brushes, paints and paper or board had to be obtained by barter. In 1998 the Royal Armoury at Leeds, Yorkshire, mounted an exhibition of Ray's Stalag IVB paintings, together with a handsome catalogue illustrating some 60 of them. Copies of many of the works are also held in the museum at Mühlberg.

4. Several first-hand accounts of brutality and the casual killings of Russians are recorded in this book.

5. The Russians, like the French and other nationals, had their own Man of Confidence.

6. See Chapter 3.

7. More of Yvonn's story is told in Chapter 12.

8. Another found his wife there.

9. As well they might have been. As Ervin Szpek noted later: "There were cases of our guys being rounded up and shot. The most publicized was the massacre at Malmédy. It was there that 85 out of a group of 120 U.S. prisoners were marched into the woods and executed by the SS."

10. The soup was made from kohlrabi, a sort of cross between turnip and cabbage, which can tolerate harsh winter conditions.

11. An intangible, extremely elastic facility encountered in most military situations, and especially in the prisoner-of-war camps, the grapevine fed upon rumour, on reports from newly arrived batches of POWs, on snippets of information gleaned from broadcasts, from other nationals returning from work details outside the camp, and so on. Grapevine news would spread through a camp at bewildering speed by word of mouth and the experienced, knowing its capacity for hope-based delusion and humbug, learned to extract its sometimes remarkably accurate grains of truth.

12. Sergeant Tom Nelson of 51 Squadron, RAF, who contributed the information for this story, added that he doubted whether the Americans were aware of the background to this windfall of food. The RAF's own Christmas dinner consisted of the ration issue of millet soup and rye bread.

Chapter 3

1. War Office UK document (declassified).

2. "Other ranks" (below officer rank).

3. "Very nourishing."

4. After this the dogs were trained not to go beyond the gate of the Russian compound.

5. The International Red Cross (now embracing Red Cross and Red Crescent).

6. Clothing, books, sports gear of all types, music scores, orchestral instruments and more.

7. Other examples of Gargini's versatility are recorded in Chapters 5 and 6.

8. "Bombay Belle" was the familiar, if not specially affectionate, name applied by POWs to the Scheissenwagens, of which several were to be seen trundling round the compounds.

Chapter 4

1. "Many of you will have seen films about POW life ... of other camps with Savoy Hotel conditions. Not so IVB!" (Wilf Sutton during an illustrated talk on Mühlberg.)

2. A play on the name Rudyard Kipling, substituting the indispensable Klim (milk) tin.

3. Reprinted in the Stalag IVB reunion brochure, Edinburgh 1996.

4. A reference to the so-called Legion of St. George, formed by the Germans from British prisoners who had volunteered to fight for them on the Russian front, with the guarantee that they would not have to fight against their own side. There were similar setups for U.S. and other nationals.

5. Spiritual care was in the hands of the padres captured at Sidi Rezegh: Major Robert McDowall, (Presbyterian), Captain Charles Willis (Church of England) and Captain Sam Day (Church of England), together with others from different denominations whom they joined in Stalag IVB. Their work is dealt with in detail by Douglas Gillam in "Doug's Story" (Chapter 7).

6. The "Major Ochse" of the Red Cross report.

Chapter 5

1. Erv Szpek Jr., chairman of the IVB Association, Chicago.

2. Bicycle story contributed by John Williams.

3. In postwar years Bill Rae served for a time as a president of the Stalag IVB Association in the U.K. and at the annual reunions was always obliged to encore some of his famous jokes first told in 1944–45.

4. Additional information about Robertson is given in Chapter 7.

5. Gargini also built several brilliant electrical devices, described in other chapters.

6. The motorless Mühlberg Motor Club flourished in Stalag IVB. After the war the superb book *Flywheel* reproduced a facsimile collection of the magazines drawn and scripted by hand in the camp. The substantial royalties from sales of this publication were donated to the British Red Cross.

7. Attested to by Gunner Ray Newell, RA, and Sergeant Harry McLean, 427 Squadron, RCAF.

Chapter 6

1. MIS-X was subsequently set up as a U.S. counterpart to MI 9. It got under way late in 1942, and the two organizations worked in close cooperation.

2. POW camps for officers.

3. For code use with special parcels see Chapter 10.

4. The report was published by the Belgian espionage group Service Clarence in a resistance newsletter of November 1943 and sent to England: de Zitter was executed by the Belgians after the war (Fred Heathfield).

5. "McAlpine," or sometimes "Alpine Willy," was so known because of the small ice ax he carried and used during searches to dig up the hut floor. An older man, a strict disciplinarian and addicted to shouting, he was a Stabsfeldwebel (staff sergeant major).

6. The German term for illicit camp radio was Schwarzradio.

7. See photograph in Chapter 11.

8. For logical reasons of risk to the whole message system, MI 9 applied also the reverse principle of not using it to include disinformation which could be "leaked" to the Germans by POWs.

Chapter 7

1. See also Chapter 10.

2. Also referred to in Chapter 9.

3. This policy was not applied in the case of British army or Commonwealth prisoners of war.

4. Flight Sergeant M.M. "Robbie" Robertson.

5. See Chapter 6.

6. See Chapter 8.

7. Thirty-five years later, at a reunion in Edinburgh, Doug met a man he'd not seen since 1945. He remembered the occasion and described how Doug ran up and down the hut, shouting at the top of his voice, "I'm a father! I'm a father!"

Chapter 8

1. The swapping of identities with another prisoner. To be effective the change needed to be complete in every detail — personal effects including family photographs, identification tags, uniform, a working knowledge of each other's service background, etc. Many escape attempts failed because of a lack of care at this preparatory stage.

2. The official food parcels packed in a number of countries for the International

Red Cross were too important for prisoners' well-being ever to be used for the delivery of escape materials. Other parcels sent by family or IS 9, though delivered via the International Red Cross, were always separate and may have been coded or used in some way for escape aid purposes.

3. Tins in Red Cross food parcels were later punctured in IVB for a time (see Chapter 3).

4. Six weeks in the cooler gave Alex time to think up another dodge. He simply "doctored" his paybook, promoting himself to sergeant. The Germans did not question this and he remained in camp, a member of John's hut, until liberation by the Russians.

5. Padre McDowall and the other chaplains would certainly have known of the existence and progress of the tunnel, but he made no reference to it in his diary in case this was read by Germans.

6. In fact, in the final weeks of the war, because of the numbers involved and the continuous movement of men into and out of the camp, it was thought advisable for U.S. personnel to have their own Man of Confidence. Elected to this role was 1st Sergeant Gleon Philipps.

7. It's believed all of these were recaptured.

8. Punishment barrack.

9. Sergeant Les Goldwyn, a navigator with RAF 83 Squadron, was commissioned while in Stalag IVB and moved to Luft VII Bankau. He escaped from there and reached Switzerland near the end of the war.

10. Confirmed in WO 208/325. (MBE = Member of the Order of the British Empire; BEM = British Empire Medal).

11. Courtesy Sergeant Sam Gillette, 242 Combat Infantry Regt, U.S. 42nd Division.

12. Incidents recorded in detail in Chapter 14.

Chaper 9

1. From British War Office report WO 208/3274 *Secret Camp Histories*, Appendix C.

2. According to both Mickey Read and Fred Heathfield, Corporal Brown was reaching under the tripwire to recover a ball when he was shot. Their accounts agree with Wally's in all other respects. Mickey added that it was learned later that Nordmann had lost his family the night before in an air raid. Perhaps he was exacting some kind of revenge.

3. Probably "Blondie" of the Tom Barker incident, but perhaps a different man from the one referred to in incidents in the RAF compound. It was a common nickname for a particular type of German guard.

4. Such incidents were not unknown in the Arbeitskommandos. An example following the bombing of Dresden was recorded by Kurt Vonnegut and Ervin Szpek of S5. A member of their work group had found a teapot in the rubble, was arrested by SS for plundering, was summarily tried and executed there in the ruins by a firing squad. Two other members of the group were forced to dig his grave.

5. The incident is described in greater detail in Chapter 7.

6. Gene got no medical treatment at the time and still has a scar under his chin where the guard hit him.

Chapter 10

1. Described by Doug Gillam in Chapter 7.

2. Who would want scent, spurs, or white collars in a prisoner-of-war camp? Many of the other items might be swappable — e.g., boots for a pen and pocket book — but food was a high-value commodity and could only be purchased with the prime currency, cigarettes.

Chapter 11

1. According to Andy Anderson one wing also took a window out of the sentry box and he (the sentry) promptly fainted.

2. The fracture to Massie's leg was not properly set at the time, and it was not until Joe Seddon of the Escape Committee (see Chapter 8), who had been a medical student before the war, treated him with massage that he was able to walk again.

3. This incident is described in greater detail in Chapter 13.

4. Years after the war Ward recorded that he still suffered discharges from one of the cuts above his lip.

5. The prisoner who had swapped identities with Florence was later recaptured and given some rough treatment. However, the Germans never found out about the woman who had lived in the camp for five months (Mickey Read says).

6. Bill Oxley, CADS' make-up artist, gave Florence her five o'clock shadow each evening.

7. In 1980, a book by Jack Stoneley, giving a fictionalized account of Florence Barrington's remarkable story, was published under the title *Jenny's War*. Subsequently the film rights to this were sold to a television film company and the "adjustments" à la Hollywood which it then received incensed British veterans of Stalag IVB. Stoneley himself attended the 1985 reunion at Edinburgh to explain (excuse?) the film's distortions, but few members attending the reunion were impressed by what they considered little more than soft soap.

Chapter 12

1. This cynically arrogant maxim translates literally as "Work makes free."

2. The "tahl" of Jacobstahl is believed to be an old spelling for "tal" (valley). Spelling variants in some accounts are Jacobsthal and Jacobstal.

3. Sergeant Tom Swallow, RASC, recalls names scribbled on the walls in Jacobstahl. The language seemed familiar but was certainly not Russian.

4. In the book *Robert Lee, Artist Craftsman*, John Sheeran writes of this work: "The supreme human tragedy of war as a destructive force for civilisation is considered in *The Burden of Dreams* 1984. Robert Lee's own war, taking part in the North African campaign and later imprisoned in camps in Italy and Germany, provided horrific, surreal scenes of human destruction which haunt his mind: a soldier's eyeball stuck to the side of a railway wagon; scorched naked figures fleeing Dresden; an abandoned train from the Russian Front packed with dying German troops; the inhumanities of a Jewish labour camp compound. At first sight *The Burden of Dreams* appears comforting, a doll's house in cross-section, playfully reinterpreted as an Escher-like puzzle, punctuated with everyday objects: a bowl of fruit, a jug, a plate, a kettle. On closer inspection, the harrowing collaged image of a doll's face, with razor teeth and fixed eyes, looms on a massive scale as if back-projected onto the wall. Broken staircases cut across her face. She seems possessed, and transfixed in death. The work can perhaps be seen as an attempt to exorcise the recurring nightmares that the artist has had concerning his experiences of the last days of the Third Reich. It vividly recalls the scenes he witnessed at Freital, where homes opened up by Allied bombing revealed the detritus of human habitation perched precariously amid the ruins. This vision of hell has become a metaphor for the hopelessness man feels when there is no escape, and no direction. Ladders, a possible reference to one of the instruments of the Passion, move in directions but lead nowhere. The apocalyptic scene is confined within a cruciform shape related to early Sienese crucifixion paintings and is equally potent an image of sacrifice."

5. A chapter of the author's earlier book, *Yesterday's Drums*, describes his experiences at the Meissen Arbeitskommando.

6. Sixty years later the knee still troubles Bas, requiring occasional surgery.

7. Some of these experiences are recounted in Chapter 14.

Chapter 13

1. Campbell had written material critical of the U.S. and its servicemen. After the war, while awaiting trial as a war criminal, he hanged himself.

2. Probably not correct: see the report by Robert Lee in Chapter 12. Henri may have interpreted "open" from the German view that Dresden was a "safe" city.

3. A comment made by Leon at a Chicago IVB reunion following a lively discussion about the camp.

4. Near the end, some of the guards at Stalag IVB, in German uniform, were found to be Hungarian. Generally they seemed nervous.

5. This translation by Roger W. Sampson was quoted by Achim Kilian at the British Stalag IVB reunion, Peterborough, April 1999.

Chapter 14

1. Possibly the guards from IVB, seen also by Mickey Read.

2. Several explanations for this stalemate situation have been advanced. There is evidence to support two of them: 1) The Russians were only prepared to release British and American personnel as the Allies handed over Russians, on a one-to-one basis. 2) At one of the pre-armistice meetings of U.S., British and Russian leaders, it had been agreed that Allied POWs released by the Russians should be repatriated via Odessa on the Black Sea. In fact both methods were applied on quite a large scale.

3. General Petrov, one of Marshal Koniev's corps commanders.

4. The same story is published in the book *Soldiers of Misfortune*, by Sanders, Sauter and Kirkwood (National Press Books, Washington 1992). It is possible that these men were Belorussians (known also as White Russians) for whom the Soviets had a deep and abiding antipathy. Belorussians forced by the Germans to serve in the Wehrmacht were pursued relentlessly by the Soviets and received no mercy if caught.

Bibliography

Books

Bryant, Frank. *There's Always Bloody Something*. Benalla, Australia: Samaria Concepts, 1991.
Calvey, Robert. *Name, Rank and Number*. Lewes, England: Book Guild, 1998.
Cawthorne, Nigel. *The Iron Cage*. London: Fourth Estate, 1993.
Fielder, Thomas L. *I Flew, I Fell, I Survived*, 3d ed. Kilsyth, Australia: T.L. Fielder, 2001.
Foot, M.R.D., and J.M. Langley. *MI9: Escape and Evasion 1939–1945*. London: Bodley Head, 1979.
Greaves, David. *Inside Story*. London: Capella Publications, 1989.
Gruzewski, Jan, and Stanislaw Kopf. *Dni Powstania*. Warszawa, Poland: Instytutu Wydawniczego Pax, 1957.
Harding, Robert. *Copper Wire*. New Milton, U.K.: R.W. Harding, 1999, 2000.
Hill, Fred. *Prisoner of War: The Experiences of a Young Salvation Army Officer in WWII*. Wootton, U.K.: Avon Books, 1994.
Jenkins, Cyril George. *P.O.W. Number 226022 — And That Is Now My Identity*. Ringwood, U.K.: Cavalry Publishing, 1997.
Kilian, Achim: *Mühlberg 1939–1948*. Köln-Weimar, Germany: Böhlau Verlag, 2001.
Kozaczuk, Wladyslaw. *Enigma*. London: Arms and Armour Press, 1984.
McKee, Alexander. *The Devil's Tinderbox*. London: Souvenir Press, 1982.
Masterman, J.C.: *The Double-Cross System in the War of 1939 to 1945*. New Haven, CT: Yale, 1972.
Rolf, David. *Prisoners of the Reich*. Barnsley, U.K.: Leo Cooper/Heinemann, 1988.
Sheeran, John. *Robert Lee, Artist Craftsman*. Otley, U.K.: Smith Settle, 1990.
Stoneley, Jack. *Jenny's War*. Watford, U.K.: Hamlin, 1980.
Stooke, Gordon. *Flak and Barbed Wire*. Loftus, Sydney, Australia: Australian Military History Publications, 1997.
Swallow, Tom, and Arthur Pill. *Flywheel*. Exeter and London: Webb & Bower/Michael Joseph, 1987.
Tagg, Mary A. *The Prisoner Padre*. Hamilton, New Zealand: University of Waikato, 1997.
Taylor, Frederick. *Dresden*. London: Bloomsbury, 2004.
Taylor, Geoff. *A Piece of Cake*. London: Corgi Books, 1981.
_____. *Return Ticket*. Oxford, England: Heinemann, 1972.

Van Maarseveen, Dick. *Fotograaf in Krÿgsgevangenschap*. Amsterdam: Rijksmuseum Amsterdam, 1984.
Vercoe, Tony. *Yesterday's Drums*. Wellington, New Zealand: Steele Roberts, 2001.
Vonnegut, Kurt. *Slaughterhouse 5*. London: Jonathan Cape, 1970.
Wolhuter, S.G. *The Melancholy State*. Cape Town, South Africa: Howard Timmins, 1984.
Zak, George K. *Soldier Boy*. Willowbrook, IL: Venture Press, 1998.

Manuscripts and Diaries (All Unpublished)

Anderson, A.F. *Memoirs of Warrant Officer A.F. Anderson, or "What Did Your Grandfather Do in the War?"* Romford, U.K., 2001.
Brokensha, David. *Paul and Dave in the War*. Sherborne, South Africa, 1993/96.
Franks, Alex W., transcribed and edited by Tom Swallow. *Non-Combatant*. Wheaton Aston, U.K., 1991.
Gillam, Douglas J. *University to University*. Peterborough, U.K., 1998.
Hall, Richard, edited by Brian W. Sims. *With the 4th Battalion, the Green Howards*. Redcar, U.K., 1997/98.
Heathfield, Fred. *Diary and Recollections of Stalag IVB*. Farndon, U.K., postwar.
Hedges, Frederick. *Six Months to Freedom*. Colchester, U.K., 1996.
McDowall, Major the Rev. R.G. *Prisoner of War Diary, 1941–1945*. (The original diary booklets, handwritten in standard Red Cross issue POW exercise books, and the 1946 typescript are held by the Auckland War Memorial Museum Library, New Zealand — MS No. 874 [two boxes, eight files]. A copy of the 1946 transcript is held by "Padre" McDowall's daughter, Dr. Mary A. Tagg of Auckland, who edited and printed the work in three bound manuscript volumes in 1996.)
Parsons, Lewis P. *Wartime Memoir*. Vange, Basildon, U.K., 2004.
Read, Reg. "Mickey." *Just a Few Ups and Downs*. Fakenham, U.K., 1996.

Other Sources

British War Office Report W/O 208/3274, *Secret Camp Histories* (declassified), Appendix D.
Canadian Legion Magazine, June 1985.
The Secret War, part 2, BBC-TV, 1988.

Contributors

I am more grateful than I can say to the following veterans of Stalag IVB and some associated *Arbeitskommandos* for so readily offering their recollections or unreservedly allowing me access to diaries, manuscripts or published works for this retrospective.

A.F. ("Andy") Anderson
Tom Barker
James Branford
David Brokensha
Jack Davis
Douglas Denton
Wesley Eckblad
Larry Falstein
Tom Fielder
Alex. Franks

Douglas Gillam
Sam Gillette
Richard Hall
Fred Heathfield
Heinz L. Herz
Fred Hill
Russell Kuehn
Robert H. Lee
Harry McLean
John McMillan

Wally Martin
Harry Muse
Tom Nelson
Ray Newell
Norman Page
Lew Parsons
Wilf. Rapson
Reg. ("Mickey") Read
Alex. Shand
Yvonn Stevenson

Wilf. Sutton
Tom Swallow
Ervin Szpek
Joe Tombling
Bas van der Laan
Kurt Vonnegut
Fred W. Ward
S.G. ("Wally") Wolhuter
Eugene Wopata
George K. Zak

Also to the following who, as relatives of former POWs, or in a personal capacity, have most willingly provided valuable information or help.

Contributors

Robert Anderson
Cheryl Cerbone
George Duncan
Peggy Gibbons
Gaynor Greenwood
Sharon Haslam
Nancy Hedges
Robert Jamieson
  (ex Repat. Report)

Achim Kilian
John Kline
Freda Lockett
M.M. Robertson
Brian W. Sims
Jeremy Sutton-Pratt
Dr. Mary A. Tagg
John Williams
Erv. Szpek Jr.

Index

Adelstein 18, 24
Afrika Korps 147, 183
Allied bomber fleets 161
The Alps 79
Altenburg 149
Altstadt 145
American Eighth Air Force 98
American fighter aircraft 165
American National Red Cross 117
American zone 175, 178
Americans 13, 27, 28, 30, 47, 59, 60, 86, 93, 99, 145, 146, 150, 151, 155, 159, 163, 184, 188
Anderson, Warrant Officer A.F. (Andy) 14, 32, 42, 51, 71, 109, 123, 128, 136, 190, 194, 195
Anderson, Robert 196
Annaburg 8, 31, 187
Appells 15, 16, 17, 50, 56, 57, 110, 111, 114, 141, 142, 183
Arbeitskommandos 52, 63, 102–103, 117, 143, 145, 147, 148, 150, 151, 156, 157, 159, 169, 170, 173, 183, 191
Ardennes 26, 98, 183
Argentine 84
Arnhem 48, 98, 158, 159
Astrakhan 21, 22
Attila 178
Auf wiedersehen 169
Augustus Bridge 145
Australia 30, 44, 92
Austria 67, 102
Ausweis 116
Autobahnen 170
AVA Radio Manufacturing Company 68

Bahnhof 147
Balalaikas 23
Ballauff, Lance Sergeant 69
Baltic 10
Banks, Captain 80, 81

Bard, Jim 154, 172, 173
Barker, Private Tom 121, 177
The Barretts of Wimpole Street 60, 82, 85
Barrington, Florence 141, 142
Barrington, Winston 142
Barth 8, 10, 11
Base Records, New Zealand 138
Bassin des Chasses 46
Bastogne 26, 27
Battle of El Alamein 136
Battle of the Bulge 26, 42, 48, 59
Battle of the Ruhr 10
BBC 18, 71, 82, 95, 96, 168, 175, 176
Belgian 14, 19, 70, 109, 129
Belgium 18, 70, 98
Benghazi 89
Berga-am-Elster 150
Berlin 7, 8, 32, 109, 115, 116, 150, 174, 175, 177
BIA 68
Biggs, Sergeant Walter 72
Birmingham 74, 93
Bitterfeld 115
Black U.S. soldier (Alabama) 153
Blighty 172
Blitz 11, 15
Blondie (German guard) 17, 83, 88, 121, 122, 175, 177
The Blower 87, 88
"Bombay Belle" 39
Borna 149
Börners (factory) 146
Boult, Alan 62
Brand Erbisdorf 154, 172
Branford, Warrant Officer James 16, 33, 49, 114
Brenner Pass 21
Bristol, Private D. 101
Bristol Beaufighter (aircraft) 74
Britain 68, 114, 133, 142, 163, 179
British Army 79, 80, 129, 137

British Commonwealth 34, 47, 89, 100, 180
British Consul 117
British Man of Confidence 24, 80, 105
British Military Attaché 115
British paratroopers 158
British Red Cross 88, 106
British Secret Service 70
Brokensha, Lance Corporal David 150, 154, 159, 173
Brokensha, Sergeant Paul 147
Brown, Corporal 120, 124
Brown, "Zulu" 151
"Brown jobs" 16, 98
Brownshirts 147
Brühl Terraces 145
Brussels 70
Brüx 152, 153, 154, 173
"Brylcreem Boys" 16
"Bubbly Boys" 37
Bulgaria 18, 21, 129
Bülzig 148, 149, 150, 171
Burxdorf 133, 167
Bushell, E. 39
Bushell, John 128

C North Compound 20, 76
CADS (Camp Amateur Dramatic Society) 53, 55, 82
Cairo 55
Cameron Highlanders 95
Camp Leader 11, 57, 70, 151, 152, 164
Camp Lucky Strike 173
Camp radio 141
Campbell, Howard W., Jr. 159
Campo 70 11
Canada 30, 36
Casablanca 21
Chaplains 80, 91, 104
Chemnitz 151, 154, 163
China 18, 22, 80
Christmas Day 153
Christmas 1943 23, 42, 43
Chu Chin Chow 62
Churchill, Winston 149, 176
City of London 62
Code-users 69
Colbert, Leon (GI) 166
Colditz 8
Collet, Nurse 70
Cologne 115
Comité International de la Croix Rouge 34
Commonwealth (British) 20, 41, 50, 52, 56, 68, 77, 80, 89, 134
Congregational Church 89
Copenhagen 116, 117
Cossacks 61, 62, 176
Crete 21, 54, 57, 78

"La Cumparsita" 135
Cyprus 18
Czechoslovakia 7, 18, 67, 143, 145, 172, 173, 174

D-Day landings 55, 162
D North Compound 14, 52, 59, 163
Danish Police Force 26, 39, 128
Danish policeman 129
Davis, Flight Sergeant Jack 34, 109, 121, 166, 176
Day, Captain Sam 80
Denmark 18, 26, 115, 116
Denton, Private Douglas 62, 63, 66, 109–110
de Zitter, Prosper 70
Dodecanese 72
Dolmetschers 21, 105
Dresden 7, 8, 48, 108, 114, 115, 138, 145–150, 152, 153, 154, 155, 156, 159, 161, 163, 169, 173, 174
Duff, Captain A.R. 46, 47
Dulag Luft 8, 70, 71, 74, 76, 94, 95, 136
Duncan, George 176, 181
Dunkirk 19
Dutch trader 129
Dutchman 29, 72, 129

Eastern Germany 8, 178
Eckblad, Wesley (GI) 149
Edinburgh 57, 93, 96, 141
Egypt 18, 21
Eisenhower, General Dwight 55, 153
Elbe (river) 8, 52, 75, 91, 145, 148, 164, 172, 174, 176, 178
Empire Theatre 14, 52, 53, 85, 129; productions 60
England 30, 41, 44, 63, 70, 92, 97, 98, 136, 153, 171, 180
English Football League 92
Enigma machine 68
Escape Committee 63, 87, 95, 100–104, 109, 110, 111, 113, 115, 137, 142
Essex Regiment 15
Europe 7, 21, 28, 67, 71, 96, 117, 153, 174

Falkenburg 112, 171
Falstein, Larry (U.S. soldier) 13, 26
Fascist government 78
Faust 62
Feldwebel 71, 119, 130, 134
Fermo 11
Fielder, Sergeant Tom 104, 106, 107, 108, 137, 166, 167
Flensburg 115
Flywheel 61
Folk, *Oberfeldwebel* 120
Fortresses (aircraft) 98, 146, 153

Index

France 18, 67, 70, 74, 173
Franks, Driver Alex 11, 141, 143, 144, 148, 149, 150, 171
Free American Corps 159
Free British Corps 85
Freiberg 173
Freiburg 151
Freital 146, 169
French Intelligence 67
French Man of Confidence 65
Füsslappen 49
Fyn 117

Gainsborough Film Company 136
Gardiner, Flight Sergeant 110
Gargini, Eric 37, 38, 59, 71
Geneva International Convention 31
Genghis Khan 178
German Army Fiscal Service 7
German Propaganda Ministry 159
German radar 43, 153
Germany 8, 172
Gestapo 11, 56, 70, 71, 137, 142, 160
Ghurkas 30
Gillam, Warrant Officer Douglas 52, 53, 54, 74, 76, 85, 164, 175, 176
Gillette, Sergeant Sam 30, 32, 128, 163
Gleina 149
Goering (Hermann) 10, 11
Goodhind, Roy 82
"Goon-boxes" 81
"Goons" 16, 71
Gorbitz 147, 150, 154, 159
Gordon-Powell, Flight Sergeant Stanley K. 115, 116, 117
Gotha 75
Grand National 127
Gray, Benny 93
Greece 18, 21, 57, 78
Green Howards 12, 30, 134
Greenwood, Gaynor 25
Grieg (Edvard) 62
Gripsholm (ship) 133
Groh, *Obergefreiter* 107, 108
Grunes Gewolbe 145

Hale, Bob 71
"Half-a-Mo" 127
Halifax (aircraft) 70
Hall, CSM Richard 12, 30, 62, 71, 119, 134, 144, 159
Hälsingborg 117
Hamburg-Neumünster 115
Hannover 112, 113
Harding, Warrant Officer Robert W. 164, 180
Harris, "Taffy" 102
Harris, Warrant Officer 101

Haslam, Sharon 140
Heathfield, Sergeant Fred 10, 13–16, 32, 36, 44, 47, 48, 50, 55, 56, 59, 62, 70, 71, 72, 102, 105, 109, 118, 120, 122, 126, 128, 134, 137, 167, 176,
Hedges, QMS Frederick 15, 26, 33, 36, 42, 47, 48, 50, 62, 119, 127, 128, 132, 167, 174, 178
Heinkel and HE 178 (aircraft) 161
Hellendorf 173
Henri 30, 134, 159
Henschells (factory) 146
Hill, Fred 11, 12, 13, 33, 42, 44, 57, 143, 144, 145, 151, 154, 156, 172
Herz, Private Heinz L. 7
Hitler, Adolf 7, 11, 149, 161, 167
Hitler Youth 121
HM Forces 80
Hofkirche (Catholic) 145
Holland 18, 21, 112, 114
Hölzel, Oberleutnant 121, 163
Hungary 18
Hunt, Sergeant Terry 23, 38, 50, 72, 88, 123, 124, 136, 137
Hunter, Flying Officer J. 101, 164
Hurst, Eric 54, 55
Hürtgen Forest 26
Hut Commander 76, 77, 81, 85, 96, 121
Hut 47B 14, 52
Hut 53B 43

ICRC 35
Imperial War Museum 96
Indian NCOs 31
International Market 128, 129, 131
International Red Cross 8, 19, 28, 33, 34, 35, 46, 49, 55, 137
Ireland 18, 30
Irving, William 62
IS 9 100
Italy 11, 18, 20, 21, 33, 53, 63, 68, 72, 78, 79, 80, 102, 115, 136, 176

Jacobstahl 8, 11, 105, 119, 143, 144, 145
Jamieson, Sergeant Robert 120
Jenkins, Sergeant Cyril G. 23, 105, 144
Jessop, Lieutenant H.V.E. 19, 46, 62, 163, 164, 180
Jews 22, 143, 145, 172
Jones, Sergeant "Taffy" 84, 123, 124
Junkers 52 (aircraft) 96
Ju88 (aircraft) 113
Ju188 (aircraft) 114

K-rations 170, 179
Kilian, Achim 7, 9, 10, 181
King George V 82

Kitcher, Private 110
KLIM (milk) 36, 88
Klim, "Big Jim" 44
Klimtin, Ruddyot 44, 109
Kommandant 11, 56
Kommandantur 73, 102, 105
König (Koenig), Hauptmann 11, 12, 163, 164
Kossdorf 171
Kozakiewicz, Yvonn Lucyna 24, 25, 171
"Kraut" 173
Krefeld 8, 70
Kreuzkirche (Protestant) 145
Kriegsgefangene 13
Krygowski, Professor Z. 67
Kuehn, PFC Russell 48, 122, 169, 177
Kuhn, Private Alfred M. 115, 116, 117
Kultur Städte 153

Lager 39 148
Lager 41 148
Lagergeld 61, 126, 127
Lancasters (aircraft) 153
Landskrona 117
Last Post 124
Lawler, Jack 47–49
Lazarett 45–47, 90
Leckwitz 176
Lee, Signalman Robert H. 146, 147, 153, 169
Legion of St George 45
Leipzig 8, 63, 115, 130, 137, 145, 148, 149, 161, 169
Leuna 148
Liège 26
Lobau 148, 156, 159
Lonnewitz 113, 132
Lorenzkirch 178
Luft I Barth 8, 10, 11
Luft VII Bankau 8
Lührsen, *Oberst* 11, 12
Luther, Martin 145, 154
Luxembourg 26, 48

M. Stammlager 1VB 7, 9, 10, 11, 13, 15, 17
MacArthur, Signalman Malcolm R. 69
MacDonald, Captain T.L. 46
Main Street 21, 118, 128, 137
Makarewicz, Warrant Officer 100, 101
Mallory, Sergeant Herb 133
Malych 30
The Man Born to Be King 82
Man of Confidence 11, 24, 28, 33, 38, 53, 55, 65, 76–83, 89, 100–105, 115, 119, 132, 142
Marlag 8, 22
Martin, Wally 154, 172, 173
Massie, Sergeant Wally 133
McDowall, Major (Padre) R. 19–38, 56, 80, 103–109, 122–131, 159–161

McGavin, Captain J.G. 46
McGregor, Sergeant E.J. 135, 137
McIntosh, Dave 133
McKee, Captain W.P. 46
McKeeman, Alex 141
McLean, Sergeant Harry 63, 66, 177, 179
McMillan, John 46, 55
McVittie, Sergeant Jock 128, 129
ME 109 & 110 (aircraft) 161
ME 163 *"Komet"* (aircraft) 161
ME 163B *"Komet"* (aircraft) 163
ME 262 (aircraft) 161
Mediterranean 21
Meissen 149, 150, 170
Merrie England 62
Messerschmitt, Willi 161, 163
Metcalfe 68
Methodist Church 89
Mexico 18
Meyers, Flight Sergeant Jack 11, 28, 55, 77–80, 105
MI 5 & MI 6 68
MI 9 68, 69, 70, 73
Middleton, Jim 141
Minden 112
Minsk University 30
Mittellandkanal 112
"Mo" 127
Monschau 27
Montgomery (Field-Marshal Bernard) 55, 153
Morocco 18
Most (name) 152
Motor Ambulance Company 11
"Muckers" 37, 84
Mühlberg 8, 40, 45, 72, 80, 105, 128, 142, 168, 171, 181
Mühlberg-am-Elbe 8, 52, 75, 91
Mühlberg Motor Club 60, 61
Muldoon, Sam ("Paddy") 134
Müller (German soldier) 130
Mumsdorf 148, 149, 151
Munich 153
Murrell, Eric 150
Muse, Gunner Harry 147
Mustangs (P 51 aircraft) 114, 133, 163, 166

Nazi 163, 181
Neethling, Captain C.P.M. 46
Nelson, Sergeant Tom 13, 15, 34, 37, 41, 49, 62, 71, 105, 121, 156
Netherlands 174
Neuburxdorf 111, 113, 167
New Times 64–66
New Zealand 20, 30, 36, 81, 138, 140, 156
New Zealand Military Forces 136
Newell, Gunner Ray 18–22, 30, 37–43, 56,

Index

63–65, 85, 95, 103–108, 129–142, 153, 160–162
Ngaruawahia Camp 136, 140
Niehus 115
NKVD/MVD 181
Nordmann (German guard) 120, 121
Normandy 48, 55, 96, 162
North Africa 20, 136, 140
Northern Ireland 30
Novachenkov 38
Nuremberg 153
NZEF (2nd) 103, 140, 148, 149

Oberlangen 171
Ochse, Major J.Q. 46
Oflag IVC 8
O'Neill, Pipe Major M. 95

Page, Sergeant Norman 9, 26, 36, 57, 58, 60, 127, 133, 135, 165
Panzers 179
Paris 68, 70, 150
Parker, Sergeant 105
Parsons, Sergeant Lew 16, 24, 29, 37, 39, 71, 158
Phelps, Sergeant Charlie 53
Pill, Arthur 61
The Pirates of Penzance 59
Plymouth Brethren 89
Pokotny, Josef 162
Poland 18, 67, 68
Polish General Staff 67
Polish rebel 129
Polish resistance fighters 25
Polish women 24, 159
Posten 40, 45, 120, 133
Poznán University 67
Presbyterian 80
Prisoner-of-war camps 8, 21, 34, 69, 165
The Prisoner of Zenda 82
The Protecting Power 34, 85, 89

RAAF 104, 164
Rae, Corporal Bill 53, 56, 58
RAF 10, 11, 15–21, 24–33, 36–43, 50–57, 71–83, 86–98, 101–110, 113–115, 118, 120, 128–137, 142, 151–157, 160, 164, 171, 178, 180
RAF *Appell* 57
RAF Museum, Hendon 38, 72, 88
Rapson, Private Wilf 148, 149, 151
RASC 11, 73
Rathaus 145
RCAF 34, 77, 100, 101, 103, 176, 179
Read, Corporal Mickey 42, 124, 175, 178
Red Cross parcels 13, 22, 73, 84, 85, 106, 126, 144, 166
Rees, Warrant Officer J. 101

Reich, Third 7, 9, 10, 160, 166
Rejewski, Marian 68
Renkeness 116
Reveille 175
Revier 13, 45, 122
Rheims 173, 179
Rhine 7, 99, 166
Riesa 8, 115, 178–181
Ringstrasse 145
RNZAF 16
Robertson, Flight Sergeant M.M. ("Robbie") 57, 59, 75, 86, 94, 95
Roman Catholic 81, 91
Romania 18, 68
Rommel, General 20
Roosevelt, President Franklin D. 163, 169
Rouen 94
Royal Artillery 22, 42
Różycki, Jerzy 68
Russian Aid Society 50

S5 cellar 155
Sagan 8
Salvation Army 11, 131
Samuels, RSM Andy 164, 180
Sauerkraut 148
Saxony 7, 74, 75, 143, 145, 146, 161
Sayers, Dorothy 82
Scandrett, Sergeant 74
Scheissenwagen 39, 135
Schillerschule 146
"*Schlachthof-fünf*" 150
Schloss 145
Schnaps 169, 179
Schöltzel, Major 11
Schwarzradios 72
Scotland 30, 36, 92, 94
Secret Camp Histories 31, 69, 73, 100, 105, 109
Seddon, Sergeant Joe 63, 100–103, 110, 111, 115, 142
Semf, *Oberst* 11
Senior British Officer (SBO) 11
Serb 103, 129
Seychelles 18, 21
Shand, Private Alex 103, 178
Shand, Sergeant John 103, 178
Siberia 39, 167
Siemens factory 146
Silesian mines 147
Simmons, Staff Sergeant 73
Sketch Club 56
Skilly 77, 78, 121, 122, 158
"Slaughterhouse 5" 155, 174
Smith, Sergeant C.R. ("Smithy") 113, 114
Smith Settle Ltd. 147
Smuts, Jan Christian 173
"Snowshoes" 11, 28, 55, 105

Sonntag, *Feldwebel* 130
South African Forces 21
Southern Irish 135
Sperl, *Oberstleutnant* 11
SS 11, 12, 56, 121
Stabsfeldwebel "McAlpine" (or "Alpine Willy") 71
Stalag IVA 8
Stalag IVB Sketch Club 56
Stalag IVB Yacht Club 59
Stalag IVC 8, 145, 152
Stalag IVD 8
Stalag IVD/Z 8
Stalag IVF 8, 145, 151
Stalag IVG 8, 145, 149
Stalag IVH/304 8, 143
Stalag IXB 8, 150
Stalag Luft III 8
Stalin, Josef 23
Stephenson, Flight Sergeant 110
Stirling (aircraft) 74
Stockholm 115
Stossier, *Oberstleutnant* 11, 12, 56, 118
Strafebaracke 113
Strafkompanie 168
Straflager 19, 122, 123, 137, 148
Strehla 177, 178
Sudetenland 7, 67
Die Sudetenlandische Treibstaff Werke AG 152
Supreme Allied Commanders 153
Sutton, Sergeant Wilf 55, 66, 135
Sutton-Pratt, Jeremy 116
Sutton-Pratt, Colonel R. 115, 116, 117
Swallow, Sergeant Tom 60, 61, 180
Switzerland 28, 34, 81, 89, 102, 112, 117, 159
Szpek, Erv., Jr. 155, 166
Szpek, Corporal Ervin 27

Tagg, Dr Mary A. 124
Tahiti 18
Taylor, Warrant Officer Geoff 113
Teichgräber, *Gefreiter* 130
Terrorflieger Schweinhunds 110
Teuton 110
Thawley, Lance Sergeant A. 101
Thetis 62
Tobruk 78, 89, 92, 95, 96, 120, 156, 173
Tombling, Corporal Joe 23, 39–62, 123–130, 160–166, 174, 178
"Toplady" 152
Torgau 8, 163, 171, 176
Turner, Lance Sergeant 69
Turner, Sergeant Major 121
Typhus 9, 31, 45, 176

Uchtmann, N. 29
Ulbrich, *Oberfeldwebel* 29, 122
Untermenschen 22
Uzbek 21, 22

van der Laan, Bas 152, 154, 174
VE-Day 173, 179
Vercoe, Tony 149, 150, 170
Vertrauensmann 11, 22, 28
Vichy regime 101
Victory Show 164, 165
Vienna 102, 142
Vistula 23
Volksdeutscher 116
Vonnegut, PFC Kurt 12, 13, 26, 28, 59, 60, 124, 145, 150–156, 159, 174
von Runstedt 26, 98
Vorlager 27, 28, 63, 65

Wales 30
Wapenbroeders 152
Ward, Private Fred 136–138, 140–142
Warne, Flight Sergeant A.R.G. 101
Warren, Sergeant J.L. 114
Warsaw 18, 23, 24, 25, 26, 67, 68, 115, 159, 171
Watson, Harry 72, 141
Wehrkreis 7, 145
Wehrmacht 7, 10, 11, 67, 118
Weimar 170, 181
Weser (river) 112
West End 55
Whyte, Major A.G.D. 46, 47, 80, 164
Willis, Captain Charles 80, 82, 89, 91
Wolhuter, Sergeant S.G. (Wally) 21–29, 34, 39, 49, 66, 72, 105–130, 163, 166, 178
Wopata, PFC Eugene 123, 163
World War I 15, 67, 108
World War II 34, 108, 118

Yanks 99, 124, 170, 173
Yeary, Captain E.C. 46
YMCA 56
Yugoslavia 18, 68, 102

Zak, George K. 27, 28, 30, 145, 148, 150, 156, 159, 181
Zealand 117
Zeithain 11, 143, 144
Zeitz 149
Zwickau 147
Zwinger Museum 145
Zygalski, Henryk 68

www.ingramcontent.com/pod-product-compliance
Ingram Content Group UK Ltd.
Pitfield, Milton Keynes, MK11 3LW, UK
UKHW042004140426
5217IPUK00015B/977